THE
ITALIAN
BAKERY

THE
ITALIAN

BAKERY

STEP-BY-STEP
RECIPES WITH THE
SILVER SPOON

INTRODUCTION

The Silver Spoon was first published in 1950 and quickly gained popularity, becoming one of the most influential Italian cookbooks of all time. Considered by many as the bible of authentic Italian cuisine, it has sold more than three million copies in Italy and has been translated into twelve languages. From the authors of the original *The Silver Spoon*, we can now enjoy *The Italian Bakery*, an exploration of the art of pâtisserie. Bring to life the delicious edible treats that are found in bakeries across Italy, from everyday little pleasures to show-stopping celebration cakes for special occasions.

Pâtisserie can be a challenging art form combining technique, science, and creativity. This book aims to demystify the secrets of the pastry chef and be a comprehensive reference guide, which should be kept close at hand for expert instruction and inspiration. Suitable for novice and experienced home cooks alike, the chapters that follow include classic basic recipes for beginners, through to more challenging recipes and innovative ideas for accomplished bakers. Follow the in-depth instructions to master the core techniques required to create the perfect sweet treat— *dolce*—and delight your family and friends.

The introductory pages of *The Italian Bakery* give all the information on essential tools and key ingredients you need to get started, as well as useful tips, tricks, and techniques to allow you to tackle any pâtisserie recipe with confidence. The following chapters include the fifty basic recipes that every pastry chef should know—from handmade pie doughs and puff pastry doughs, through crêpe batters, enriched doughs, meringues, and crèmes, to glazes and frostings. Each recipe is accompanied with clear instructions and step-by-step photographs to illustrate the critical stages of the method, along with additional information to help you avoid the most common mistakes.

In addition to the fifty basic recipes that form the building blocks of all Italian *dolci*, there are ninety more complex, full recipes that are accompanied by full-page photographs of the finished dish and detailed instructions. As is typical of every Italian bakery, you will find pâtisserie from France, such as mille-feuille and choux buns; viennoiserie from Austria, including chocolate-filled pastries and strudel; and even sweet breads from Eastern Europe, known as babka; alongside classic Italian bakes, such as cannoncini and tiramisù. Create breakfast brioches and cookies; tarts and small cakes for a simple daytime treat; meringues, delicate mousses, and semifreddos for summer evenings; chocolate pralines and cakes; perfectly glazed desserts; and festive centrepieces. A dessert is always something special, especially when created with your own hands.

LEGEND

GLUTEN-FREE

DAIRY-FREE

VEGAN

VEGETARIAN

5 INGREDIENTS
OR FEWER

30 MINUTES
OR LESS

PREPARATION
TIME

COOKING TIME
ON STOVE

COOKING TIME
IN OVEN

RESTING TIME

STORAGE TIME
IN REFRIGERATOR

STORAGE TIME
IN FREEZER

GETTING STARTED

EQUIPMENT

WEIGHING AND MEASURING

PREPARING AND MIXING

SHAPING AND BAKING

DECORATING

WEIGHING AND MEASURING

Pâtisserie is equal parts art and science. Creativity, flair, and imagination are all important, but precisely weighing and measuring out each ingredient is imperative —even when very small quantities are being used, such as active raising agents and concentrated flavorings. When cooking some dishes, a looser approach to assessing ingredients by eye can work—a pinch of salt, a scattering of herbs, a handful of nuts—but with pâtisserie a consistently accurate approach is essential. Guessing the weight of any ingredient will rarely give the desired end result. To avoid such disappointment, weighing scales are an essential kitchen tool, just as they are in a science laboratory:

— Digital weighing scales
Modern digital weighing scales are efficient, lightweight, easy to store, and simple to wipe clean. While traditional mechanical or balance scales might look good in the kitchen, they are less accurate and leave more room for error. Digital scales with a large capacity, that can weigh up to 11 pounds/5 kg, or even 22 pounds/10 kg, will stand you in good stead for more recipes. As well as measuring solids by weight in ounces or grams, digital scales can also measure liquids by volume in fluid ounces or millilitres.

— Measuring cups, cones, pitchers (jugs), and spoons
Rather than weighing out ingredients, some pastry chefs prefer to use volumetric measurements. While it is a less accurate system, many find it easier to measure out flour in cups, for example. Essential for measuring liquids, from water and juice to milk and cream. Some measuring cups or jugs allow you to convert one unit of measurement to another, while others show units more common in other countries, which is useful when a recipe is written in a different language.

— Weights and measures
Both imperial and metric measurements are given for every recipe in this book. Always follow one set of measurements throughout, not a combination of imperial and metric, as they are not interchangeable.

PREPARING AND MIXING

The successful preparation of any dessert starts with a tried-and-tested recipe, good-quality ingredients, and all the necessary tools. First, you must weigh and measure out all the ingredients. Then you can set to work, transforming them with the help of electric mixers, whisks, and blenders, as well as other simple yet indispensable small tools that are essential in any baker's kitchen:

— Fine-mesh strainer (sieve)
Preferably one with a metal mesh. This is essential for sifting flour, raising agents, and other powdered dry ingredients; sifting dry ingredients minimizes any lumps in a mixture but it also allows air to permeate the particles as they separate. A strainer (sieve) can also be used to dust confectioners' (icing) sugar or cocoa powder over desserts, although for this a finer strainer would be even better.

— Grater
Some graters incorporate holes of different shapes and sizes, so they can be used for a variety of purposes, such as zesting citrus fruit (small holes) and shredding (grating) chocolate bars (larger oblong holes).

— Hand or electric whisk
Essential for beating eggs and whipping cream. Whisks are also more effective than a simple spoon for mixing and blending sauces, crèmes, and thick and thin batters. An electric model is often faster and more efficient than a hand whisk; they are easy to use and usually come with a range of accessories to mix even dense mixtures to perfection.

— Immersion (stick) blender
A highly practical, hand-held appliance that enables ingredients to be blended directly in a bowl or pan. The most classic ones have a blade for mixing, while others come with a whisk or a disk for whipping, and sometimes even a small accessory for mixing dough. Without doubt, it is an essential tool for any kitchen. It is best to choose one with a powerful motor, so it won't overheat with use, and with detachable accessories for easier cleaning.

— Kitchen thermometer

Preferably a digital one; this is a must-have item for any aspiring pastry chef. For many recipes, the perfect end result relies on achieving and maintaining the correct temperature during the preparation and cooking of the ingredients. Tempering chocolate, caramelizing sugar, and melting ingredients in a bain-marie are just some of the processes in which being just a few degrees out can make a big difference. For each of these techniques, a particular kind of thermometer is required with its own characteristics and temperature scales: from simple immersion thermometers to digital probes, complete with a small display screen at one end and a metal thermal probe or skewer at the other. The candy (sugar) thermometer is sometimes called a caramellometer.

— Mixer

A professional or semi-professional appliance able to work with a wide variety and large quantity of ingredients. Available as a stand mixer in its most substantial version, with many accessories, this is your best option if you are a keen baker who wants a multi-tasking appliance. Medium-sized mixers are better suited for domestic use, and are more than capable of performing a range of tasks, thanks to their interchangeable attachments. For example, the rotary motion using the hook-shaped attachment is perfect for working with thicker doughs, such as bread and brioche. There is also a paddle attachment for working softer doughs, such as pie dough and sponge cake batter. A whisk attachment can be used for whipping egg whites, cream, and meringue. Some models also have a cooking function. The choice of mixers in terms of power, size, range of attachments, and price is extensive. Instead of a stand mixer, a handheld mixer is a good option for anyone short on kitchen space.

— Spatula

Whether rubber or silicone, a spatula is an extremely flexible tool, which means it can scrape out even the smallest amounts of mixture from any awkward corners. It is also the tool of choice for incorporating whipped cream or egg whites into a mixture with no loss of volume. Metal spatulas—or palette knifes—on the other hand, are used for filling, distributing, spreading, and leveling any crème or frosting inside or on top of a cake.

SHAPING AND BAKING

Once the base mixture has been prepared, it is necessary to shape the dough or batter to transform it into its final form. This may be a tart, tartlet, cake, muffin, or pudding, depending on the consistency of the base mixture and the type of cooking required. These are baking processes that require careful handling, as well as specific types of pans (tins) and molds.

— Baking sheets, pans, and molds

Available in aluminum, as well as non-stick materials, they all have different characteristics. Therefore, the choice can be a subjective one. As for the minimum number of pans (tins) required, a round pan for tarts and other types of cake (8–10 inches/20–25 cm in diameter) is absolutely essential, with one loaf pan for loaf-shaped cakes and one Bundt pan for ring-shaped cakes. Springform pans or pans with a removable base, which make the unmolding of cakes exceptionally easy, are very useful. Baking molds made of corrugated, heat-resistant paper are also very practical as they are disposable.

— Crêpe-maker

The simplest way to make crêpes is to use an 8-inch/20-cm non-stick aluminum skillet (frying pan) with low, slightly flared sides. Crêpe-makers usually come with a batter spreader (a T-shaped double stick) and a spatula to lift the crepe once it is ready. More sophisticated versions have a non-stick electric plate and a temperature regulator.

— Pastry (piping) bags

Called a *poche à douille* in French, this is the quintessential item for pastry chefs. Once, these conical bags were made of paper or waxed cloth, but more recently disposable bags in lightweight transparent plastic have been preferred, as they are practical and hygienic. If you want to reduce your consumption of single-use plastics, reusable bags made from coated cotton that can be washed are also readily available. Filled with cream, frosting, dough, choux, or any other soft mixture, the bag is rolled or twisted at the top to close and then lightly squeezed until the contents are extruded through a narrow opening or piping tip (nozzle) at the bottom. Pastry bags are used for making cookies, profiteroles, and meringues, as well as to fill and to decorate. A wide range of decorative effects can be achieved by fitting the bag with a piping tip (nozzle). An array of different piping tips is available, from small to large, smooth or shaped.

— Pastry or cookie cutters
Available in metal or plastic, in various shapes and sizes, these cutters are used for punching out shapes from sheets of rolled-out dough to make cookies or decorations. Cutters can be smooth for a straight cut, scalloped for a wavy edge, or molded into novelty shapes, including everything from an animal to a bride and groom. As a piece of basic kitchen equipment, the round plastic cutters sold in sets of various diameters are indispensable.

— Pâtisserie grid or wire cooling rack
This is simply a wire cooling rack in the shape of a grid on which to rest pastries and cookies while they cool, and cakes when filling or decorating. When placed over a tray, a pâtisserie grid is also useful for collecting any excess frosting, glaze, or crème.

— Rolling pin
Made of wood, marble, or other materials, a rolling pin is essential for stretching and flattening pastry dough. Some rolling pins are specifically intended for pâtisserie, which are made from marble or metal, as the cold material helps to keep the pastry cool. Others are hollow and can be filled with ice.

— Silicone molds
Food-grade silicone molds are often more practical than metal pans as they don't always need to be buttered and dusted with flour. Thanks to the non-stick and flexible properties of the silicone material, removing cakes from them is easy and the shape will always be perfect. However, for an intricately shaped mold, such as for a Bundt cake, you may need to grease the mold to ensure the cake turns out cleanly. Silicone molds can be used at temperatures ranging from –40°F/–40°C to +535°F/+280°C, so they can be transferred directly from the oven to the freezer, if necessary. They can be used in both the refrigerator and the freezer, in fan-assisted and static temperature ovens, as well as in microwave ovens—but they must never be used in gas ovens.

DECORATING
The tradition of decorating desserts is an ancient one, but it was as recently as the eighteenth century when the pâtissier Antonin Carême turned it into a veritable art form. The simplest forms of decoration are chopped or sliced fresh fruit, dried or candied fruit, crystallized sugar grains, or chocolate drops (available ready-made and resistant to melting). For decoration using chocolate, it is sufficient just to melt the chocolate with a little water and then draw or write with it using a paper cone (see pages 36–7) or a pastry (piping) bag fitted with a very small piping tip (nozzle).

— Chocolate tools
As in any art form, working with chocolate requires the use of specific tools, which are used for shaving, melting, mixing, molding, and decorating. Some tools—or similar ones—can be found in an averagely equipped domestic kitchen. Others are very specific from polycarbonate molds in various sizes, for creating filled or hollow tempered chocolate shapes, to simple ramekins; from small tin or aluminum fluted containers for the preparation of chocolate candies, to praline forks for advanced practitioners.

— Piping tips or nozzles
These are additional and interchangeable accessories for use with pastry (piping) bags of frosting, chocolate, cream, and other toppings. Piping tips (nozzles) can be made of plastic or metal and have openings in different shapes and sizes to create many different types of decoration, allowing you to personalize decorations.

— Pastry brush
Very useful for soaking the bottom of desserts with flavored syrups and liqueurs, for brushing pastry surfaces with egg or milk to glaze them, and for greasing molds, baking sheets, and pans (tins) uniformly and without waste. Nowadays silicone brushes are preferred to natural bristles as they are more hygienic and practical—and without the inconvenience of it occasionally shedding the odd bristle.

— Pastry or cookie cutters
Cutters are used not only to shape cookies before baking, but also to punch out pastry or fondant shapes to decorate tarts and cakes; this is often the first form of decoration a budding pastry chef attempts when making desserts.

INGREDIENTS

FLOUR

RAISING AGENTS

SUGARS AND SWEETENERS

EGGS

CREAM, BUTTER, AND FATS

COCOA AND CHOCOLATE

SETTING AGENTS

FRESH AND DRIED FRUITS

OTHER FLAVORINGS

FLOUR

In pâtisserie, the most commonly used flour is soft wheat grain. Generally, type "00" and "0" flour and, occasionally, type "1" is used, although there is no shortage of alternatives: wholegrain, rice, oat, and spelt flours, used together with soft wheat grain flour, all impart a unique taste and texture to desserts. However, flours are not interchangeable and, even in the context of the same "type," the different soft wheat grain flours have distinct characteristics that mean each are best suited to the preparation of certain kinds of desserts.

— Soft wheat grain flour
Depending on the fiber and protein content, soft wheat grain flour is differentiated by a number. "00" flour is the whitest one but also has the least fiber and protein. "0" flour is the type most commonly used for baked goods, not only in a domestic setting but also at artisanal and industrial level. In pâtisserie, flour types "1" and "2" are used less often than the more refined flours but, thanks to their characteristic of restricting excessive rising, they are preferred for the preparation of some desserts. Because of its high gluten content, soft wheat flour cannot be replaced with oat, potato, millet, rice, or rye flours, which have little or no gluten.

— Manitoba flour
In recent times, Manitoba flour has become more popular. Obtained from the milling of a particular type of soft wheat grain (cultivated mainly in Manitoba, a Canadian region), it has the advantage of offering, with a similar level of preparation, an excellent rise, due to its gluten content that is particularly resistant and compact, and able to retain the carbon dioxide necessary for rising. It is particularly suitable for fat- and sugar-rich doughs, which require long leavening periods.

Two important considerations when choosing a flour for pâtisserie are the quality of its manufacture and its protein content. Always source the best quality flour that you can find. Many manufacturers bleach their flour with chemicals, such as chlorine dioxide and benzoyl peroxide, to artificially whiten its appearance. Check the packaging to ensure the flour contains no bleach, bromate, or artificial preservatives. Also check the packaging to know the protein content of the flour you are using—the higher the level of protein, the stronger the flour (see page 26).

RAISING AGENTS

Raising agents react with other ingredients during cooking to release the carbon dioxide necessary to increase the volume of the dough. Their effects may be similar but the different types of raising agents are certainly not interchangeable. Cell structure, softness, and elasticity, as well as flavor, are strongly affected by each agent.

— Baking powder
This chemical powder is the classic raising agent for cakes. It is generally composed of substances such as sodium bicarbonate and acid salts. It may also be known by other terms such as "baker's ammonia" or "cream of tartar." Baking powder is sifted with the flour or added to the mixture last of all; when warm or hot liquids are added, the preparation must be put into the oven immediately.

— Brewer's yeast
This owes its name to the fact that at one time it was obtained exclusively from the production of beer. It consists of *Saccharomyces cerevisiae*, a sort of microscopic fungus whose metabolism results in fermentation and the subsequent leavening of dough. Its use for bread, pizza, and cakes causes the dough to increase in volume when left to rest for a variable period. Brewer's yeast is available fresh, in small pats, or dried. As a home baker, fresh yeast is not as easy to get hold of and it deteriorates quite quickly over a few days. Dried yeast guarantees consistent results, even after is has been stored for a while. There are two types of dried yeast: active and instant. Dried active yeast is reactivated by dissolving it in a tepid liquid (never hot, or the yeast will be destroyed) with a teaspoon of sugar or honey to "feed" it; fresh yeast and instant yeast are added directly to the dough. If a recipe calls for fresh yeast, the approximate conversions to dried yeast are: ½ quantity of dried active yeast to 1 quantity of fresh yeast, or ¼ quantity of dried instant yeast to 1 quantity of fresh yeast.

— Natural yeast
Natural yeast, starter culture, or sourdough is the oldest and most natural method of leavening, much slower than that obtained with brewer's yeast. A fermented mix of water and flour, therefore already enriched with enzymes and probiotics, it is used as a raising agent. The finished product is less soft and airy than when using brewer's yeast, but it lasts longer and is more resistant to mold.

SUGARS AND SWEETENERS

Above all else, pâtisserie needs sweetness. The variety of commercially available sweeteners is considerable, given the recent proliferation of artificial sweeteners. However, pastry chefs have their preference, with sugar (or sucrose) sitting head and shoulders above the rest. As well as adding sweetness, sugar helps to bring out the natural flavors in other ingredients. Alternative natural sweeteners are mainly used in accordance with very precise culinary requirements, traditional recipes, or specific diets.

— Refined sugar

For a long time honey was the most commonly used sweetener, but is has now been superseded by refined sugar. Sucrose is the commercially available sugar, and is obtained from beet or cane. Sugar can be bought in various forms: superfine (caster) sugar (ground into very small crystals, most commonly used in cake batters, crèmes, and syrups); granulated sugar (larger crystals than superfine sugar, used for more rustic bakes, cookies, and some cakes); confectioners' (icing) sugar (superfine sugar ground into a powder, used for frostings, glazes, and when whipping cream); pearl or nib sugar (very coarse, opaque white fragments, used as decoration, does not melt when cooked). A certain quantity of sugar is needed when baking cakes to achieve a stable crumb structure. If too little sugar is added, the texture may be spoiled. However, if too much sugar is added, the bake may brown too quickly in the oven.

— Brown sugars

Brown sugars have small crystals, they are darker and softer than refined sugars, and they still contain some molasses. They can help to add a little extra color and moisture to baked goods. Brown sugars may be refined sugars that have had molasses added back or may be unrefined or refined less in the production process (these are labeled as muscovado sugars). They come in dark and light versions and also a crystallized form of cane sugar known as turbinado, demerara, or raw cane sugar. From a nutritional point of view, the extra molasses provides minimal extra minerals, so the benefits of brown sugars from a calorie and health point of view are minimal.

— Honey

Before sugar became the dominant sweetener within baking, honey was the only available alternative. Its taste was considered by some to be a bit too intense, which led to it being replaced by more neutral natural sweeteners. The nutritional properties of honey remain unrivaled. Made up of glucose, fructose, and small quantities of sucrose, the concentration of vitamins and minerals in honey make it a culinary marvel. Honey imparts a softness and characteristic caramel color to baked goods.

— Dextrose and glucose syrup

Both are obtained from cornstarch (the viscosity of the syrup is dependent on the concentration of dextrose), and are used in pâtisserie in specific preparations, mainly ice cream, crèmes, and syrups. More generally, they are used where the objective is to decrease the sweetening quality or when it is necessary to slow down the crystallization of ordinary sugar, making the mixture more fluid.

— Malt syrup

This syrup can be made from barley, rice, corn, or wheat. It has lesser sweetening power than sugar (3½ ounces/ 100 g of malt syrup corresponds to around 2¾ ounces/ 80 g of sugar), but it is very rich in vitamins and minerals such as potassium, sodium, and magnesium.

— Maple syrup

Obtained from boiling down the sap of the sugar maple and black maple trees, maple syrup has a distinct flavor with hints of caramel and vanilla. Even in modest quantities, it contains sucrose and is, therefore, not suitable for diabetics. It has a high vitamin content.

SWEETENING POWER

There is no apparatus that can objectively measure the sweetness of various types of sugar. Instead, sweetness is assessed using the relative sweetness scale: sucrose is attributed the value of 100 and the sweetness of other sugars is assessed and quantified relative to this by trained expert tasters to define the relative sweetening power (RSP) of the other "sugars":

fructose	120–170
glucose	70
honey	130
invert sugar	125
lactose	40
maltose	50
sucrose	100

EGGS

First of all, it is important to choose the right eggs, as well as to understand their significant nutritional properties. It takes a bit of art and a bit of science to use them in pâtisserie, as many of the recipes in this book will demonstrate.

— Egg classifications

Both the shells of eggs and their boxes carry numbers and symbols that reveal their classification and provenance. In the US eggs are graded AA, A, or B, with grades AA and A sold in grocery stores and lower grade B used industrially. In the UK there are two grades of eggs, A and B, with only grade A available to purchase in stores and grade B used industrially. Eggs are also classified on the basis of their weight (including the shell). In the US an egg is classified as small if it weighs between 1½ ounces and 1¾ ounces, medium between 1¾ ounces and 2 ounces, large between 2 ounces and 2¼ ounces, and extra-large if it weighs more than 2¼ ounces. In the UK an egg is small (S) if it weighs less than 53 g, medium (M) if it weighs between 53 g and 63 g, large (L) if it weighs between 63 g and 73 g, and extra-large (XL) if it weighs over 73 g. Commercial UK eggs are stamped with a traceability code, which includes the type of farming system (O = organic, 1 = free range, 2 = barn, 3 = cage), the country of origin, the farm ID number, and the best before date. All the recipes in this book call for US size large eggs and UK size medium eggs.

— Yolks and whites

When used in pâtisserie, the quantity of eggs required, rather than their weight, is usually indicated in the recipe. This is generally adequate in most cases, provided you are aware that recipes conventionally refer to medium or large eggs, with a weight of 2⅛–2½ oz/60–70 g. As well as adding color, flavor, and protein to every recipe, egg yolks are rich in fats and lecithin making them an efficient emulsifier, and an unparalleled binding agent. Egg whites do not impart a significant color or flavor to recipes and are not as nutritionally dense as yolks, but when whisked into stiff peaks they are indispensable in adding volume and softness.

CREAM, BUTTER, AND FATS

It is impossible to list all the uses of milk products in pâtisserie: they soften, they add moisture, they act as natural emulsifiers, and above all, they impart a unique flavor. Without any of the milk derivatives, especially cream and butter, pâtisserie would not be as rich and flavorful.

— Butter

The high fat content (80–85%) and minimal water content (less than 16%) of butter makes it particularly suitable for pâtisserie. From both a nutritional and culinary perspective, its proteins, fats, and minerals add to the richness of butter. Whether used cold in cubes, softened into a paste, or melted in a bain-marie, butter provides structure, consistency, and a unique flavor to baked goods.

— Cream

This is the fat component of milk (minimum 30% fat). In pâtisserie it is used in crèmes, mixes, and as decoration. Whipped cream is used a lot (directly in mixes, crèmes, mousses, and ice creams, and as decoration or filling). For cream to reach the desired consistency, it must be used straight from the refrigerator and whipped in a chilled bowl with cold utensils.

— Vegetable fats

Long before butter, olive oil was an essential ingredient in pâtisserie, especially in Italy. After a period of decline, during which it was replaced by butter or other vegetable-derived fats, olive oil is now regaining its reputation in baking, partly because of its unique nutritional and culinary qualities. It is light and easy to digest. In recent years, there has been a resurgence in the popularity of olive oil as a replacement for butter in many recipes.

COCOA AND CHOCOLATE

Chocolate is used by the world's best pâtissiers to prepare irresistible desserts. There are several types, classified by the percentage of cocoa solids they contain. During the winter months chocolate needs to be stored in a cupboard, away from light and heat sources. During warmer months it should be stored in the refrigerator. Bittersweet (dark) chocolate can be kept for three years, milk chocolate for one year, and white chocolate for eight months. If it appears opaque, with a whitish patina (bloom), it means that, while it is still edible, it has been subject to fluctuations in temperature which may have compromised its flavor.

— Cocoa powder

This is obtained from cocoa seeds, also called beans, that have been cleaned, de-husked, roasted, and pressed; what remains is ground into a powder. It has a maximum water content of 9% and a minimum content of 20% cocoa butter (less than 20% is referred to as low-fat cocoa).

— Bittersweet (dark) chocolate

This contains at least 43% cocoa solids. Extra dark chocolate is also available, which has a minimum cocoa content of 45%. Nowadays there is a type of bittersweet (dark) chocolate to suit all tastes, ranging from the minimum allowable cocoa content up to much higher percentages, through increments, from 60–70% up to an intense 99%.

— Milk chocolate

The most consumed type of chocolate and children's favorite. Milk chocolate contains at least 25% cocoa solids and 14% milk-derived products, such as milk, cream, or butter. Superior or extra-fine milk chocolate must contain at least 30% cocoa solids and 18% milk-derived products and is a "fatter," but also more satisfying, version of regular milk chocolate.

— Gianduja chocolate

This is a chocolate mix, containing a minimum of 32% each of cocoa and ground hazelnuts. As well as hazelnuts, it is possible to find variants with chopped almonds or walnuts.

— White chocolate

This contains a maximum of 55% sucrose, at least 20% cocoa butter and at least 14% milk or dried milk-derived products. In practice, white chocolate does not contain cocoa solids and, in effect, it is not a real form of chocolate.

SETTING AGENTS

Setting or gelling agents are used to thicken a preparation.

— Sheet gelatin

Gelatin is derived from pork or beef collagen. There are different grades and types. The most readily available are: platinum, gold, silver, bronze, and titanium. The term "bloom" refers to the strength of the gelatin. If the bloom is higher, it is stronger and produces a firmer set. Platinum is the highest in strength, decreasing to the lowest, titanium. The recipes in this book call for platinum gelatin sheets, but other grades can be substituted without affecting the end result. Platinum and gold sheets weigh less per sheet than bronze or titanium sheets, but they are stronger. Gelatin does vary between manufacturers and countries, so check the instructions on the packaging when judging the amount needed.

Sheet gelatin is popular as it dissolves quickly in warm liquids, when making cooked preparation. Although it is important not to boil a preparation once the gelatin has been added, as that reduces its setting power. When soaking gelatin sheets before adding them to any preparation, always soak the sheets in ice-cold water before using. If you soak the sheets in warm water, the gelatin will start to melt and some of the weight will be lost.

— Powdered gelatin

Gelatin is available in powdered form. Like sheet gelatin, powdered gelatin also needs to be soaked in cold water before using. However, powdered gelatin absorbs the water like a sponge before being added to a preparation. When soaking powdered gelatin, use the ratio 1 part powdered gelatin to 5 parts water. Powdered gelatin can be used instead of sheet gelatin, but you will need to convert according to the relative strength of both the sheet gelatin and powdered gelatin.

— Agar agar

For a vegetarian or vegan substitute to gelatin, agar agar provides a plant-based alternative. Agar agar is derived from a variety of seaweed. It is available in various forms: bars, strands, flakes, and powder. Simply follow the manufacturer's instructions on the packaging when using.

— Pectin

Pectin is a naturally occurring starch found in fruits. It is the key setting agent in preserves, jams, and jellies.

FRESH AND DRIED FRUITS

Whether in the form of fruit preserves, jams, or jellies, ice creams, or mousses, as a filling for a tart, when folded through a loaf cake, or simply used in its natural, fresh state as decoration, the use of fruit in pâtisserie is essential.

— Citrus fruits
Their collective name is synonymous with the tart, sour flavor typical of these fruits. Among the most widely used citrus fruits within pâtisserie are lemons, limes, citrons, oranges, mandarins, tangerines, clementines, grapefruit, and tangelos (a cross between a tangerine and a pomelo).

— Fruit purees
Among those fruits most commonly used in pâtisserie, both cooked and raw, are apples, pears, peaches, apricots, cherries (also used for liqueurs and schnapps, and in herbal medicine), figs (fresh or dried), pomegranate (the fruit contains fleshy and juicy seeds), prunes or plums. These fruits are also used to make preserves, jams and jellies, or dried fruit.

— Forest fruits and berries
No longer foraged wild, small forest fruits and berries are now cultivated in greenhouses. Strawberries, raspberries, blueberries, and blackberries have long been used as much more than just simple decoration. Also classified as a forest fruit are Cape gooseberries, which can be used fresh but are mainly found in preserves (jams) and gelatines (jellies).

— Tropical fruits
Once grown only in far-flung regions of the globe, a wide variety of tropical and subtropical fruits, are now cultivated around the world and are available all year round.
— Avocado: the creamy flesh of an avocado can be used in desserts, such as chocolate mousse (see page 290).
— Banana: a popular fruit, bananas can be eaten raw or cooked (see page 270).
— Kiwi: also known as Chinese gooseberry, the kiwi has a high vitamin C content, yet it is not classified as a citrus fruit.
— Mango: the sweet flesh of a ripe mango has a distinct floral flavor.
— Papaya: as well as eaten raw, papaya can be used to prepare mousses, semifreddos, and ice creams.
— Pineapple: can be used fresh, but it is more frequently used cooked.

OTHER FLAVORINGS

The core ingredients of any dessert are flour, sweeteners, fats, and raising agents, but other ingredients are necessary to bring something extra; these are flavorings.

— Nuts
In the case of nuts like walnuts and almonds, the shell is removed and the seed inside is the nut that is consumed. The most commonly used nuts include: almonds (used in sugared almonds, brittle, and nougat), cashews, chestnuts (used in marron glacé (candied chestnuts) and ground into flour), groundnuts (peanuts), hazelnuts (commonly used in desserts, ice cream, and gianduja chocolate), pistachios, and walnuts.

— Seeds
A concentrated source of nutrients, seeds lend a crunchy texture to cakes, mousses, and ice creams. Sesame seeds have a really high calcium content. Hemp seeds contain iron, phosphorus and omega-3 and represent a complete protein food. Similar qualities are offered by poppy seeds, which contain phytosterols able to reduce cholesterol levels.

— Spices and vanilla
Some people think that spices are best used in savory recipes. However, they can also be used to create delicious desserts. Among the most common is vanilla, which can be used to flavor cakes, crèmes, ice creams, blancmange, and other desserts. Also popular is cinnamon, obtained from the bark of the tree of the same name, mainly in Sri Lanka. Originally from Asia, ginger and turmeric are obtained from roots, which are left to dry and then finely ground. Cardamom is a seed harvested from small pods. These spices are excellent for giving a special flavor to cakes, crèmes, and cookies. Lastly, it would be remiss not to mention cloves; used to flavor tarts, preserves (jams), and chestnut desserts.

COOKING METHODS

BAKING IN AN OVEN

COOKING WITH A BAIN-MARIE

BAKING IN AN OVEN

Every modern oven incorporates a thermostat, which accurately indicates the internal temperature of the appliance. A functioning thermostat is important to ensure consistently accurate heat levels during precise cooking times. Even though today's ovens are incredibly advanced, perfect baking is a skill that needs to be learned and practiced. The recipes, techniques, and tips found in reputable baking books provide invaluable information when learning the art of pâtisserie. However, there is no substitute for experience—a practiced baker can gauge the quality of a bake either by eye or by touch.

— Correct oven placement

Fan or convection ovens circulate the hot air around the oven, so the temperature should be constant throughout without any "hot spots." However, the action of the warm air being forced around the oven causes food to brown more quickly, which is why fan ovens are usually set at a lower temperature. Each type of dessert needs to be cooked in the correct position within the oven. Cake pans (tins) must always be placed on a wire shelf, never on a solid shelf or on the base of the oven, because overheating could burn the bottom of the cake. To ensure even cooking, it is also important to position the cake pan correctly inside the oven. If, for example, you are cooking a tart with a filling, you need to place the wire shelf on the second level up from the base of the oven, so that the heat is higher at the bottom of the pan and the pastry can cook to perfection, despite being in contact with a moist filling. However, cakes that must rise during cooking must always be placed in the central part of the oven.

— Monitoring the oven temperature

For desserts that need to rise during cooking, never open the oven door before two-thirds of the cooking time has passed as the sudden drop in temperature could either make the dessert sink or slow down its cooking. Sometimes when a cake rises during cooking it forms a dome or cracks in the center: this happens because the temperature is too high and the crust forms very quickly. It is best to check with an oven thermometer that the temperature indicated by the thermostat corresponds to the actual temperature of the oven; if not, adjust it to take into account any discrepancy.

— Checking progress

Keep in mind that every oven is different and therefore the results will vary. To ensure that a cake is cooked, check that it is shrinking away from the edges of the pan (tin) or test it by inserting a wooden skewer into the middle: the skewer must be completely dry and free of crumbs when pulled out. You can also use a digital probe thermometer, inserting it into the cake: the temperature could vary from 197.5°F/92°C to 208.5°F/98°C depending on the type of cake mixture.

Lastly, take into account something that may seem obvious but that is often overlooked: when using a smaller cake pan (tin) and less mixture, the cooking will take less time. Conversely, a larger quantity of mixture will cook more slowly, so keep this in mind when multiplying quantities.

THE CORRECT TEMPERATURE

Low, medium, hot, or very hot: occasionally recipes can be somewhat vague about cooking temperatures. The table below can be used as a guide to help you set the correct oven temperature for recipes where only a general indication of temperature is given. Getting the temperature right is an essential step to achieving a perfect cake:

LOW HEAT			
225°F—250°F	110°C—130°C	110°C—130°C Fan (convection)	Gas ¼—Gas ½

MEDIUM HEAT			
250°F—350°F	130°C—180°C	110°C—160°C Fan (convection)	Gas ½—Gas 4

HOT			
350°F—400°F	180°C—200°C	160°C—180°C Fan (convection)	Gas 4—Gas 6

VERY HOT			
400°F—475°F	200°C—240°C	180°C—220°C Fan (convection)	Gas 6—Gas 9

— Removing from the oven
When cooked, it is best not to remove the cake from its pan (tin) as soon as it comes out of the oven, but rather to leave it to rest for at least ten minutes. Removing a cake from its pan too soon risks breaking it because, when hot, cakes are very fragile. Once the cake has been taken out of the pan, it is best to serve it immediately if it is to be enjoyed warm; otherwise, place it on a wire cooling rack to cool before transferring it to a serving plate.

COOKING WITH A BAIN-MARIE

This piece of equipment dates back to the Roman Empire, is far removed from the technology used in the most modern ovens. Special sets of saucepans are commercially available for bain-marie cooking or you can use a double-boiler (a semi-spherical container with a handle and a hook) suspended over a pan of simmering water. However, it is just as easy to use utensils that are already available in a reasonably well-equipped kitchen: two saucepans or two baking dishes, the smaller of which can be placed inside the larger. When it comes to perfecting pâtisserie, the use of a bain-marie is essential.

— Delicacy, precision, and safety
This type of cooking involves the immersion of one container, holding the ingredients to be heated, into a larger container holding the water, which is kept at simmering point. In particular, this method is used for delicate sauces or, more frequently, to reheat a preparation without altering its taste and texture. Bain-marie cooking allows greater control over the precise temperature at which mixtures are cooked, particularly ones that are sensitive to sudden jumps in temperature, such as those based on eggs, honey, and sugar. It is a type of cooking that works by conduction: the container with the ingredients or mixture is not heated by direct contact with a heat source, but by the heat of the simmering water. This allows better control over the temperature and cooking, especially for those preparations that suffer when exposure to intense heat.

— Not just on the stove
Bain-marie cooking on the stove is particularly recommended for the preparation of sauces and crèmes, which require constant attention and stirring, or for melting butter or pasteurizing eggs. However, the same cooking technique can also be used in the oven to cook a mixture.

One or more smaller containers are placed in a larger, deep baking dish, which is filled with water almost up to the rim of the smaller containers.

— Cooking "dry" or "by immersion"
Bain-marie cooking is called "dry" when the double-boiler insert or saucepan is positioned so that it is not in direct contact with the simmering water and the ingredients are heated by steam only. In this way, greater control can be maintained over the temperature, which can be kept lower so that the particular characteristics of the ingredients are not lost. However, when the receptacle containing the ingredients is immersed in the hot water of the larger container, this is known as "bain-marie by immersion." This method is particularly useful when reheating food, but when certain precautions are taken, it can also be used to prepare mousses and sauces.

USING A COLD BAIN-MARIE

A cold bain-marie can be used to quickly cool preparations: in this case the smaller pan containing the ingredients to be cooled is immersed in a large pan containing water, ice, and coarse salt. The salt increases the thermal capacity of the water, allowing the water to maintain a low temperature.

THE SCIENCE OF PÂTISSERIE

FLOUR STRENGTH

The natural properties of the original grain determines the nutritional content of each flour and also its possible uses in a culinary context, particularly in the case of pâtisserie.

— Proteins

As with breadmaking, in pâtisserie an important property of flour is its "strength." Every type of flour is milled to have a specific protein content—the higher the protein, the stronger the flour. The strength of flour is expressed by the indicator W, and it defines many of the characteristics of the final baked product: from its friability to elasticity, texture to shine, roughness to softness. Gliadin and glutenin are the two simple proteins in flour that, when in contact with water and worked into a dough, form an elastic structure called gluten. The higher the level of these two proteins, the higher the W strength on the index. However, the W rating is not printed on packages of flour for general retail, so look at the nutritional content panel on the package to find the protein content per 4 ounces/100 g. It's important to use the right flour with the appropriate protein content for the recipe you are making. Some brands allow wide fluctuations in the protein content of their flour, meaning slightly different result each time you use a new package of flour. By choosing a reputable flour brand that maintains consistent protein levels, will give you the most consistent results.

— Gluten

The gluten level in flour determines a dough's ability to retain the gases formed during the fermentation process triggered by raising agents. Higher levels of gluten result in a compact, elastic dough with greater capacity to absorb water, thereby promoting a slow leavening. A lower gluten content results in the lesser absorption of water and a faster leavening: in practice, this means a lighter, less compact dough.

— The lowest-strength flours can be used for cookies, wafers, and crackers.
— Medium strength flours can be used for classic pie doughs (shortcrust pastry), choux pastry, sponge mixtures, waffle batters, and crêpe batters.
— Puff pastry works best when made with strong flour with a W of 280–300: in fact, it must be easy to stretch and withstand being worked for long periods.
— Strong flours are also needed for leavened doughs, such as croissants, brioche, and traditional festive Italian favourites including Pandoro, Panettone, and Colomba.

— Flours with a strength higher than 400 (the most frequently used is Manitoba flour) are special soft grain flours, characterized by a high protein content: by adding them to weaker flours, they can increase the strength of those flours. As the packaging of flour for home cooking rarely displays the strength or W value of the flour, relying on your baking experience is essential. A good test is to squeeze a handful of flour in the palm of your hand: weak flour will remain compacted once you open your hand; strong flour will appear more fragmented. It is simply a question of the absorption of moisture.

The strength index

SPECIAL FLOURS

W 360 and higher	13.5% protein and higher	During mixing this flour absorbs up to 90% of its weight in water

STRONG FLOURS

W 270–350	12.5%–13.5% protein	During mixing this flour absorbs approximately 65–75% of its weight in water

MEDIUM STRENGTH FLOURS

W 180–260	10.5%–12.5% protein	During mixing this flour absorbs approximately 50–65% of its weight in water

WEAK OR FLAT FLOUR

W 90–170	9%–10.5% protein	During mixing this flour absorbs approximately 50% of its weight in water

— Stability, tenacity, and extensibility

The stability of flour—that is to say the working time a dough can tolerate before the softening phase of the dough starts, with the consequent loss of texture—is in itself an index of the flour quality. For low-quality flours, a working period of only three minutes is enough to cause their "degrading," while high-quality flours have a stability period that can last up to fifteen minutes. It is important to consider this factor in the preparation of puff pastry. No less relevant, in relation to the strength of flour, is the ratio between the tenacity (P) and extensibility (L) of its gluten: for breadsticks or cookies, both the strength and the P:L ratio of the flour used can be low, while in flour for leavened products, they must be high.

RAISING AGENTS

Even though microbiological leavening using natural yeasts and chemical leavening using baking powder both trigger the development of carbon dioxide in a dough, modern pâtisserie has been searching for a simpler, easier-to-use raising agent; an ingredient that does not alter the flavor of the preparation, but ensures a consistent rise to make a difference.

— A controlled rise

Since industrial production began in the nineteenth century, sodium bicarbonate has been overwhelmingly used in pâtisserie production. Originally added to buttermilk and then later to other acidic ingredients, sodium bicarbonate seemed able to develop the carbon dioxide necessary for leavening. However, as it is impossible to measure the natural acidity of ingredients in a home kitchen, it was difficult to know precisely how much bicarbonate was necessary to trigger the required rise. A solution was promptly found by replacing all the other acidic ingredients with an acid salt—cream of tartar (acid potassium tartrate)—obtained mainly from grapes and tamarind. The ability to measure exactly the quantities of cream of tartar and sodium bicarbonate necessary to trigger leavening, and the advantage of the former in not leaving any aftertaste, led to the production of a prepacked powdered raising agent for baking.

— The search continues

The only downside of using cream of tartar with sodium bicarbonate is the rapid reaction of the two components in water. Within minutes of mixing the ingredients together, around 80% of the carbon dioxide will be released, well before baking the mixture has hardened the external structure of the dough. In doughs containing little gluten, only the thickness of the dough can retain the residual carbon dioxide, and only for a limited time. The need arose for a new acidic substance that could cause a controlled reaction and slow down the dispersion of carbon dioxide. Nowadays, many instant chemical raising agents of different compositions can be found on supermarket shelves.

MAKING YOUR OWN RAISING AGENT

There are many acidic ingredients that react with sodium bicarbonate to produce carbon dioxide, which is at the root of leavening. Among these, some of the most frequently used are: lemon juice, vinegar, yogurt, molasses, raw sugar, fruit juice, honey, raw cocoa, yogurt, buttermilk, and sour cream.

SUGAR

When you consider a sweet treat, your mind instinctively thinks of sugar. But from a scientific point of view, things are a little more complicated, both in terms of the variety of sweeteners available and their properties. It is this variety and these chemical and molecular properties that help to achieve unique and irresistible flavors, colors, and textures in baking.

— A molecular question

The sweetening power of a "sugar" depends on one or more molecules made of carbon, hydrogen, and oxygen. In some cases, it is a matter of a single molecule, as in glucose and fructose; in others, it is a combination of molecules, as in the case of sucrose, composed of one glucose molecule and one fructose molecule linked to each other. Sucrose is the common table sugar and the one most used in pâtisserie.

— The secret of sugar's "success"

Sucrose has many characteristics, and a lot of these are interesting from a culinary point of view. It is very widely available, a result of the global spread of sugar cane and beet cultivation, and it has some peculiar properties. One of the most surprising is sucrose's solubility, which can reach up to 2 lb 3 oz per pint (2 kg per litre), but perhaps even more important in pâtisserie is its melting point: sucrose breaks down at a temperature of between 363°F/184°C and 367°F/186°C. Heating sucrose gives rise to an "apparent melting": that is to say, the sugar crystals don't melt, but cause a reaction called "inversion," whereby the sucrose breaks down into its two constituent molecules (fructose and sucrose). As the temperature increases, sugar changes its structure: it breaks down first, and then, with the elimination of the water molecules, it darkens and acquires a caramel flavor. The "inversion" of sucrose causes the formation of sugars with high hygroscopic properties, capable of absorbing many molecules of water, that are extremely useful in soft mixtures. Nor do the sugars dry out too much when exposed to air. A spontaneous "inversion" process, brought about by some temperatures or certain conditions, can be obtained through acids or enzymes. An example of an invert sugar is golden syrup. The use of sugar, in combination with the proteins in any dough, is also responsible for the Maillard reaction, one that gives a "golden" color to baked products.

Lining a deep cake pan (tin)

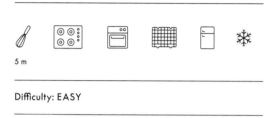

5 m

Difficulty: EASY

EQUIPMENT NEEDED
Parchment paper
Pencil
Scissors

Take a sheet of parchment paper just wider than the base of the cake pan (tin). Place the pan near one of the edges of the sheet. Using a sharp pencil, draw a circular outline on the parchment paper around the base of the pan (1).

Using scissors and following the pencil line as a guide, cut out the disk of parchment paper to line the base of the pan (2).

From the remaining parchment paper, cut a strip that is about 2 inches/5 cm wider than the depth of the pan and long enough to line the inner sides (3).

Fold 1 inch/2.5 cm of this strip over along its length (4).

Using scissors, cut little snips along the folded edge of the parchment paper up to the crease (5).

Place the long parchment paper strip inside the pan so that the snipped edge sits on the base of the pan (6–7).

At this point, place the paper disk you cut earlier on the base of the pan so that it sits on top of the strip that lines the sides (8). Make sure the snips and the base form a sharp corner and won't allow any mixture to leak through the parchment paper lining.

For square tins, follow the same instructions as above, but fold the long strip that covers the sides at the four corners to fit neatly inside the pan.

TIPS AND TRICKS

A quick way to line a cake pan (tin) is to wet some parchment paper under running water and then pat it dry with a clean tea towel. In doing this the paper becomes softer and clings more easily to the sides of the pan. The only downside of using this method is that the sides of the cake will never be as smooth as a cake cooked in a pan lined using the method described above.

Lining the bottom
of a springform cake pan (tin)

5 m

Difficulty: EASY

EQUIPMENT NEEDED
Parchment paper
Scissors

Take a sheet of parchment paper slightly bigger than the base of the springform cake pan (tin) (1).

Unclip the sides of the pan and remove the base. Place the parchment paper over the base (2).

Place the unclipped sides of the springform pan back over the base so that it sits on top of the parchment paper (3).

Close the clip on the side of the springform pan so that the parchment paper is stretched well over the base (4–5).

Using scissors, cut away the excess parchment paper (6).

TIPS AND TRICKS
Lining a springform cake pan (tin) makes it easier to remove the cake from the bottom of the pan when it has not been greased and dusted with flour, as is the case with sponge cake.

How to achieve an even rise

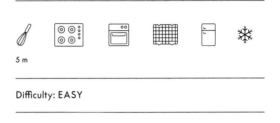

5 m

Difficulty: EASY

EQUIPMENT NEEDED
Kitchen foil

Take a sheet of kitchen foil that is slightly longer than the total circumference of the cake pan (tin) (1).

Along one long side, fold down the foil so you have a strip slightly taller than the sides of the pan (2).

Continue folding the edges of the foil down (3) until you end up with a strip that is just slightly taller than the sides of the pan (4).

Wrap the foil strip around the outside of the pan, pressing well with your fingertips (5–6).

To stop the strip shifting around, fold the foil that extends above the pan over the top edge and down towards the inside (7).

TIPS AND TRICKS
In order to achieve a more even bake, slow the rise of a cake that uses a chemical raising agent by dampening a sheet of kitchen paper, then lightly wringing it out and inserting it between the layers of foil. This trick helps to distribute the heat in a slower and more uniform manner within the pan (tin), preventing the cake from rising too much at the center and forming a dome—the result is a cake with a flatter surface, which is less likely to crack. Some retailers sell reusable fabric "bake-even" cake strips, which are dampened and wrapped around the pan before baking, and promise level cakes with no crowns, cracked tops, or crusty edges.

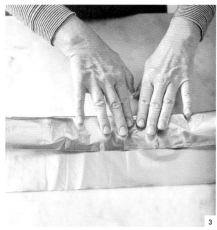

Blind baking

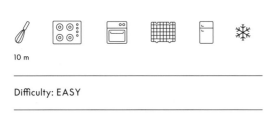

10 m

Difficulty: EASY

EQUIPMENT NEEDED
Scissors
Parchment paper
Ceramic baking beans, dried pulses, or coarse salt

Take a square of parchment paper that is larger than the cake pan (tin) you are going to use. Fold the paper into a rectangle (1).

Fold the paper rectangle in half (2) to form a square (3). Fold the smaller square along its diagonal to obtain a triangle with two equal sides (4) and then again to obtain another triangle (5).

Using scissors, cut across the base of the triangle to neaten (6).

Place the tip of the paper triangle at the center of the pan; the wide base of the triangle should extend above the side of the pan by an inch or a few centimeters (7); once you have measured it, trim away any excess.

Make small cuts along the wide base of the paper triangle of the same length as the depth of the sides of the pan (8).

Unfold the paper triangle (9), place the sheet of parchment paper in the pan over the pastry.

Press the parchment paper down gently so that it clings to the edges of the pan (10).

Fill the lined pan with ceramic baking beans, dried pulses, or coarse salt (11) and spread them evenly over the base, so that the pastry doesn't lose its shape during cooking.

TIPS AND TRICKS
For the best results, after two-thirds of the recommended cooking time for the pastry you are using, remove the baking beans, pulses, or salt, and parchment paper from the tart pan (tin), and then return to the oven to finish cooking.

How to make
a paper cone

5 m

Difficulty: AVERAGE

EQUIPMENT NEEDED
Parchment paper or silicone paper
Scissors, sharp knife, or scalpel

Take a rectangle of parchment paper that measures 13¾ × 17¾ inches/30 × 45cm and fold it carefully along its diagonal so that you have two triangles of the same size (1).

Using a sharp knife or scalpel, cut the paper along the fold (2). Try to slide the sharp blade through the paper to get as clean a cut as possible. You can make a paper cone out of each triangle.

Take one of the resulting paper triangles and hold it at the middle of the longest side between thumb and index finger (3).

Using your other hand, hold the point on the opposite side. The longer side of the triangle should be on your left. Curl the shorter corner on your right over to the corner that is pointing towards you, so that it forms a cone. With your left hand, wrap the longer corner on the left around the tip of the cone twice and then join it together with the other two corners at the back of the cone. (4–5–6).

If the bag still has an open tip at the front, you can close it by wiggling the inner and outer layers of paper back and forth, until the cone forms a small, sharp point (7).

Fold the corners at the open end into the inside of the cone twice to prevent it from unravelling (8–9).

At this point you can fill the paper cone with royal icing or melted chocolate (10). Only ever half-fill the paper cone, otherwise the contents will ooze out of the top when you squeeze on the cone to pipe your decorations. Close the top opening of the cone by folding the side with the seam over to the plain side twice (11).

Using scissors, snip away the tip of the paper cone. Depending on the decorations you are piping, adjust the size of the opening at the tip of the cone—keep the opening small when piping fine decorative lines and make the opening larger when piping frostings and fillings (12).

TIPS AND TRICKS
In the absence of a piping bag or pâtisserie syringe, a paper cone is very useful for creating intricate decoration and lettering. The thumb of one hand pushes on the closed top, allowing the contents to be squeezed out, while the other hand guides the paper cone while decorating.

How to fill a pastry (piping) bag

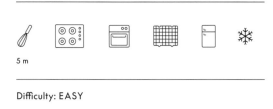

5 m

Difficulty: EASY

EQUIPMENT NEEDED
Disposable pastry (piping) bag
Piping tip (nozzle) in your chosen size and shape
Sharp knife or scissors
Measuring cup, jug, or other container with straight sides
Spatula or spoon

Insert your chosen piping tip (nozzle) into the pastry (piping) bag and push it firmly down into the point (1).

Using a sharp knife or scissors, cut away the point of the pastry bag at about one-third of the way down from the tip of the piping tip (2).

Push the part of the pastry bag near the piping tip inside the piping tip itself, so that the mix does not escape while you are filling the bag (3).

Place the pastry bag inside the straight-sided measuring cup, jug, or container and fold the edges of the bag outwards (4–5).

Fill the pastry bag with the mixture to be piped using a spoon or a spatula (6).

Carefully remove the pastry bag from the cup, jug, or container (7).

Twist the empty top section of the pastry bag in order to push the mixture to be piped down towards the piping tip and expel any air pockets (8).

TIPS AND TRICKS
Using a pastry bag requires some manual dexterity when following the proper technique—it is a good idea to practice your piping before attempting to decorate a full cake. The first step to creating perfect piped decorations is to exert a steady, even pressure on the bag with one hand while you guide the tip of the bag with the other.

Dissolving gelatin

15 m

Difficulty: EASY

INGREDIENTS
Sheet gelatin

EQUIPMENT NEEDED
Pitcher (jug), bowl, or other measuring container

Pour cold water into a pitcher (jug), bowl, or container and place the sheet gelatin in the water (1).

Ensure that the sheets are completely immersed in the water (2).

Leave the sheets to soak in the water for 5 minutes, until they are completely rehydrated and soft (3).

Drain the sheets and squeeze them with your hands to remove as much water as possible (4).

At this point, the gelatin is ready to be added to the warm mixture that is to be thickened (5). Stir until the gelatin has completely dissolved.

TIPS AND TRICKS
Once the soaked sheets are added to a warm mixture, continue to cook the mixture for a few seconds, stirring continuously, without letting the mixture come to the boil. In fact, gelatin starts to dissolve at 98°F/37°C, but its ability to set a mixture and the final result will be compromised if the temperature exceeds 158°F/70°C. When cooling a mixture to which gelatin has been added, the longer this cooling stage takes, the better the mixture will thicken. Therefore, it is not advisable to cool any mixture quickly in the freezer to speed up the setting process.

How to use a
vanilla bean (pod)

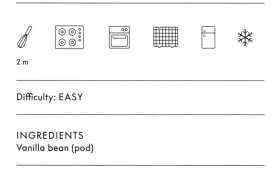

2 m

Difficulty: EASY

INGREDIENTS
Vanilla bean (pod)

EQUIPMENT NEEDED
Chopping board
Sharp knife

Soften the vanilla bean (pod) by pressing on it gently with your fingertips and rolling it between your fingers (1).

Place the vanilla bean on a chopping board, press on it gently and make an incision along its length with a sharp knife (2).

Gently open the vanilla pod along the incision, using your fingers and the knife (3).

Scrape the inside of the pod with the blade of the knife (4) to collect all the dark vanilla seeds, which are now ready to be used (5).

TIPS AND TRICKS
Once the seeds have been removed, do not discard the empty vanilla bean (pod) but instead place it in a jar of sugar to make vanilla sugar. Alternatively, use it to infuse alcohol along with the peel of an unwaxed lemon for a week: the infusion can be used to flavor crèmes and other mixtures.

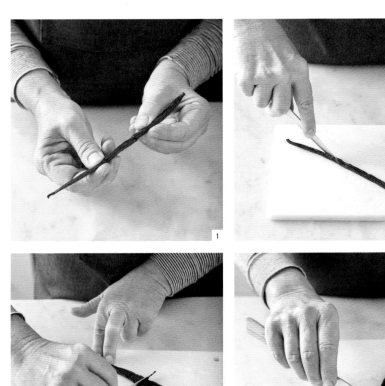

FOR THE BEST RESULTS

SIFTING

MIXING

WHIPPING

WHISKING

SIFTING
— Sifting flour

When you add flour to a mixture that must rise—thanks to the presence of a raising agent or whisked egg whites—the flour must always be sifted to ensure there are no lumps and to incorporate air, making the mixture lighter and more likely to achieve a good rise. Yeast, baking soda (bicarbonate of soda), or other powdered raising agents must always be sifted to eliminate small lumps and to evenly distribute them in the mixture.

MIXING
— Mixing

When you incorporate dry ingredients, such as flour or cocoa, into ingredients full of air, such as whisked egg whites or whipped cream, it is essential to add the sifted dry ingredients a little at a time and blend with the mixture with a silicone spatula using circular movements from the bottom towards the top. This will prevent the air bubbles in the whipped mix from bursting; otherwise, you risk the mixture deflating and not rising as it should during baking, which will affect the final result. When blending mixtures with a spatula, rotate the bowl in a clockwise direction and blend from the edge as well as in the center of the container to avoid the formation of clumps.

WHIPPING
— Whipping cream

In all the recipes that follow, whipping cream always refers to fresh cream and never to long-life (UHT) cream. When whipping cream, it needs to be cold in order to get the best results; keep it at refrigerator temperature—that is, between 35°F/2°C and 39°F/4°C. It is even better still if the mixing bowl and electric whisk attachments have also been chilled in the refrigerator. Start whisking at a low speed and then gradually increase to a faster speed. It is essential not to overwhip the cream—stop when the cream is firm but still smooth. If you go past this point, the cream becomes lumpy and then separates into a liquid and a solid part, becoming unusable. If you add sugar before you start whipping, the cream will not achieve the same volume. For best results, it is advisable to add the sugar towards the end once the cream is partially whipped.

WHISKING
— Whisking egg whites

Whether you whisk egg whites by hand or use an electric whisk or stand mixer, the temperature of the egg whites does not have an impact on the final result. If cold from the refrigerator, egg whites will take longer to whisk than those at room temperature, but at the end of the process the volume and stability will be the same in both cases. At a temperature of between 86°F/30°C and 122°F/50°C, which can be obtained by slightly warming the egg whites in a bain-marie, they will whisk faster and incorporate more air. It is not advisable to add a pinch of salt to the egg whites: salt does make the egg whites foam at the start of the whisking process but then has a negative impact on the final result because, by removing water from the foam, it makes the fragile structure less stable. On the other hand, adding an acidic element—such as a few drops of lemon juice, vinegar, or cream of tartar—helps the whisked egg whites to achieve a more stable structure during cooking and a greater volume. The presence of any fat in the egg whites, caused by a drop of egg yolk or by using a bowl or whisk that is not completely grease-free, reduces the volume obtained at the end of the whisking process by about two-thirds. When the egg whites are whisked with an electric whisk or a stand mixer, you must always start at a low speed, increasing it gradually to the maximum speed as the egg whites are whisked.

HOW TO READ THE RECIPES

BASE PREPARATIONS AND
MAIN RECIPES

PREPARATION, COOKING, AND
STORAGE TIMES

SERVINGS

INGREDIENTS AND EQUIPMENT

FURTHER ADVICE

BASE PREPARATIONS AND MAIN RECIPES

With every baking recipe it is essential to adopt a comprehensive, clear, and intuitive approach. This objective has been the driving force when devising all the recipes in this book; a pâtisserie course in which the base preparations lay the foundation for the main recipes or finished dishes.

In the main recipes, the base preparations are clearly cross-referenced, including the relevant page number so you can find each one easily. In cases where the base preparation has been used without any variation in weight and ingredients, the main recipes will call for "1 quantity" or a simple multiple of the base preparation: for example, listed under ingredients will be "1 quantity of choux pastry" or "2 quantities of tempered milk chocolate." In all other cases the precise weight of the base preparation is given; in these instances, you will need to prepare a sufficient quantity of the base recipe to achieve the weight needed.

In those base preparations that are later subject to significant changes in ingredients or weights when incorporated into a particular recipe, reference will be made to the basic procedure to be followed and the relative ingredients and weights to be used only for that recipe will be given.

PREPARATION, COOKING, AND STORAGE TIMES

Preparation times are calculated to exclude cooking time, unless the cooking phase requires the active presence of the person preparing it. The cooking time on the stove is the total of all the cooking times on the stove and the same applies to cooking time in the oven. For base preparations, the storage times in the refrigerator or freezer are those for the pre-cooked dough or mix. For the other recipes, strict safety margins have been observed: when recipes include creams or crème, this results in shorter storage times.

SERVINGS

Almost all the main recipes serve 8 people, and very occasionally 6 people. This is considered to be the most useful number of portions for a celebration cake. For some recipes, where a substantial number of individual items are made, such as cookies and croissants, an approximate quantity is given. A quantity is given for all the base preparations along with information on whether they can be stored in the refrigerator or freezer and used later.

INGREDIENTS AND EQUIPMENT

With very rare exceptions, the ingredients and equipment required for each base preparation and main recipe have been listed in order of use. Where greater clarity is necessary, ingredients have been divided by preparation: "For the base," "For the crème," "For the frosting," "For decoration," etc. Each equipment list indicates what is needed for mixing, cutting, sifting, etc. The quantities of ingredients need for each recipe are given in imperial or metric measurements, or in volumetric cups. When measuring out your ingredients, do not mix and match but always follow a single set of measurements as the imperial, metric, and cups are not interchangeable.

FURTHER ADVICE

For every basic technique and for many recipes, there is a brief and useful tip or trick for saving time or for making a difficult step easier, to avoid the most common errors and to vary a recipe.

BASIC PREPARATIONS
AND RECIPES

PASTRY

Classic pie dough (shortcrust pastry)

Pasta frolla classica a mano

15 m   1 h   24 h   60 d

Difficulty: AVERAGE

MAKES 1 QUANTITY
(APPROXIMATELY 1 POUND/450 G DOUGH
OR ENOUGH TO LINE A 10-INCH/25-CM TART TIN
OR MAKE A 7-INCH/18-CM DOUBLE CRUST PIE)

FOR THE DOUGH
10½ ounces/2½ cups/300 g type "00" flour or
   all-purpose (plain) flour
5 ounces/½ cup plus 3 tablespoons/150 g cold
   unsalted butter
3 ounces/⅓ cup/80 g superfine (caster) sugar
Grated zest of 1 unwaxed lemon
Pinch of salt
1 egg
2 egg yolks

EQUIPMENT NEEDED
Fine-mesh strainer (sieve)
Zester
Plastic wrap (cling film)

AS USED IN
– Apple and Cinnamon Lattice Pie
   (see page 68)
– Ricotta and Black Cherry Tart with Chocolate
   (see page 70)
– Pistachio Tart with Ruby Chocolate
   (see page 72)
– Chocolate Tartlets with Caramel Mousse
   (see page 74)

Sift the flour into a mound on a clean work surface and make a well in the middle. Cut the cold butter into small cubes and place in the well along with the sugar, lemon zest, and a pinch of salt (1).

Working quickly to ensure the ingredients do not become too warm, rub everything together using your fingertips. (See tricks and tips on page 54.) Starting from the center and working outwards, gradually incorporate all the flour into the butter until the mixture resembles coarse breadcrumbs (2).

Rub the mixture between the palms of your hands (3) to break it down into fine crumbs. When the mixture resembles sand, heap it back into a mound and make a well in the middle, then add the egg and two additional yolks to the well (4).

Using your fingertips, combine all the ingredients (5) then shape the dough (pastry) into a ball, work quickly and do not handle the dough more than necessary (6).

Gently flatten the ball of dough slightly, then wrap it in plastic wrap (cling film) (7). Leave to rest in the refrigerator for at least 1 hour.

If you often use pie dough, you can multiply the ingredients to make more dough and divide it into individual portions. Wrap each portion individually, and place in a freezer bag for freezing.

HOW TO USE
When it is time to use the pie dough, roll it out to ⅛ inch/3 mm thick on a lightly floured surface, then carefully lift the rolled-out dough and transfer it to a prepared pan (tin). Press down firmly on the base and sides and trim away any excess dough with a small sharp knife. Bake as instructed in your recipe.

VARIATIONS
A classic pie dough (shortcrust pastry) can be varied in many ways, for example, by changing the ratio of butter to flour used, the type and quantity of sugar, or replacing some of the flour with ground nuts.

Sweet pie dough is prepared by mixing 9 ounces/2 cups/250 g type "00" flour or all-purpose (plain) flour with 3½ ounces/ 7 tablespoons/100 g unsalted butter, 3 ounces/⅓ cup/80 g confectioners' (icing) sugar, 2 eggs, and a pinch of salt.

Chocolate pie dough is made with 9 ounces/2 cups/250 g type "00" flour or all-purpose (plain) flour, 5 ounces/½ cup plus 2 tablespoons/140 g unsalted butter, ¾ ounce/2 tablespoons/ 20 g sifted unsweetened cocoa powder, 3 ounces/⅓ cup/80 g superfine (caster) sugar, 1 egg, and 1 additional yolk.

Pie dough with nut flour (ground nuts) is made by mixing 9 ounces/ 2 cups/250 g type "00" flour or all-purpose (plain) flour with 3½ ounces/1 cup/100 g nut flour (such as ground almonds, hazelnuts, pistachios, or walnuts), 3½ ounces/1 cup/100 g confectioners' (icing) sugar, 5 ounces/½ cup plus 2 tablespoons/ 140 g unsalted butter, 1 egg, and a pinch of salt.

Pie dough (shortcrust pastry) with egg yolks

Pasta frolla con tuorlo sodo

15 m   1 h   24 h   60 d

Difficulty: AVERAGE

MAKES 1 QUANTITY
(APPROXIMATELY 14 OUNCES/380 G DOUGH
OR ENOUGH TO LINE A 9-INCH/23-CM TART TIN)

FOR THE DOUGH
8 ounces/1⅔ cups/230 g type "00" flour or all-purpose
  (plain) flour
5 ounces/½ cup plus 3 tablespoons/150 g cold
  unsalted butter
2 ounces/½ cup/60 g confectioners' (icing) sugar
Pinch of salt
1 vanilla bean (pod)
3 yolks from hard-boiled eggs

EQUIPMENT NEEDED
Fine-mesh strainer (sieve)
Plastic wrap (cling film)

AS USED IN
– Vanilla Cheesecake with Peaches
  (see page 82)

Sift the flour into a mound on a clean work surface and make a well in the middle (1). Cut the cold butter into small cubes and place in the well along with the sugar, a pinch of salt and the seeds from the vanilla bean (pod).

Working quickly to ensure the ingredients do not become too warm, rub everything together using your fingertips. Starting at the center and working outwards, gradually incorporate all the flour into the butter until the mixture resembles coarse breadcrumbs (2–3).

Gather the mixture back into a mound and make a well in the middle. Using the back of a teaspoon, push one hard-boiled egg yolk at a time through the fine-mesh strainer (sieve) and let it fall straight into the mixture (4). Add all of the hard-boiled egg yolks in the same way.

Using your fingertips, combine the yolks (5) then work the mixture with your hands (6) to form a very soft dough. Work quickly and do not handle the dough more than necessary.

Shape the dough into a ball then gently flatten it slightly (7) and wrap it in plastic wrap (cling film) (8). Leave to rest in the refrigerator for at least 1 hour.

HOW TO USE
When it is time to use the pie dough, on a lightly floured surface, roll it out to ⅛ inch/3 mm thick. Carefully lift the rolled-out dough and transfer it to a prepared pan (tin). Press down firmly on the base and sides and trim away any excess dough with a small sharp knife. Bake as instructed in your recipe.

TIPS AND TRICKS
For all types of classic pie dough (shortcrust pastry), it is very important to prevent the mixture from becoming too warm while it is being worked. Always use cold butter from the refrigerator and handle the dough as little as possible, to ensure it does not become sticky. Instead of using your fingertips, you can use a metal dough scraper or pastry cutter to incorporate the flour into the butter to help keep the mixture cool.

Whipped cookie dough

Pasta frolla montata

15 m			1 h	24 h	60 d

Difficulty: AVERAGE

MAKES 1 QUANTITY
(APPROXIMATELY 28 OUNCES/750 G DOUGH
OR ENOUGH TO MAKE 25 MEDIUM COOKIES)

FOR THE DOUGH
9 ounces/1 cup plus 1 tablespoon/250 g unsalted butter
4 ounces/1 cup plus 2 tablespoons/130 g confectioners'
    (icing) sugar
Grated zest of 1 unwaxed lemon or seeds of 1 vanilla
    bean (pod)
2 eggs
13½ ounces/3 cups/380 g type "00" flour or all-purpose
    (plain) flour
1 egg yolk
Pinch of salt

EQUIPMENT NEEDED
Bowl
Fine-mesh strainer (sieve)
Zester (if using lemon zest)
Stand mixer fitted with whisk attachment or
    electric whisk and bowl
Silicone spatula
Pastry (piping) bag
Baking sheet
Parchment paper

Cut the butter into small cubes, place in a bowl, and bring to room temperature to soften. When the butter is soft, sift the confectioners' (icing) sugar into the bowl with the butter (1). Add the lemon zest or the vanilla seeds and beat the ingredients together, using an electric whisk or stand mixer, until you obtain a smooth cream (2–3).

Add the first egg (4) and a tablespoon of the flour and mix with a spatula until completely incorporated (5).

Add the second egg and the additional egg yolk and quickly mix with the spatula to combine. Sift the remaining flour directly into the mixture (6), add a pinch of salt and quickly mix with the spatula until the dough becomes smooth (7).

Transfer the dough to a pastry (piping) bag (8). Pipe the cookie dough into your desired shape directly onto a baking sheet lined with parchment paper. Before baking, leave the cookies to rest for at least 1 hour in the refrigerator. Bake as instructed in your recipe.

HOW TO USE

Whipped cookie dough is prepared in a very different way to a classic pie dough (shortcrust pastry); here, soft butter is beaten with the other ingredients to obtain a very soft, light dough. This dough can't be rolled out with a rolling pin, like other types of pie dough. Instead, it is mainly used for cookies. Rather than resting in the refrigerator, this dough must be shaped or piped immediately and then chilled in the refrigerator before baking. Shape the cookies using a pastry (piping) bag or a cookie press—allow the mixture to drop directly onto a lined baking sheet. Bake the cookies at 350°F/180°C/160°C Fan/Gas 4 for 10–15 minutes depending on their size, or until set and lightly golden around the edges. The cookies can be dipped in melted chocolate or sandwiched together with buttercream before serving.

Crumble mix
Impasto per crumble

10 m   30–35 m   24 h   60 d

Difficulty: EASY

MAKES 1 QUANTITY
(APPROXIMATELY 14 OUNCES/400 G MIXTURE
OR ENOUGH TO COVER A 10-INCH/25-CM DISH)

FOR THE CRUMBLE TOPPING
9 ounces/2 cups/250 g type "00" flour or all-purpose
   (plain) flour
2 ounces/¼ cup/50 g turbinado (demerara) sugar
5 ounces/½ cup plus 3 tablespoons/150 g cold unsalted
   butter
Pinch of salt
Grated zest of ½ unwaxed orange or lemon, or seeds of
   1 vanilla bean (pod)

FOR THE FRUIT BASE
1 pound 4 ounces/1 kg fruit of your choice
2–4 ounces/¼–½ cup/50–100 g turbinado (demerara)
   sugar, depending on the natural sweetness of the fruit

EQUIPMENT NEEDED
Bowl
10-inch/25-cm ovenproof dish or 8 individual
   ovenproof dishes

AS USED IN
– Plum Crumble
   (see page 92)
– White Chocolate Cremoso with Grapefruit
   (see page 266)

Cut the butter into small cubes place in a bowl. Add the flour to the bowl with a pinch of salt (1).

Working quickly to ensure the ingredients do not become too warm, rub everything together using your fingertips (2).

Gradually incorporate all the flour into the butter until the mixture resembles coarse breadcrumbs (3) and then add the sugar and mix until well combined.

HOW TO USE
Bake as instructed in your recipe. Alternatively, preheat the oven to 400°F/200°C/180°C Fan/Gas 6. Chop your chosen fruit into small chunks and sprinkle with the sugar, if using. Add any flavorings, such as citrus zest. Spoon the fruit into a single ovenproof dish or divide it equally between individual ovenproof dishes (4).

Spoon the crumble mixture onto the fruit pieces, covering them completely (5). Bake in the preheated oven for 30–35 minutes, or until the crumble topping is lightly golden and the fruit is soft and its juices are bubbling around the edges.

MISTAKES TO AVOID
As with other types of dough (pastry), it is very important to prevent the crumble mix from becoming too warm while it is being worked. Always use cold butter from the refrigerator and do not overwork the dough. If soft butter is used or the crumble mix is allowed to get too warm, you will end up with a smooth dough, instead of the characteristic crumb-texture. If this happens, wrap the dough in plastic wrap (cling film) and leave to cool in the refrigerator for 1–2 hours or until firm, then grate it directly onto the fruit using a grater with large holes.

All-butter pie dough (pastry)
Pasta brisée

10 m   25–40 m 1 h   24 h   60 d

Difficulty: AVERAGE

MAKES 1 QUANTITY
(APPROXIMATELY 10 OUNCES/300 G DOUGH
OR ENOUGH TO LINE AN 8-INCH/20-CM TART TIN)

FOR THE DOUGH
7 ounces/1⅔ cups/200 g type "00" flour or all-purpose
   (plain) flour
1 ounce/2 tablespoons/30 g superfine (caster) sugar
Pinch of salt
3½ ounces/7 tablespoons/100 g unsalted butter
1¾ fl oz/3 tablespoons/50 ml water

EQUIPMENT NEEDED
Fine-mesh strainer (sieve)
Metal dough scraper
Measuring cup or jug
Plastic wrap (cling film)

AS USED IN
– Fig-Filled Spelt Cookie Bars
  (see page 80)
– Pineapple Tarte Tatin with Lemon Balm Sorbet
  (see page 86)
– Tartlets with Caramelized Pineapple Compote
  (see page 88)
– Lemon Tart with Sage and Blueberries
  (see page 90)

Sift the flour into a mound on a clean work surface and make a well in the middle. Add the sugar and a pinch of salt (1). Cut the cold butter into small cubes and place in the well along with the sugar and salt (2).

Working quickly to ensure the ingredients do not become too warm, mix the ingredients together using a metal dough scraper (3–4). Starting from the center and working outwards, gradually incorporate all of flour into the butter until the mixture resembles coarse breadcrumbs.

Heap the crumbs back into a mound and make a well in the middle, then add the cold water to the well (5).

Using your fingertips, combine all the ingredients (6) then shape the dough (pastry) into a small block of even thickness (7). Again, work quickly and do not handle the dough more than necessary to prevent it becoming too warm.

Wrap the dough in plastic wrap (cling film) and leave to rest in the refrigerator for at least 1 hour.

HOW TO USE
When ready to use, on a lightly floured surface, roll out the pie dough to ⅛ inch/3 mm thick. Use the rolled-out dough to line a greased or lined pan (tin). Press down firmly on the base and sides, then prick the base of the dough with a fork. Using a sharp knife, trim away any excess dough that is overhanging the sides of the tart pan to neaten. Bake the pastry case as instructed in your recipe. Alternatively, line the pastry case with parchment paper, then fill with baking beans and place in the lower part of the oven preheated to 350°F/180°C/160°C Fan/Gas 4 for 15–25 minutes to blind bake. After 15–25 minutes, remove the baking beans and parchment paper and return to the oven for a further 10–15 minutes or until the pastry case has dried out.

VARIATIONS
For a variation add an egg to the dough: mix 7 ounces/1⅔ cups/ 200 g flour with 3¼ ounces/6 tablespoons/90 g butter, 1 egg, 1 ounce/2 tablespoons/30 g superfine (caster) sugar and a pinch of salt. Once the all-butter pie dough (pastry) has been placed in the pan (tin), leave it to rest in the refrigerator for at least 10 minutes before baking at 350°F/180°C/160°C Fan/Gas 4.

TIPS AND TRICKS
If you often use pie dough, you can multiply the ingredients to make more dough and divide it into individual portions. Wrap each portion individually, and place in a freezer bag for freezing.

Puff pastry
Pasta sfoglia

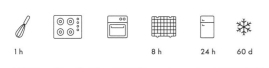

1 h · 8 h · 24 h · 60 d

Difficulty: ADVANCED

MAKES 1 QUANTITY
(APPROXIMATELY 1 POUND 14 OUNCES/850 G
DOUGH OR ENOUGH TO TOP 3 × 8-INCH/
20-CM PIE DISHES)

FOR THE DOUGH
3½ ounces/½ cup/110 g unsalted butter
5 fl oz/scant ⅔ cup/150 ml water
Pinch of salt
12 ounces/2¾ cups/350 g type "00" flour or all-purpose
　(plain) flour
1 tablespoon white wine vinegar or lemon juice

FOR THE BUTTER PASTE
5 ounces/1¼ cups/150 g type "00" flour or all-purpose
　(plain) flour
13½ ounces/1½ cups plus 1 tablespoon/380 g cold butter,
　cut into cubes

EQUIPMENT NEEDED
Bain-marie or double boiler
Measuring cup or jug
Bowls
Plastic wrap (cling film)
Metal dough scraper
Parchment paper
Rolling pin

AS USED IN
– Mille-Feuille with Vanilla Cream
　(see page 94)
– Almond and Chocolate Sfogliata
　(see page 96)
– Classic Cannoncini with Chantilly Cream
　(see page 98)

To make the dough, melt the butter in a bain-marie or double boiler and leave to cool. Measure out the water and add the salt. Place the flour in a bowl and pour in the water. Add the vinegar and melted butter (1). Work the ingredients with your hands to bring them together into a dough (2), then shape into a block (3). Wrap in plastic wrap (cling film) (4) and refrigerate for 2 hours.

To make the butter paste, sift the flour into a mound on a clean surface and make a well in the middle. Place the butter in the well (5). Rub the flour and butter together using your fingertips or a dough scraper, until you obtain a very soft paste (6).

Place the butter paste between two sheets of parchment paper and roll it out with a rolling pin to form a rectangular block (7). Wrap in plastic wrap and let rest in the refrigerator for 2 hours.

Using a rolling pin, roll the chilled dough out on a lightly floured surface to form a rectangle ¼ inch/½ cm thick with the short side of the rectangle facing towards you (8). Flatten the butter paste into a rectangle the same width as the rolled-out dough but a third of its length. Place the butter on top of the dough in the center (9).

Take the short side of the dough closest to you and fold it up and over the butter paste. Fold the other short side of the dough up and towards you to cover the first fold of dough. Turn the dough through 90° so the folds no longer face you and roll the dough out again to form a rectangle just under ½ inch/1 cm thick (10).

Take the short side of the dough closest to you and fold it up and over into the middle of the rectangle, then do the same with the other side, folding the dough up and over so the short sides meet in the center of the rectangle (11). Fold the rectangle in half again, wrap it in plastic wrap, and let rest in the refrigerator for 2 hours.

Position the dough with the short side closest to you and roll it into a rectangle ½ inch/1 cm thick (12). Fold the lower third of the dough up and away from you, then fold the upper third up and towards you to cover the first fold of dough. Wrap the block in plastic wrap and let rest in the refrigerator for 1 hour. Repeat this stage a further 4 times, to make a total of 6 stages, and always leave the dough to rest in the refrigerator between each stage.

HOW TO USE
When it is time to use the dough, bake as instructed in your recipe.

MISTAKES TO AVOID
When folding the dough for the first time, it can be difficult to keep the butter paste inside. When rolling out the dough, leaving it a little thicker in the middle helps to hold the butter in its center. If the butter escapes, refrigerate the dough for 2 hours then start the folding process again. Allow adequate chilling time between each stage so the dough is firm but not solid, and do not repeat the process more than 6 times. After this, the butter and dough merge and cannot achieve the desired flaky texture. The flakiness is due to the water contained in the butter. When heated, it creates a vapor that remains trapped between the layers of dough. This causes the individual layers of dough to delaminate and the pastry to puff up.

Rough puff pastry

Pasta sfoglia veloce

1 h   1 h 30 m   24 h   60 h

Difficulty: ADVANCED

MAKES 1 QUANTITY
(APPROXIMATELY 2 POUNDS 6 OUNCES/1.1 KG
DOUGH OR ENOUGH TO TOP 3 × 10-INCH/
25-CM PIE DISHES)

FOR THE DOUGH
1 pound 2 ounces/2 cups plus 2 tablespoons/
   500 g unsalted butter
3½ fl oz/scant ½ cup/100 ml ice-cold water
1 pound 2 ounces/4 cups/500 g type "00" flour or
   all-purpose (plain) flour
Pinch of salt

EQUIPMENT NEEDED
Measuring cup or jug
Metal dough scraper
Rolling pin
Plastic wrap (cling film)

Cut the butter into small cubes and bring to room temperature to soften. Measure out the water and place in the refrigerator to chill. Sift the flour into a mound on a clean work surface and make a well in the middle. Add the butter and a pinch of salt (1).

Using your fingertips, rub everything together. Starting from the center and working outwards, gradually incorporate all the flour into the butter until the mixture resembles coarse breadcrumbs, but leave some small lumps of butter that are not completely incorporated (2).

Add the very cold water to the crumbly mixture. Working quickly to ensure the ingredients do not become too warm, mix the ingredients together to form a dough, using your hands or a metal dough scraper (3).

Lightly dust a clean surface with flour (4). Roll out the dough with a rolling pin (5). Flatten the dough further with the palms of your hands to approximately 1 inch/2.5cm thick and shape it into a rectangle (6).

Roll out the dough into a rectangle ½ inch/1 cm thick so the short side of the rectangle faces towards you (7).

Taking hold of the short side that is furthest away from you, fold the upper third of the dough up and towards you to cover the middle third of the rectangle. Then fold the lower third up and away from you to cover the first fold of dough (8). Wrap the block in plastic wrap (cling film) and leave to rest in the refrigerator for 30 minutes.

Once chilled, unwrap the dough and return it to the lightly floured surface. Position the dough so the short side of the rectangular block faces towards you (9). Roll out the dough to form a rectangle ½ inch/1 cm thick (10).

Taking hold of the short side that is nearest to you, fold the lower third of the dough up and away from you to cover the middle third of the rectangle (11). Then fold the upper third up and towards you to cover the first fold of dough (12). Wrap the block in plastic wrap and leave to rest in the refrigerator for 30 minutes.

Repeat this stage 2 more times, to make a total of 4 stages, and always leave the dough to rest in the refrigerator for 30 minutes between each stage.

HOW TO USE
When it is time to use the dough, bake as instructed in your recipe.

TIPS AND TRICKS
Rough puff pastry can be made ahead, then stored in the freezer or refrigerator to use at a later date. When the dough is thawed, you can shape and bake the dough as instructed in your recipe. Rough puff pastry is usually baked at 400°F/200°C/180°C Fan/Gas 6 or above. To prevent the pastry from shrinking during baking, leave it to rest in the refrigerator for 30 minutes after rolling and shaping.

Strudel dough (pastry)

Pasta da strudel

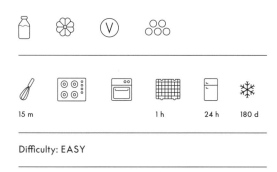

15 m

1 h

24 h

180 d

Difficulty: EASY

MAKES 1 QUANTITY
(APPROXIMATELY 10½ OUNCES/300 G DOUGH
OR ENOUGH TO MAKE A 16-INCH/40-CM STRUDEL)

FOR THE DOUGH
9 ounces/2 cups/250 g type "00" flour or all-purpose
    (plain) flour
Pinch of salt
1 tablespoon extra-virgin olive oil
4 fl oz/½ cup/125 ml water

EQUIPMENT NEEDED
Bowls
Fine-mesh strainer (sieve)
Measuring cup or jug
Plastic wrap (cling film)
Rolling pin
Dish towel (tea towel) or parchment paper

AS USED IN
– Mille-Feuille with White Chocolate and Apricots
  (see page 100)
– Classic Apple Strudel
  (see page 102)

Sift the flour directly into a bowl and add a pinch of salt and a tablespoon of extra-virgin olive oil (1).

Add the water to the bowl (2).

Using your hands, mix the ingredients, first in the bowl (3) and then on a clean work surface (4), until you obtain a smooth, soft dough (pastry).

Place the dough in a clean bowl, cover it with plastic wrap (cling film) and leave to rest for 1 hour at room temperature. (Do not refrigerate the dough as it will become too cold to stretch.)

On a lightly floured surface, slightly flatten the dough (5) and start to roll it out using a rolling pin (6).

When the dough starts to get thinner, move it onto a large, clean dish towel (tea towel), lightly dusted with flour (7), or a large sheet of parchment paper.

Keep rolling out the dough until it is very thin and transparent–to the point you can almost see your hands through it.

HOW TO USE
When it is time to use the dough, bake as instructed in your recipe. Alternatively, wrap the strudel around a savory or sweet filling and shape into one long roll or use the dough to make individual samosa-style parcels. Bake in a 400°F/200°C/180°C Fan/Gas 6 oven until lightly golden and crisp.

TIPS AND TRICKS
Like other flour-based doughs, leaving the strudel dough to rest is essential to ensure the gluten matrix activated during the dough's preparation becomes more elastic—this makes the dough easier to roll out. Without this resting time, when the dough is rolled out, it will not be as elastic and is likely to shrink. If a hole forms when you roll out the strudel dough, lightly dampen the edges of the tear, overlap them and gently press with floury fingers to seal.

As it is rolled out very thinly, this strudel pastry dries out very quickly once rolled out and so it needs to be covered with either plastic wrap (cling film) or a clean, non-terry cloth dish towel (tea towel) and should then be used as quickly as possible.

APPLE AND CINNAMON LATTICE PIE

Pie di mele e canella intrecciato

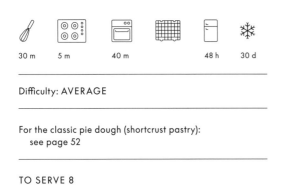

30 m   5 m   40 m   48 h   30 d

Difficulty: AVERAGE

For the classic pie dough (shortcrust pastry):
see page 52

TO SERVE 8

FOR THE PASTRY SHELL (CASE)
Butter, for greasing
1½ quantities (23 ounces/650 g) of classic pie dough
(shortcrust pastry) prepared following the base recipe
on page 52
Flour, for dusting

FOR THE PIE FILLING
½ ounce/1 tablespoon/15 g unsalted butter
2 ounces/1 cup/60 g fresh breadcrumbs
1 teaspoon ground cinnamon
3 ounces/¾ cup/80 g shelled walnuts
Grated zest of 1 unwaxed lemon
2½ ounces/½ cup/70 g turbinado (demerara) sugar
1 pound 2 ounces/500 g Golden Delicious apples
1 egg yolk

EQUIPMENT NEEDED
Small saucepan
Rolling pin
7-inch/18-cm loose-bottomed, fluted tart pan (tin)
with deep sides
Food processor
Zester
Apple corer
Pastry wheel with smooth blade
Pastry brush
Cooling rack

Preheat the oven to 350°F/180°C/160°C Fan/Gas 4 and grease the tart pan (tin) with a little butter.

To make the pie filling, melt the butter in a small saucepan, add the breadcrumbs and sauté them over medium heat until they start to brown. Add the cinnamon to the pan, stir, and set aside to cool.

On a lightly floured surface, roll out half of the pie dough (pastry) to ⅛ inch/3 mm thick. Carefully lift the rolled-out pie dough and use it to line the prepared tart pan. Press down firmly on the base and sides, then prick the base of the dough with a fork. Using a sharp knife, trim away any excess dough that is overhanging the sides of the tart pan to neaten. Sprinkle the toasted breadcrumbs over the base.

Finely chop the walnuts in the food processor, then combine with the lemon zest and 2 ounces/⅓ cup/50 g of the sugar. Peel the apples, use the corer to remove the core, then slice them thinly. Place a layer of apple slices over the breadcrumbs in the pastry shell (case) and sprinkle with a little of the walnut mixture. Repeat the layers until all the ingredients have been used.

Roll out the remaining pie dough and any scraps to ⅛ inch/3 mm thick. Using the pastry wheel, cut into strips about 1 inch/3 cm wide. Weave the pastry strips into a lattice pattern over the top of the apples, leaving even spaces between each strip. Trim the pastry lattice and then stick the ends of the strips onto the pastry shell edges, pressing down with a finger, and cut away any excess.

To make an egg wash, mix the egg yolk with a few drops of cold water. Using a pastry brush, glaze the pastry with the egg wash and then sprinkle over the remaining sugar. Place the pie in the lower part of the preheated oven and bake for 40 minutes, or until golden. Let cool for 15 minutes in the tart pan, then remove from the pan, and transfer to a cooling rack to cool completely before serving.

RICOTTA AND BLACK CHERRY TART WITH CHOCOLATE

Crostata di ricotta e amarene con cioccolato

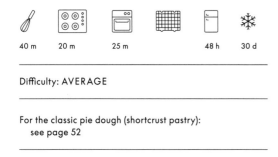

40 m   20 m   25 m   48 h   30 d

Difficulty: AVERAGE

For the classic pie dough (shortcrust pastry):
see page 52

TO SERVE 8

FOR THE BASE
Butter, for greasing
1 quantity (14 ounces/400 g) of classic pie dough (shortcrust
pastry) prepared following the base recipe on page 52

FOR THE FILLING
10½ ounces/generous 2 cups/300 g black cherries
3½ ounces/scant ½ cup/100 g superfine (caster) sugar
17½ ounces/2 cups/500 g whole (full-fat) sheep's
or cow's milk ricotta
3½ fl oz/scant ½ cup/100 ml heavy (whipping) cream
1 vanilla bean (pod)
2 ounces/⅓ cup/50 g bittersweet (dark) chocolate,
finely chopped

EQUIPMENT NEEDED
Pitting tool
Saucepan
Skimmer
Fine-mesh strainer (sieve)
Silicone spatula
Rolling pin
3 × 14-inch/8 × 34-cm loose bottomed
rectangular tart pan (tin)
Baking beans
Cooling rack

Preheat the oven to 350°F/180°C/160°C Fan/Gas 4. Grease the tart pan (tin) with a little butter.

On a lightly floured surface, roll out the pie dough (pastry) to ⅛ inch/3 mm thick. Carefully lift the rolled-out pie dough and use it to line the prepared tart pan. Press down firmly on the base and sides, then prick the base of the dough with a fork. Using a sharp knife, trim away any excess dough that is overhanging the sides of the tart pan to neaten.

Line the pastry case with parchment paper, fill with baking beans, and place in the lower part of the preheated oven for 20 minutes to blind bake. After 20 minutes, remove the baking beans and parchment paper and return to the oven for a further 5 minutes, or until the pastry case is golden. Remove from the oven and leave to cool in the pan for 10 minutes, then remove the pastry case from the pan and leave to cool completely on a cooling rack.

Meanwhile, to make the filling, wash and pit (stone) the black cherries using the pitting tool, remove the stalks and place in a saucepan with the sugar. Bring to a boil over medium heat and cook for 10 minutes. Remove the cherries with a skimmer and set aside. Leave the cooking juice to reduce to a syrup that thinly coats the back of a spoon. Add the cherries back to the syrup, remove from the heat and leave to cool.

Pass the ricotta through a fine-mesh strainer (sieve) into a bowl, pressing down with a silicone spatula to form a smooth, uniform cream. Add the cream and seeds from the vanilla bean (pod) to the ricotta and whisk until light and creamy. Gently fold the chopped chocolate through the ricotta cream.

Spoon the ricotta mix into the baked pastry case and spread it evenly into all corners. Top with the cooked cherries and drizzle over the remaining syrup.

PISTACHIO TART WITH RUBY CHOCOLATE

Torta al pistacchio con cioccolato rosa

40 m   5 m   35 m   2 h   48 h   30 d

Difficulty: AVERAGE

For the classic pie dough (shortcrust pastry):
   see page 52 for the method, but use the ingredients
   listed below to make a pistachio pie dough

TO SERVE 8

FOR THE BASE
7 ounces/1¼ cups/200 g type "00" flour or all-purpose
   (plain) flour
3½ ounces/⅔ cup/100 g shelled pistachios
3½ ounces/7 tablespoons/100 g unsalted butter,
   plus extra for greasing
3 ounces/⅔ cup/80 g confectioners' (icing) sugar
Pinch of salt
1 egg

FOR THE GANACHE
6½ ounces/180 g ruby chocolate
7 fl oz/scant 1 cup/200 ml heavy (whipping) cream
1½ ounces/3 tablespoons/40 g unsalted butter
1 ounce/30 g beaten egg
1 egg yolk

TO DECORATE
¾ ounce/20 g ruby chocolate
¾ ounce/2½ tablespoons/20 g shelled pistachios

EQUIPMENT NEEDED
Food processor
Rolling pin
8-inch/20-cm round loose-bottomed tart pan (tin)
Baking beans
Parchment paper
Bowls
Measuring cup or jug
Small saucepan
Silicone spatula
Grater with large holes

Preheat the oven to 350°F/180°C/160°C Fan/Gas 4. Grease the tart pan (tin) with a little butter.

Blitz the flour and pistachios in the food processor to a fine, smooth powder. Use this, plus the ingredient quantities listed on this page, to prepare the pistachio pie dough (shortcrust pastry) following the method given on page 52.

On a lightly floured surface, roll out the pie dough (pastry) to ⅛ inch/3 mm thick. Carefully lift the rolled-out pie dough and use it to line the prepared tart pan. Press down firmly on the base and sides, then prick the base of the dough with a fork. Using a sharp knife, trim away any excess dough that is overhanging the sides of the tart pan to neaten.

Line the pastry case with parchment paper, fill with baking beans, and place in the lower part of the preheated oven for 20 minutes to blind bake. After 20 minutes, remove the baking beans and parchment paper and return to the oven for a further 5 minutes, or until the pastry case has dried out and is golden. Remove from the oven and reduce the oven temperature to 325°F/160°C/140°C Fan/Gas 3.

To make the ganache, finely chop the ruby chocolate and set aside in a bowl. Pour the cream into a small saucepan, set over low heat and bring almost to boiling point, then pour it over the chocolate, continuously stirring with a silicone spatula until it has melted. Cut the butter into small cubes and add, along with the beaten egg and the yolk, and mix to combine.

Pour the ganache onto the pie dough base and spread evenly. Bake in the middle part of the oven for 10 minutes. Remove from the oven and leave to rest in the pan for 10 minutes, then place in the refrigerator for 2 hours. Once cool, remove from the pan and slice to serve or slice while still in the pan. To serve, decorate with more grated ruby chocolate and some finely chopped pistachios.

CHOCOLATE TARTLETS WITH CARAMEL MOUSSE

Tartellette al cacao con mousse al caramello

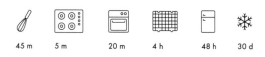

45 m   5 m   20 m   4 h   48 h   30 d

Difficulty: ADVANCED

For the chocolate pie dough (shortcrust pastry):
  see page 52 for the method, but use the ingredients
  listed below to make a chocolate pie dough
For the decorative caramel:
  see page 324 for the method, but use the ingredients
  listed below to make a decorative caramel

MAKES 8 TARTLETS

FOR THE BASE
10 ounces/2¼ cups/280 g type "00" flour or all-purpose
  (plain) flour
4 ounces/½ cup/120 g unsalted butter, plus extra
  for greasing
1½ ounces/⅓ cup/40 g unsweetened cocoa powder
3 ounces/⅓ cup/80 g superfine (caster) sugar
Pinch of salt
1 egg
1 egg yolk

FOR THE MOUSSE
¹⁄₁₄ ounce/2 g platinum gelatin sheets
4 fl oz/½ cup/120 ml heavy (whipping) cream
3¼ ounces/scant ½ cup/90 g superfine (caster) sugar
2 ounces/3 tablespoons/50 g unsalted butter
7 ounces/¾ cup plus 1 tablespoon/200 g cream cheese

FOR THE DECORATIVE CARAMEL
2 ounces/¼ cup/50 g sugar
1 tablespoon/12 ml water

TO DECORATE
3 ounces/80 g bittersweet (dark) chocolate

EQUIPMENT NEEDED
Small baking sheet
Parchment paper
Bowl
Saucepans
Measuring cup or jug
Immersion (stick) blender
Silicone spatula
6 × 5-inch/12-cm round loose-bottomed tartlet pans (tins)
Rolling pin
6-inch/15-cm round pastry cutter
Baking beans
Cooling rack
Squeeze bottle or pastry (piping) bag
Bain-marie or double boiler

Using the ingredients quantities listed on this page, prepare the caramel following the instructions on page 324, pour onto a small baking sheet lined with parchment paper, and leave to cool.

To make the mousse, soak the gelatin in cold water for 5 minutes. Pour the cream into a saucepan, place over low heat and bring almost to boiling point. Place the sugar in a separate small saucepan and cook over low heat until completely melted and then increase the heat to medium until the sugar forms an amber-colored caramel. Remove from the heat and gradually add the hot cream, then mix, taking care to avoid splashes. Cut the butter into small cubes, add to the pan and blitz with an immersion (stick) blender. Drain the water from the gelatin and squeeze it dry, add to the pan and stir until it has dissolved. Leave to cool slightly.

Place the cream cheese in a bowl and stir with a silicone spatula until smooth. Slowly drizzle the caramel into the cream cheese and blitz with an immersion blender. Place the mousse in the refrigerator for 4 hours.

Preheat the oven to 350°F/180°C/160°C Fan/Gas 4. Grease the tartlet pans (tins) with a little butter.

Using the ingredient quantities listed on this page, prepare the chocolate pie dough (pastry) following the instructions on page 52.

On a lightly floured surface, roll out the pie dough (pastry) to ⅛ inch/3 mm thick. Using the pastry cutter, cut out pastry disks slightly larger than the prepared tartlet pans. Place a pastry disk into each pan. If necessary, re-roll any scraps to give enough disks. Press down firmly on the base and sides, then prick the base of the dough with a fork. Using a sharp knife, trim away any excess dough that is overhanging the sides of the tart pan to neaten.

Line the pastry cases with parchment paper, fill with baking beans, and place in the lower part of the preheated oven for 15 minutes to blind bake. After 15 minutes, remove the baking beans and parchment paper and return to the oven for a further 5 minutes, or until the pastry cases have dried out. Remove from the oven. Remove from the pans and leave to cool completely on a cooling rack.

Fill the pastry cases with the caramel mousse using a squeeze bottle or pastry (piping) bag, then place them in the refrigerator for 30 minutes or until ready to serve. Finely chop the chocolate, melt it in a bain-marie or double boiler and pour it into a paper cone made with parchment paper. Drizzle the melted chocolate in fine lines over the prepared tartlets and decorate with small pieces of broken caramel. Serve when the chocolate has set.

SPICED OAT COOKIES

Biscotti speziati all'avena

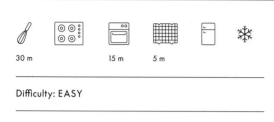

30 m   15 m   5 m

Difficulty: EASY

MAKES 24 COOKIES

FOR THE COOKIES
3½ ounces/¾ cup/100 g type "00" flour or all-purpose
   (plain) flour
3½ ounces/¾ cup/100 g organic whole-wheat
   (wholemeal) flour
½ ounce/2 teaspoons/10 g baking soda (bicarbonate
   of soda)
Pinch of salt
9 ounces/2¾ cups/250 g quick cooking oats (rolled oats)
3 ounces/generous ⅓ cup/80 g superfine (caster) sugar
1 teaspoon ground cinnamon
1 teaspoon ground ginger
3½ ounces/7 tablespoons/100 g unsalted butter
1 lemon
2 eggs
1½ ounces/2 tablespoons/40 g acacia honey
26 almonds with skins on

EQUIPMENT NEEDED
Bowl
Fine-mesh strainer (sieve)
Juicer
Rolling pin
2½-inch/6-cm round pastry cutter
Baking sheet
Parchment paper

Preheat the oven to 350°F/180°C/160°C Fan/Gas 4.

Sift both the flours into a bowl with the baking soda (bicarbonate of soda) and pinch of salt. Add the oats, sugar, and spices. Cut the cold butter into small cubes and add to the bowl. Working quickly to ensure the ingredients do not become too warm, rub everything together using your fingertips until the mixture resembles breadcrumbs.

Juice the lemon and pour through a fine-mesh strainer (sieve) into the bowl, add the eggs and honey, and work quickly into a smooth dough. On a lightly floured surface, roll out the dough to ½ inch/ 1 cm thick. Use the pastry cutter to cut out 24 circles, place them on a baking sheet lined with parchment paper and leave to rest for 5 minutes at room temperature.

Gently press an almond into the top of each cookie. Bake the cookies in the preheated oven for 15 minutes and leave to cool on the baking sheet before serving.

These cookies can be stored in an airtight container for up to 3–4 days.

TIPS AND TRICKS
If you would rather use skinned (blanched) almonds, soak them in cold water for 20 minutes before placing them on the cookies, this will prevent them from darkening too much during baking.

RHUBARB TART WITH ROBIOLA CREAM

Tarte al rabarbaro con crema di robiola

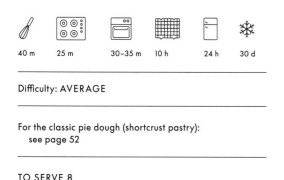

40 m   25 m   30–35 m   10 h   24 h   30 d

Difficulty: AVERAGE

For the classic pie dough (shortcrust pastry):
    see page 52

TO SERVE 8

FOR THE BASE
¾ quantity (12 ounces/350 g) of classic pie dough
    (shortcrust pastry) prepared following the base recipe
    on page 52

FOR THE COMPOTE
½ ounce/10 g platinum gelatin sheets
1 vanilla bean (pod)
14 ounces/400 g rhubarb
4½ ounces/⅔ cup/140 g superfine (caster) sugar
3 tablespoons/40 ml water

FOR THE CREAM
½ ounce/10 g platinum gelatin sheets
10½ ounces/1⅓ cups/300 g Robiola cheese (or use
    full-fat cream cheese)
2 ounces/scant ½ cup/50 g confectioners' (icing) sugar
1 vanilla bean (pod)
7 fl oz/scant 1 cup/200 ml heavy (whipping) cream
½ ounce/10 g bittersweet (dark) chocolate, to decorate

EQUIPMENT NEEDED
Rolling pin
Parchment paper
9-inch/23-cm loose-bottomed fluted tart pan (tin)
    with deep sides
Baking beans
Bowls
Peeler
Saucepan
Measuring cup or jug
Immersion (stick) blender
Silicone spatula
Small saucepan
Spatula or palette knife
Vegetable peeler

Preheat the oven to 350°F/180°C/160°C Fan/Gas 4. Grease the tart pan (tin) with a little butter.

On a lightly floured surface, roll out the pie dough (pastry) to ⅛ inch/3 mm thick. Carefully lift the rolled-out pie dough and use it to line the prepared tart pan. Press down firmly on the base and sides, then prick the base of the dough with a fork. Using a sharp knife, trim away any excess dough that is overhanging the sides of the tart pan to neaten.

Line the pastry case with parchment paper, fill with baking beans, and place in the lower part of the preheated oven for 25 minutes to blind bake. After 25 minutes, remove the baking beans and parchment paper and return to the oven for a further 5–10 minutes, or until the pastry case has dried out and is golden. Remove from the oven and leave to cool.

To make the rhubarb compote, soak the gelatin in cold water for 5 minutes. Split the vanilla bean (pod) lengthwise and scrape out the seeds and set aside. Peel the rhubarb, cut it into small chunks and place in a saucepan with the sugar, water, and the empty vanilla bean. Cook over medium heat for 20 minutes, stirring often, until you obtain a smooth mixture, then remove the vanilla bean. Squeeze the water from the gelatin, add to the pan and stir until it has dissolved. Turn the heat off and blitz with an immersion (stick) blender. Leave to cool, then pour the compote on the tart base. Leave in the refrigerator for 2 hours, or until set.

To make the topping, beat the Robiola cheese with the confectioners' (icing) sugar and the reserved seeds from the vanilla bean until you obtain a smooth consistency. Using a silicone spatula, pile the topping on top of the set rhubarb compote, spreading it out to the edges of the tart in an even layer.

To serve, remove from the tart pan and place it on a serving plate and shred (grate) over some bittersweet (dark) chocolate. Leave to reach room temperature for 30 minutes before serving.

FIG-FILLED SPELT COOKIE BARS

Biscotti al farro ripieni ai fichi

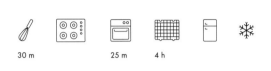

30 m   25 m   4 h

Difficulty: AVERAGE

For the all-butter pie dough (pastry):
    see page 60 for the method, but use the ingredients
    listed below to make a spelt pie dough

TO SERVE 8 (MAKES 16 COOKIES)

FOR THE DOUGH
12 ounces/3 cups/350 g organic spelt flour
¼ ounce/2 teaspoons/7 g baking powder
3 ounces/⅓ cup/80 g superfine (caster) sugar
Pinch of salt
3 ounces/5 tablespoons/80 g unsalted butter
3½ fl oz/½ cup/125 ml whole (full-fat) milk

FOR THE FILLING
10½ ounces/2 cups/300 g dried figs
2½ ounces/¼ cup/70 g acacia honey
Grated zest and juice of 1 unwaxed lemon

TO DECORATE
¾ ounce/5 teaspoons/20 g turbinado (demerara) sugar

EQUIPMENT NEEDED
Bowls
Food processor
Zester
Juicer
9-inch/23-cm square cake (pan) with deep sides
Parchment paper
Rolling pin
Silicone spatula
Chopping board

To make the filling, soak the dried figs in cold water for 4 hours. Drain, remove the stalks, cut into small pieces and place in the food processor with the honey. Add the grated zest from the lemon, then juice the lemon and pour the juice into the processor a little at a time as you blitz, until you obtain a thick paste.

Using the ingredients and quantities listed on this page, prepare the all-butter pie dough (pastry) following the instructions on page 60.

Preheat the oven to 400°F/200°C/180°C Fan/Gas 6. Line the cake pan (tin) with parchment paper.

Divide the dough into two equal pieces. On a lightly floured surface, roll out one piece into a rectangle the same size as the cake pan and place in the bottom of the pan. Trim off any excess dough with a small sharp knife then spread the fig puree filling over the dough. Roll out the other portion of dough to a rectangle the same size as the cake pan and place on top of the fig puree. Press down gently with the palms of your hands to seal, and trim off any excess dough around the edge of the pan.

Sprinkle the turbinado (demerara) sugar over the top layer of dough and cook in the preheated oven for 25 minutes until golden. Leave to cool completely in the baking sheet, then transfer to a chopping board and cut into 16 bars.

These cookie bars can be stored in an airtight container for up to 3–4 days.

VANILLA CHEESECAKE WITH PEACHES

Cheesecake alla vaniglia e pesche

30 m   1 h 45 m   4 h 15 m   48 h   30 d

Difficulty: AVERAGE

For the pie dough (shortcrust pastry) with egg yolks:
   see page 54

TO SERVE 8

FOR THE BASE
1 quantity (14 ounces/380 g) pie dough (shortcrust pastry)
   with egg yolks prepared following the base recipe
   on page 54

FOR THE FILLING
14 ounces/1¾ cups plus 2 tablespoons/400 g cream cheese
   (at room temperature)
5 ounces/⅔ cup/150 g well-drained Greek yogurt
   (at room temperature)
4 ounces/½ cup/120 g superfine (caster) sugar
1 vanilla bean (pod)
2 eggs
1 egg yolk
1½ ounces/⅓ cup/40 g cornstarch (cornflour)

TO DECORATE
1 white peach
1 yellow peach
Edible lavender flowers

EQUIPMENT NEEDED
7-inch/18-cm round springform pan (tin)
Parchment paper
Rolling pin
Baking beans
Bowl
Silicone spatula

Preheat the oven to 325°F/160°C/140°C Fan/Gas 3. Line the base of the springform pan (tin) with parchment paper.

On a lightly floured surface, roll out the pie dough (pastry) into a 7-inch/18-cm round, that is ½ inch/1 cm thick. Cut out a disk from the dough using the springform pan as a cutter.

Assemble the springform pan by clipping the sides around the lined base. Carefully lift the dough disk and use it to cover the base of the pan. Prick the dough with a fork, cover it with parchment paper, and cover with baking beans. Place in the lower part of the preheated oven for 35 minutes to blind bake. After 35 minutes, remove the baking beans and parchment paper and return to the oven for a further 15–20 minutes, or until the pastry base has dried out and is golden. Remove from the oven and reduce the oven temperature to 300°F/150°C/130°C Fan/Gas 2.

To make the filling, beat the cream cheese with the spatula until it is smooth, then add the yogurt, sugar, the seeds from the vanilla bean (pod), the eggs and the additional yolk. Mix with the spatula until combined. Mix in the cornstarch (cornflour), then pour the filling onto the cheesecake base.

Bake in the preheated oven for 50 minutes, or until the cheesecake is just set. Leave to rest in the turned-off oven for 15 minutes before removing to cool completely. When cool, refrigerate the cheesecake for at least 4 hours.

To serve, remove the cheesecake from the springform pan and place it on a serving dish. Decorate with the sliced peaches and lavender flowers.

TIPS AND TRICKS
If you want a lighter, more airy cheesecake, separate the egg whites from the yolks and, using an electric whisk, beat the whites with the sugar to soft peaks. (Do not whisk the egg whites to stiff peaks as the mixture will be too stiff to fold in easily and the extra air could cause the cheesecake to puff up and then sink back down.) Add the egg whites to the cream cheese and yogurt mixture and gently fold in.

The cream cheese and yogurt should both be at room temperature as generally this gives a smoother cheesecake filling once baked.

WAFERS WITH PISTACHIO CREAM AND FOREST FRUITS

Cialdine con crema di pistacchi e frutti di bosco

20 m   5–6 m

Difficulty: EASY

TO SERVE 8

FOR THE WAFERS
2 ounces/¼ cup/60 g unsalted butter
2 ounces/generous ¼ cup/60 g superfine (caster) sugar
2 ounces/60 g egg whites (approximately 2 large
  egg whites)
2 ounces/½ cup/60 g type "00" flour or all-purpose
  (plain) flour
Pinch of salt

FOR THE PISTACHIO CREAM
2 ounces/¼ cup/60 g unsweetened pistachio paste
7 fl oz/scant 1 cup/200 ml heavy (whipping) cream

TO DECORATE
3½ ounces/⅔ cup/100 g mixed berries (forest fruits)
2 tablespoons dried rose petals

EQUIPMENT NEEDED
Bowl
Electric whisk
Fine-mesh strainer (sieve)
Pastry (piping) bag
⅛-in/3-mm plain piping tip (nozzle)
Baking sheet
Parchment paper
1-inch/3-cm round petit-fours silicone molds
Immersion (stick) blender

Preheat the oven to 400°F/200°C/180°C Fan/Gas 6. Line the baking sheet with parchment paper. Cut the butter into small cubes, place in a bowl, and bring to room temperature to soften.

Using an electric whisk, beat the softened butter with the sugar until smooth and creamy. Add the egg whites, sift the flour into the bowl, add a pinch of salt, and mix until you have a smooth, runny mixture. Transfer to the pastry (piping) bag fitted with a ⅛-inch/3-mm plain piping tip (nozzle).

Working in batches, pipe the mixture onto the prepared baking sheet in very thin disks, about 2½ inches/6 cm in diameter, and leaving a 2-inch/5-cm space between each disk to allow for them to spread during baking. Bake the wafers in the preheated oven for 5–6 minutes, until they start to turn golden at the edges.

While still warm, carefully remove the wafers from the parchment paper and place in the silicone molds, gently shaping them into cups with your fingers. Leave to cool.

To make the pistachio cream, place the pistachio paste and cream in a bowl and blitz together with an immersion (stick) blender to make a smooth cream. Place half a teaspoon of pistachio cream into each wafer. Top with one or two berries or forest fruits, then scatter over the dried rose petals. Serve immediately.

MISTAKES TO AVOID
The wafer dough tends to harden as it cools, so bake the piped disks in small batches and set the cooked wafers in the silicone molds as soon as they are cool enough to handle safely. If you find they have cooled too much and are no longer pliable, place the wafers back in the oven for 30 seconds to soften.

TIPS AND TRICKS
To make your own pistachio paste, place shelled and skinned pistachios in a high-speed blender or food processor and blitz briefly. Do not process the nuts for too long, though, as they can turn oily.

PINEAPPLE TARTE TATIN WITH LEMON BALM SORBET

Tatin di ananas con zenzero e sorbetto

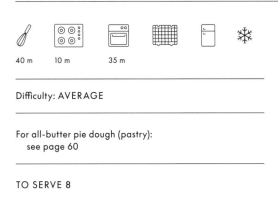

40 m   10 m   35 m

Difficulty: AVERAGE

For all-butter pie dough (pastry):
  see page 60

TO SERVE 8

FOR THE PASTRY SHELL (CASE)
Butter, for greasing
1 quantity (9 ounces/250 g) all-butter pie dough (pastry),
  prepared with eggs and following the base recipe
  on page 60

FOR THE FILLING
1 pineapple, approximately 3 pounds 5 ounces/1.5 kg
1 ounce/2 tablespoons/30 g unsalted butter
2 ounces/¼ cup/50 g superfine (caster) sugar
1 ounce/1½-inch piece/30 g fresh ginger
2 lemon balm sprigs (or use a mixture of lemon verbena
  and mint sprigs)

FOR THE SORBET
4 lemon balm sprigs (or use a mixture of lemon verbena
  and mint sprigs)
2½ fl oz/5 tablespoons/80 ml water
3 ounces/⅓ cup/80 g superfine (caster) sugar
14 ounces/1⅔ cups/400 g whole-milk (full-fat) Greek yogurt

EQUIPMENT NEEDED
Small saucepan
Measuring cup or jug
Bowl
Fine-mesh strainer (sieve)
Silicone spatula
Food processor or blender
Peeler
8-inch/22-cm round tart tatin pan (tin) or similar solid-
  bottomed pan that can go on the stove and in the oven
Fine Microplane grater or grater with fine holes
Rolling pin

Preheat the oven to 350°F/180°C/160°C Fan/Gas 4.

To make the sorbet, place the lemon balm leaves in a saucepan and pour in the water. Add the sugar to the water, bring to a boil over medium heat to dissolve the sugar, then turn off the heat and set aside to cool. Place the yogurt in a freezer-safe container and strain the cooled syrup into the container, mixing it into the yogurt with a silicone spatula. Place the container in the freezer until the sorbet mixture is firm. Once firm, remove the container from the freezer and blitz the sorbet in a food processor or blender to break up any ice crystals but without letting the mixture melt. Return the sorbet to the freezer for 2–3 hours.

To make the filling, peel the pineapple and slice the flesh into ⅛-inch/3-mm slices, removing the core. Butter the bottom of the tart pan (tin), sprinkle it with sugar and arrange the pineapple slices on top, overlapping them slightly. Peel and shred (grate) the ginger and finely chop the lemon balm leaves. Sprinkle a little ginger and lemon balm over the layer of pineapple. Repeat with several layers of pineapple, alternating with the ginger and lemon balm. Place the tart pan over the lowest heat possible, cover, and cook the pineapple for 5 minutes. Uncover and cook until the juice from the pineapple has evaporated and the sugar has caramelized. Leave to cool.

On a lightly floured surface, roll out the pie dough (pastry) into a 10-inch/26-cm round. Carefully lift the rolled-out dough and place it over the pan to cover the pineapple. Tuck the edges of the dough in towards the bottom of the pan to seal the edges. Place the pan in the preheated oven and bake for 35 minutes, or until the pastry is golden. Turn the tart tatin out by inverting the pan onto a serving plate. If preferred, add more color to the pineapple by using a cook's blowtorch. Serve warm or cold with the yogurt sorbet.

MISTAKES TO AVOID
Aluminum can react with highly acidic fruit, such as pineapple, and give the dish a metallic taste, so avoid using an aluminum tart pan.

TARTLETS WITH CARAMELIZED PINEAPPLE COMPOTE

Tartellette con composta di ananas caramellata

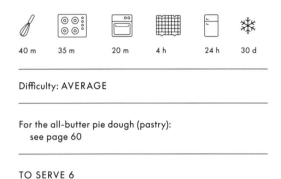

40 m   35 m   20 m   4 h   24 h   30 d

Difficulty: AVERAGE

For the all-butter pie dough (pastry):
   see page 60

TO SERVE 6

FOR THE BASE
1 quantity (9 ounces/250 g) all-butter pie dough (pastry)
   prepared following the base recipe on page 60

FOR THE COMPOTE
2 pounds 11 ounces/1.2 kg pineapple
2 ounces/¼ cup/50 g granulated white sugar
2 allspice berries
Grated zest of 1 unwaxed lime

TO DECORATE
9 ounces/1 cup/250 g mascarpone
1½ fl oz/3 tablespoons/50 ml heavy (whipping) cream
2½ ounces/¾ cup/75 g confectioners' (icing) sugar
Grated zest of 1 unwaxed lime

EQUIPMENT NEEDED
6 × 5-inch/12-cm round loose-bottomed tart pans (tins)
Rolling pin
6-inch/15-cm round pastry cutter
Parchment paper
Baking beans
Bowls
Immersion (stick) blender
Mortar and pestle
Saucepan
Silicone spatula
Zester
Hand whisk

Preheat the oven to 350°F/180°C/160°C Fan/Gas 4. Grease the tartlet pans (tins) with a little butter.

On a lightly floured surface, roll out the pie dough (pastry) to ⅛ inch/3 mm thick. Using the pastry cutter, cut out pastry disks slightly larger than the prepared tartlet pans. Place a pastry disk into each pan. If necessary, re-roll any scraps to give enough disks. Press down firmly on the base and sides, then prick the base of the dough with a fork. Using a sharp knife, trim away any excess dough that is overhanging the sides of the pans to neaten.

Line the pastry cases with parchment paper, fill with baking beans, and place in the lower part of the preheated oven for 15 minutes to blind bake. After 15 minutes, remove the baking beans and parchment paper and return to the oven for a further 5 minutes, or until the pastry cases have dried out. Remove from the oven and leave to cool completely on a cooling rack.

To make the compote, prepare the pineapple by removing the skin, then cut off the top and base, and remove the central core. Cut 1 pound 2 ounces/500 g of the flesh into small chunks then blitz to a fine puree with an immersion (stick) blender. Crush the allspice berries using a mortar and pestle and set aside.

Place the sugar in a saucepan, add 2 tablespoons of water, and cook over low heat until the sugar has dissolved, then increase the heat to medium and cook until you have an amber-colored caramel. Add the pineapple a little at a time, taking care not to splash, then add the crushed allspice berries. Continue to cook over medium–low heat for 25 minutes, stirring occasionally, until the mixture resembles a thick compote. Add the lime zest and stir. Leave the compote to cool in the refrigerator, then spoon it into the prepared pastry cases.

Place the mascarpone, cream, and confectioners' (icing) sugar in a bowl and whisk until smooth. To serve, make a quenelle of the whipped cream using two soup spoons (dessertspoons) and place on top the of the compote on each tart. Decorate each tart with some freshly grated lime zest.

LEMON TART WITH SAGE AND BLUEBERRIES

Pie al limone e salvia con mirtilli

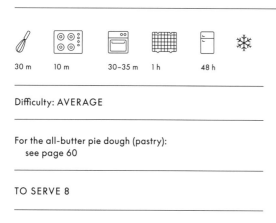

30 m   10 m   30–35 m   1 h   48 h

Difficulty: AVERAGE

For the all-butter pie dough (pastry):
   see page 60

TO SERVE 8

FOR THE BASE
1 quantity (9 ounces/250 g) all-butter pie dough (pastry)
   prepared following the base recipe on page 60
Butter, for greasing

FOR THE FILLING
4 unwaxed lemons
4 ounces/generous ½ cup/120 g superfine (caster) sugar
1 ounce/¼ cup/25 g cornstarch (cornflour)
6 egg yolks
7 fl oz/scant 1 cup/200 ml whole (full-fat) milk
2 ounces/3 tablespoons/50 g unsalted butter
3 sage leaves
3 tablespoons heavy (whipping) cream

TO DECORATE
4 ounces/¾ cup/120 g blueberries
2 sage leaves, finely shredded
Confectioners' (icing) sugar, for dusting

EQUIPMENT NEEDED
7-inch/18-cm round loose-bottomed tart pan (tin)
   with deep sides
Rolling pin
Parchment paper
Baking beans
Bowls
Zester
Juicer
Fine-mesh strainer (sieve)
Hand whisk
Measuring cup or jug
Saucepans
Silicone spatula
Spatula or palette knife
Small strainer or dusting spoon

Preheat the oven to 400°F/200°C/180°C Fan/Gas 6. Grease the tart pan (tin) with a little butter. Cut the butter into small cubes, place in a bowl, and leave to soften.

On a lightly floured surface, roll out the pie dough (pastry) to ¼ inch/5 mm thick. Carefully lift the rolled-out pie dough and use it to line the prepared tart pan. Press down firmly on the base and sides, then prick the base of the dough with a fork. Using a sharp knife, trim away any excess dough that is overhanging the sides of the tart pan to neaten. Line the pastry case with parchment paper, then fill with baking beans and place in the lower part of the preheated oven for 25 minutes to blind bake. After 25 minutes, remove the baking beans and parchment paper and return to the oven for a further 5–10 minutes or until the pastry case has dried out and is golden. Remove from the oven and leave to cool.

To make the filling, grate the zest of the lemons and set aside. Place the sugar in a bowl with the cornstarch (cornflour). Juice all the lemons and pour through a strainer (sieve) into the bowl. Add the egg yolks, and mix all the ingredients together using a hand whisk, until the sugar has dissolved.

Finely chop the sage leaves. Heat the milk with the butter, lemon zest and chopped sage leaves in a saucepan over low heat until just below boiling point. Turn off the heat and leave to infuse for 5 minutes. Pour through a strainer into a bowl, then slowly add to the sugar and egg yolk mix, stirring continuously with a silicone spatula. Transfer to a saucepan and cook over low heat for 5 minutes, stirring continuously, until it thickens. Add the cream, mix and pour into the tart base, using a spatula or palette knife to spread it out evenly.

Leave the filling to cool, then place the tart in the refrigerator for 1 hour. To serve, decorate with the blueberries, finely shredded sage leaves, and a dusting of confectioners' (icing) sugar.

PLUM CRUMBLE

Crumble di prugne

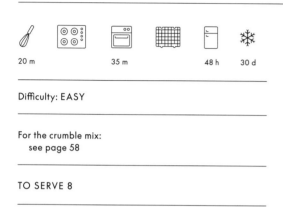

20 m   35 m   48 h   30 d

Difficulty: EASY

For the crumble mix:
   see page 58

TO SERVE 8

FOR THE CRUMBLE

2 pounds 4 ounces/1 kg ripe plums
2 ounces/¼ cup/50 g superfine (caster) sugar
1 heaping teaspoon ground cinnamon
1 quantity (10 ounces/300 g) of crumble topping prepared
   following the base recipe on page 58
Butter, for greasing

EQUIPMENT NEEDED

Bowls
10-inch/25-cm round ovenproof dish
   or 8 individual ovenproof ramekins
Baking sheet
Parchment paper

Preheat the oven to 400°F/200°C/180°C Fan/Gas 6. Grease the ovenproof dish with a little butter.

To make the fruit filling, wash and dry the plums, cut them in half, pit (stone) them, then roughly chop. Mix the sugar with the cinnamon. Fill the prepared ovenproof dish with enough chopped plums to cover the base. Sprinkle over some of the sugar cinnamon mix then continue alternating with a layer of chopped plums and a layer of sugar until all the ingredients have been used. Top with the crumble mix so that it completely covers the fruit.

Place the ovenproof dish on a baking sheet lined with parchment paper and bake in the preheated oven for 35 minutes. The crumble is perfectly done when the top is golden and the juice from the cooked fruit starts to bubble and seep out around the sides of the dish. Leave to cool slightly and serve with crème fraîche, softly whipped cream, crème anglaise (custard), or ice cream, according to taste.

MILLE-FEUILLE WITH VANILLA CREAM

Millefoglie in piedi con crema alla vaniglia

30 m 　 5 m 　 1 h 10 m 　 50 m 　 24 h

Difficulty: ADVANCED

For the puff pastry:
　 see page 62

TO SERVE 8

FOR THE PUFF PASTRY
½ quantity (1 pound/450 g) puff pastry prepared following
　 the base recipe on page 62
1 ounce/¼ cup/30 g confectioners' (icing) sugar

FOR THE CREAM
½ ounce/15 g platinum gelatin sheets
3 eggs
3 tablespoons/40 ml orange liqueur
5 egg yolks
3 ounces/⅓ cup/80 g superfine (caster) sugar
Grated zest of 1 unwaxed orange
½ fl oz/3 tablespoons/50 ml water
10 fl oz/1¼ cups/300 ml heavy (whipping) cream

TO DECORATE
Small edible flowers such as violets
Candied orange peel, cut into fine strips

EQUIPMENT NEEDED
2 baking sheets
Parchment paper
Rolling pin
Fine-mesh strainer (sieve)
Bowls
Bain-marie or double boiler
Measuring cup or jug
Zester
Electric whisk
Small saucepan
Pastry (piping) bag
¾-inch/2-cm plain piping tip (nozzle)

Preheat the oven to 350°F/180°C/160°C Fan/Gas 4 and line one of the baking sheets with parchment paper.

Divide the dough equally into two pieces. On a lightly floured surface, roll out one piece into a 13 × 9-inch/32 × 24-cm rectangle, that is ⅛ inch/3 mm thick. Carefully lift the rolled-out dough and transfer it to the lined baking sheet. Prick it all over with a fork and trim off any excess to neaten the edges. Cover the dough with a sheet of parchment paper, then place the second baking sheet on top. Bake in the preheated oven for 30 minutes. Remove the top baking sheet and parchment paper, then set aside the cooked puff pastry sheet. Repeat for the second half of the dough.

Increase the oven temperature to 475°F/240°C/220°C Fan/Gas 9. Place each cooked puff pastry sheet onto a baking sheet and dust with the confectioners' (icing) sugar. Return the pastry to the oven for 5 minutes, or until the sugar has caramelized. Remove from the oven and leave to cool.

To make the cream, soak the gelatin in cold water for 15 minutes. Place the eggs in a bain-marie or double boiler, making sure the bottom of the bowl does not touch the hot water. Add the orange liqueur, egg yolks, sugar, and orange zest. Beat with an electric whisk until the mixture is dense and mousse-like. Remove from the heat and continue whisking the mixture until cooled to room temperature.

Heat the water in a small saucepan until it is very hot but not boiling. Squeeze the water from the gelatin, add it to the pan, and stir until it has dissolved. Add the gelatin to the whisked egg mixture and stir until incorporated.

In a separate bowl, whip the cream to soft peaks and then fold it into the whisked egg and gelatin mixture. Leave to cool in the refrigerator for 20 minutes until it starts to set.

Transfer the cream to a pastry (piping) bag fitted with a plain piping tip (nozzle). Cut the puff pastry sheets into 24 rectangles of equal size. Place 8 rectangles of puff pastry on the work surface, caramelized side down, and pipe on the cream. Continue with another layer of puff pastry and cream, then finish with one rectangle of puff pastry with the caramelized side up. Leave to set in the refrigerator for 30 minutes, then arrange the mille-feuille on individual serving plates. Pipe the remaining cream on top and decorate with the edible violets and strips of candied orange peel.

ALMOND AND CHOCOLATE SFOGLIATA

Sfogliata alle mandorle e cioccolato

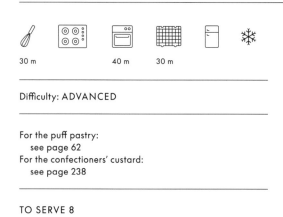

30 m   40 m   30 m

Difficulty: ADVANCED

For the puff pastry:
   see page 62
For the confectioners' custard:
   see page 238

TO SERVE 8

FOR THE CHOCOLATE FRANGIPANE
4 ounces/½ cup plus 1 tablespoon/130 g unsalted butter
7 ounces/1¾ cups/200 g ground almonds
5 ounces/1¼ cups/150 g confectioners' (icing) sugar
1 ounce/¼ cup/30 g flour
2 eggs
¼ quantity (2 ounces/¼ cup/60 g) of confectioners' custard
   prepared following the base recipe on page 238
2 ounces/⅓ cup/50 g bittersweet (dark) chocolate chips

FOR THE PASTRY
½ quantity (1 pound/450 g) of puff pastry prepared
   following the base recipe on page 62
1 egg yolk
1 teaspoon whole (full-fat) milk
Confectioners' (icing) sugar, for dusting

EQUIPMENT NEEDED
Stand mixer fitted with flat beater attachment
Rolling pin
Baking sheet
Parchment paper
Silicone spatula
Side of an 8-inch/20-cm round tart pan (tin)
Pastry brush
Fine-mesh strainer (sieve)

Preheat the oven to 475°F/240°C/220°C Fan/Gas 9.

To make the chocolate frangipane cream, beat the butter in a stand mixer with a flat beater, until it has a creamy consistency. Mix the ground almonds and confectioners' (icing) sugar in a bowl, then, with the mixer running, add to the butter. Next, add the flour followed by the eggs, one at a time, and mix until fully incorporated. Add the custard and chocolate chips and mix to combine.

Divide the puff pastry dough into two pieces, one slightly larger than the other. On a lightly floured surface, roll out the smaller piece of dough to a 8-inch/20-cm round, that is 1⁄16 inch/2 mm thick. Next, roll out the larger piece of dough to a 10-inch/25-cm round, that is ⅛ inch/3 mm thick.

Line a baking sheet with parchment paper and place the smaller disk of dough on the sheet. Spoon the chocolate frangipane cream in the middle and spread it over the dough, leaving a 1½-inch/4-cm border around the edge of the pastry.

Beat the egg yolk with the milk to make a glaze. Using a pastry brush, brush the pastry border with the egg mixture. Carefully place the larger disk of dough over the smaller disk and chocolate frangipane cream, making sure no air is trapped under the pastry.

Press the edges of both disks together to seal. Leave the pastry parcel in the refrigerator for 30 minutes. Press the edge of the tart pan (tin) down onto the edges of the pastry to cut it into a neat circle. Trim away any excess pastry and firmly crimp the edges of the dough disks together using the tines of a fork. Brush the surface of the pastry with the rest of the egg glaze. Using a sharp knife, make a small hole in the center to let steam escape during baking. Lightly score some curved lines on the pastry surface, starting at the center of the disk and working outwards to the edge, but taking care not to cut all the way through the dough.

Bake the pastry in the preheated oven for 10 minutes, then lower the temperature to 400°F/200°C/180°C Fan/Gas 6 and bake for a further 25 minutes. Increase the temperature back to 475°F/240°C/220°C Fan/Gas 9, dust the pastry with the confectioners' (icing) sugar and bake for 5 minutes, or until the sugar caramelizes. Serve the pastry either warm or cold.

This sfogliata can be stored in an airtight container for up to 2 days.

CLASSIC CANNONCINI WITH CHANTILLY CREAM

Cannoncini classici con chantilly

20 m   5 m   15–20 m   24 h

Difficulty: AVERAGE

For the puff pastry:
    see page 62
For the Chantilly cream:
    see page 246

TO SERVE 8 (MAKES 16 SMALL CANNONCINI)

FOR THE CANNONCINI
5 ounces/⅔ cup/150 g superfine (caster) sugar
1¾ fl oz/3 tablespoons/50 ml water
½ quantity (10½ ounces/300 g) of puff pastry prepared
    following the base recipe on page 62
½ quantity (14 ounces/400 g) of Chantilly cream prepared
    following the base recipe on page 246

EQUIPMENT NEEDED
2 baking sheets
Parchment paper
Small saucepan
Measuring cup or jug
Rolling pin
Smooth pastry wheel
Bowl
16 metal cannoncini or cream horn tubes
Pastry brush
Cooling rack
Pastry (piping) bag fitted with ½-inch/1-cm star
    piping tip (nozzle)

Preheat the oven to 400°F/200°C/180°C Fan/Gas 6 and line the baking sheets with parchment paper.

Place 2 ounces/¼ cup/50 g of the sugar in a small saucepan, add the water and bring to boiling point over medium heat to make a syrup. Continue to cook until all the sugar has dissolved then set aside to cool.

On a lightly floured surface, roll out the puff pastry dough into a 13 × 9-inch/32 × 24-cm rectangle, that is ⅛ inch/3 mm thick. Using a pastry wheel, cut the rolled-out dough into 16 strips, each measuring ¾ inch/2 cm wide.

Pour the remaining sugar into a bowl. Hold a metal cannoncini tube in one hand and, starting at one end, wrap it with a strip of pastry, overlapping each wrap slightly, so as not to leave any gaps. Brush each pastry with the sugar syrup and roll it in the remaining sugar, making sure it is completely covered. Place on the lined baking sheets and continue preparing the rest. Depending on how many metal tubes you have, make and bake the cannoncini in batches.

Bake in the preheated oven for 15–20 minutes, or until the pastry is puffed, golden, and starting to release from the cannoncini tubes. Leave to cool for 15 minutes, then slide the pastries off the cannoncini tubes and let cool completely on a cooling rack.

To serve, fill a pastry (piping) bag fitted with a star piping tip (nozzle) with the Chantilly cream and fill each cannoncini. To ensure the pastry remains crisp, fill the cannoncini immediately before serving.

VARIATIONS
Instead of filling the cannoncini with Chantilly cream, pipe them full of confectioners' custard (see page 238) for a richer filling.

MILLE-FEUILLE WITH WHITE CHOCOLATE AND APRICOTS

Millefoglie di pasta da strudel con albicocche

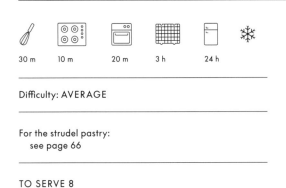

30 m   10 m   20 m   3 h   24 h

Difficulty: AVERAGE

For the strudel pastry:
  see page 66

TO SERVE 8

FOR THE DOUGH
½ quantity (5 ounces/150 g) of strudel pastry prepared
  following the base recipe on page 66
1½ ounces/3 tablespoons/50 g unsalted butter, melted

FOR THE WHITE CHOCOLATE CREAM
½ ounce/15 g platinum gelatin sheets
3 ounces/80 g white chocolate
10 fl oz/1¼ cups/300 ml heavy (whipping) cream
5 fl oz/scant ⅔ cup/150 ml whole (full-fat) milk
Grated zest of 1 unwaxed lemon
¾ ounce/5 teaspoons/20 g superfine (caster) sugar

FOR THE CARAMELIZED APRICOTS
10½ ounces/1⅓ cups/300 g apricots
1 ounce/2 tablespoons/30 g unsalted butter
1½ ounces/scant ¼ cup/40 g turbinado (demerara) sugar

TO DECORATE
2 apricots, quartered
Small edible flowers
Confectioners' (icing) sugar, for dusting

EQUIPMENT NEEDED
Bowl
Small saucepan
Measuring cup or jug
Zester
Silicone spatula
Immersion (stick) blender
2 baking sheets
Parchment paper
Non-stick skillet (frying pan)
Baking sheet
Rolling pin
3-inch/8-cm round pastry cutter
Pastry (piping) bag fitted with ½-inch/1-cm plain piping
  tip (nozzle)
Small strainer or dusting spoon

To make the white chocolate cream, soak the gelatin in cold water for 5 minutes. Finely chop the white chocolate and set aside in a bowl. Whip the cream in a bowl to soft peaks and set aside.

Pour the milk into a small saucepan, add the grated zest of the lemon and the sugar, and bring almost to boiling point over low heat. Remove the saucepan from the heat. Squeeze the water from the gelatin, add the gelatin to the pan, and stir until it has dissolved.

Pour the hot milk over the chopped white chocolate, stirring with a silicone spatula until the chocolate has melted. Leave to cool, then blitz with an immersion (stick) blender until smooth then fold in the whipped cream. Leave to cool in the refrigerator for 3 hours.

Preheat the oven to 350°F/180°C/160°C Fan/Gas 4.

To make the caramelized apricots, pit (stone) the apricots and chop into quarters. Melt the butter in a non-stick skillet (frying pan), add the sugar and apricots and cook over high heat for 5 minutes, until they start to caramelize. Place on a baking sheet and leave to cool.

On a sheet of parchment paper, roll out the strudel dough until roughly the thickness of a sheet of paper. Using the pastry cutter, cut out 24 disks of dough. Remove the excess pastry from around the cut-out disks and then lift the parchment paper onto the baking sheet. Use two baking sheets, if necessary. Melt the remaining butter in a small saucepan. Brush the strudel dough disks with the melted butter.

Bake in the preheated oven for 20 minutes or until starting to turn golden. Remove from the oven and leave to cool. Fill the pastry (piping) bag, fitted with a plain tip (nozzle), with the cream. Place 8 strudel pastry disks on individual plates, pipe each disk with a swirl of cream, spoon over some apricots and cover with another strudel disk. Repeat with another layer of cream and apricots and top off with another strudel disk.

Decorate each mille-feuille with an apricot quarter, a few small edible flowers, and a dusting of confectioners' (icing) sugar.

TIPS AND TRICKS
To prevent the first strudel pastry disk sliding around on the serving plate, place a teaspoon of cream in the middle of the plate to help the pastry adhere to the plate.

CLASSIC APPLE STRUDEL

Strudel di mele classic

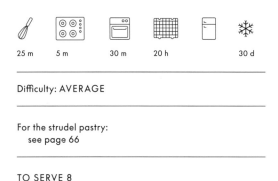

25 m	5 m	30 m	20 h		30 d

Difficulty: AVERAGE

For the strudel pastry:
    see page 66

TO SERVE 8

FOR THE DOUGH
1 quantity (10½ ounces/300 g) strudel pastry prepared
    following the base recipe on page 66
1 egg yolk

FOR THE FILLING
1 ounce/3 heaping tablespoons/30 g raisins
2 pounds 4 ounces/1 kg Reinette (Russet) or
    Golden Delicious apples
1½ ounces/scant ¼ cup/40 g superfine (caster) sugar
1 teaspoon ground cinnamon
1 ounce/¼ cup/30 g pine nuts
Grated zest of 1 unwaxed lemon
5 ounces/½ cup plus 3 tablespoons/150 g unsalted butter
2½ ounces/1 cup/70 g fresh breadcrumbs

TO DECORATE
¾ ounce/3 tablespoons/20 g confectioners' (icing) sugar

EQUIPMENT NEEDED
Bowls
Paper towels
Peeler
Corer
Zester
Non-stick skillet (frying pan)
Baking sheet
Parchment paper
Rolling pin
Dish towel (tea towel)
Pastry brush
Small saucepan
Small strainer or dusting spoon

To make the filling, soak the raisins in warm water for 20 minutes, then drain and pat dry with paper towels. Peel the apples, remove the cores, and chop into small cubes. Place in a bowl with the soaked raisins and add the sugar, cinnamon, pine nuts, and lemon zest. Stir until well combined.

Melt 1½ ounces/3 tablespoons/40 g of the butter in a non-stick skillet (frying pan), add the breadcrumbs and toast them over a moderate heat until they start to turn golden. Transfer to a plate and leave to cool.

Preheat the oven to 425°F/220°C/200°C Fan/Gas 7 and line the baking sheet with parchment paper. Prepare an egg glaze by mixing the egg yolk with a few drops of water.

On a lightly floured surface, roll out the strudel dough into a large 24 × 16-inch/50 × 40-cm rectangle. When the dough starts to get thinner, move it onto a large, clean dish towel (tea towel), lightly dusted with flour and continue rolling out the dough until it is very thin and transparent—to the point you can almost see your hands through it.

Melt the remaining butter in a small saucepan. Brush the rolled-out strudel dough with the melted butter. Scatter the toasted breadcrumbs over two-thirds of the dough, starting from one of the long edges and leaving a 1½-inch/4-cm border along the short edges. Pile the filling onto the long side of the dough without breadcrumbs.

Using the dish towel to help you, roll up the strudel to enclose the filling in the dough, starting from the long edge with the filling and tucking in the sides of the dough as you roll.

Place the strudel seam-side down on the lined baking sheet and brush all over with more melted butter. Bake in the preheated oven for 15 minutes, then brush the strudel with the egg wash and bake for a further 15 minutes, or until the pastry is golden and crisp. Serve while still warm, dusted with confectioners' (icing) sugar and accompanied by crème anglaise (custard), cream, or ice cream, according to taste.

SPONGE

Classic whisked sponge
Pan di Spagna

20 m — 40 m

Difficulty: EASY

MAKES 1 QUANTITY
(ENOUGH TO MAKE AN 8-INCH/20-CM ROUND
DEEP SPONGE)

FOR THE SPONGE
6 eggs
4 ounces/⅔ cup/120 g superfine (caster) sugar
Flavoring to taste (seeds of 1 vanilla bean (pod) or
    the grated zest of ½ unwaxed lemon)
Pinch of salt
5 ounces/1¼ cups/150 g type "00" flour or all-purpose
    (plain) flour
1 ounce/4 tablespoons/30 g cornstarch (cornflour)

EQUIPMENT NEEDED
8-inch/20-cm round springform cake pan (tin)
    with deep sides
Parchment paper
Stand mixer fitted with whisk attachment or
    electric whisk and bowl
Bowl
Fine-mesh strainer (sieve)
Silicone spatula
Cooling rack

AS USED IN
– Chestnut Mini Sponge Cakes
  (see page 114)
– Forest Fruits Pudding
  (see page 116)

Preheat the oven to 350°F/180°C/160°C Fan/Gas 4 and line the cake pan (tin) with parchment paper. Do not butter or flour the pan, simply line it with parchment paper.

Break the eggs into the bowl of the stand mixer (1). Add the sugar, any flavoring, and a pinch of salt (2). Start the mixer on a slow speed and start to beat the ingredients together, gradually increase the speed, and continue to beat for 10 minutes (3), until the mixture falls from the whisk in wide ribbons and leaves a visible trace on the mixture below (4).

Combine the flour and cornstarch (cornflour) in a bowl then sift one-third directly onto the whisked egg mixture (5). Using a silicone spatula, gently fold the flour into the mixture with an upwards motion, taking care not to knock any air out of the mixture (6).

Sift in the remaining flour, one-third at a time (7), and gently fold in to combine. Pour the sponge mixture into the lined pan.

Bake the sponge in the preheated oven for 40 minutes, or until golden, risen, and firm on top—the sponge should be starting to shrink away from the pan and a skewer inserted into the center comes out clean. Do not open the oven door until the end of the cooking time to prevent the cake from sinking in the center. Let the sponge cool for 20 minutes before removing it from the pan. If necessary, run a spatula in between the pan and cake to loosen the sponge. Place the sponge on a cooling rack to cool completely.

The sponge can be stored for 48 hours when wrapped in plastic wrap (cling film) and kept at room temperature. As there is no fat in the mixture, It is susceptible to drying out.

HOW TO USE
The sponge can be sliced and layered with any filling. In which case, it is best to bake the sponge the day before as it is easier to cut the day after baking. It should never be cut while still warm, as it will be too soft and crumbly.

TIPS AND TRICKS
To whisk eggs perfectly, they must be at room temperature and not cold from the refrigerator. It is possible to mix the eggs and sugar, then start to whisk in a bain-marie or double boiler with gently simmering water, without letting the temperature exceed 120°F/50°C, then transfer to the stand mixer and continue to beat until pale and mousse-like and falling in ribbons. It is also advisable to use this bain marie method if using only a hand mixer.

VARIATIONS
For a chocolate sponge, replace the cornstarch with the same weight of unsweetened cocoa powder, then prepare the sponge following the instructions given above.

Genoise sponge

Pasta génoise

20 m   15 m   40–45 m

Difficulty: AVERAGE

MAKES 1 QUANTITY
(ENOUGH TO MAKE AN 8-INCH/20-CM ROUND
DEEP SPONGE)

FOR THE SPONGE
6 eggs
4 ounces/⅔ cup/120 g superfine (caster) sugar
Pinch of salt
1¾ ounces/3 tablespoons/45 g unsalted butter
5 ounces/1¼ cups/150 g type "00" flour or all-purpose
(plain) flour
Flavoring to taste (seeds of 1 vanilla bean (pod) or
grated zest of ½ unwaxed lemon)

EQUIPMENT NEEDED
8-inch/20-cm round springform cake pan (tin)
with deep sides
Parchment paper
Bain-marie or double boiler
Electric whisk
Kitchen thermometer
Bowls
Fine-mesh strainer (sieve)
Silicone spatula
Cooling rack

AS USED IN
– Pistachio and Passion Fruit Pudding
(see page 118)
– Candied Orange and Ginger Syrup Cake
(see page 120)
– Tea Cake with Apricot Compote and Cream
(see page 122)

Preheat the oven to 350°F/180°C/160°C Fan/Gas 4 and line the cake pan (tin) with parchment paper (see page 28).

Break the eggs into a bain-marie or double boiler over gently simmering water. Add the sugar and a pinch of salt and beat together with an electric whisk (1). Use a kitchen thermometer to check the temperature of the mix, ensuring that it never exceeds 120°F/50°C (2). If the temperature is too high the eggs will begin to scramble and stick to the bottom of the bowl. Continue until you obtain a dense but very fluffy and frothy mix. Remove from the heat and whisk until the mix has cooled, then transfer to a large bowl (3).

Meanwhile, melt the butter in a bain-marie or double boiler and set aside to cool slightly.

Sift one half of the flour directly onto the whisked mixture (4). Using a silicone spatula, gently fold the flour into the mixture with an upwards motion, taking care not to knock any air out of the mixture. Sift in the remaining half of the flour and add your preferred flavoring, then gently fold in to combine.

Pour the melted butter slowly around the edges of the bowl (5), then quickly fold the butter into the mixture (6) until just incorporated.

Pour the sponge mix into the lined cake pan and bake in the preheated oven for 40–45 minutes, or until golden, risen, and firm on top—the sides of the sponge should be starting to shrink away from the sides of the pan and a skewer inserted into the center comes out clean. Do not open the oven door until the end of the cooking time to prevent the cake from sinking in the center. Let the sponge cool for 20 minutes before removing it from the pan. If necessary, run a spatula in between the pan and the cake to loosen the sponge. Place the sponge on a cooling rack to cool completely.

The sponge can be stored for 72 hours when wrapped in plastic wrap (cling film) and kept at room temperature.

HOW TO USE
The sponge can be sliced and layered with any filling. In which case, it is best to bake the sponge the day before as it is easier to cut the day after baking. It should never be cut while still warm, as it will be too soft and crumbly.

VARIATIONS
The butter in this sponge gives it a melt-in-the-mouth texture. To obtain a sponge with a more crumbly texture, substitute one-third of the flour with potato starch or cornstarch (cornflour).

TIPS AND TRICKS
As for all other whipped mixes, the temperature and cooking time for Genoise sponge differs depending on the depth of the cake pan (tin). When cooked in a deep springform pan, bake the sponge for 40–45 minutes at 350°F/180°C/160°C Fan/Gas 4. When cooked in a shallow jelly roll pan (Swiss roll tin), bake the sponge for 6–7 minutes at 400°F/200°C/180°C Fan/Gas 6.

Roulade sponge
Pasta biscuit

15 m   7–10 m

Difficulty: EASY

MAKES 1 QUANTITY
(ENOUGH TO MAKE A 15 × 10-INCH/35 × 28-CM
RECTANGULAR SPONGE)

FOR THE SPONGE
4 eggs
4 ounces/⅔ cup/120 g superfine (caster) sugar
Pinch of salt
4 ounces/1 cup/125 g type "00" flour or all-purpose
(plain) flour

EQUIPMENT NEEDED
15 × 10-inch/38 × 25-cm jelly roll pan (Swiss roll tin) or
baking sheet
Parchment paper
Bowls
Electric whisk
Silicone spatula
Fine-mesh strainer (sieve)

AS USED IN
– Chocolate Cake with Cherries in Barolo Chinato
(see page 124)
– Banana, Mango, and Mint Charlotte
(see page 126)

Preheat the oven to 425°F/220°C/200°C Fan/Gas 7 and line the jelly roll pan (Swiss roll tin) or baking sheet with parchment paper.

Separate the egg yolks from the whites and place the whites in a grease-free bowl (1). Add half the sugar and a pinch of salt to the egg whites and beat with an electric whisk until the mixture reaches soft peaks, and the sugar has completely dissolved (2).

Add the remaining sugar and a tablespoon of water to the egg yolks in a separate bowl (3). Beat with an electric whisk, until the mixture is light and frothy (4).

Add a quarter of the egg whites whisked with the sugar to the beaten yolk mixture and then gently fold it into the mix using a silicone spatula (5).

Sift all the flour directly onto the beaten yolk mixture (6) and gently fold it into the mix using a silicone spatula. Add the remaining whisked egg whites and gently fold in until fully combined (7).

Pour the sponge mixture into the lined baking sheet, spreading it evenly (8). Place the baking sheet in the preheated oven and bake for 7–10 minutes, or until lightly golden, risen, and just firm to the touch—a skewer inserted into the center comes out clean. Let the sponge cool slightly in the pan, then turn it out onto a sheet of parchment paper dusted with superfine (caster) sugar.

HOW TO USE
To make a classic roulade, roll up the sponge while it is still warm and then leave it to cool completely while rolled into a spiral. If you try to roll the sponge when cold, it is more likely to crack. Once cool, unroll the sponge, cover it with any filling and then roll the sponge back up.

TIPS AND TRICKS
As well as the preparation of roulades with different fillings, this type of sponge can also be used for the base and layers of a cake (see page 124). It can also be used in a charlotte (see page 126). In this case, you can make the sponge more decorative by piping the mixture onto a lined baking sheet using a pastry (piping) bag fitted with a ½-inch/1-cm plain piping tip (nozzle), creating oblique lines close to each other. Bake for 8–10 minutes at 350°F/180°C/160°C Fan/Gas 4. Cut the sponge to fit the bottom and sides of the pan (tin) for the charlotte.

Savoiardi sponge fingers
Impasto per savoiardi

15 m   10 m   20 m

Difficulty: EASY

MAKES 1 QUANTITY
(8 OUNCES/225 G OF MIXTURE BEFORE BAKING
OR ENOUGH TO MAKE 12 MEDIUM SAVOIARDI)

FOR THE SPONGE
2 eggs
3 ounces/⅔ cup/80 g type "00" flour or all-purpose
   (plain) flour
3 ounces/⅓ cup/80 g superfine (caster) sugar
1 ounce/¼ cup/30 g confectioners' (icing) sugar
1 vanilla bean (pod)
Pinch of salt

EQUIPMENT NEEDED
Bowls
Electric whisk
Silicone spatula
Fine-mesh strainer (sieve)
Pastry (piping) bag fitted with ½-inch/1-cm plain piping
   tip (nozzle)
Baking sheet
Parchment paper
Small strainer or dusting spoon

AS USED IN
– Summer Tiramisù
  (see page 128)

Preheat the oven to 400°F/200°C/180°C Fan/Gas 6 and line the baking sheet with parchment paper.

Separate the egg yolks from the whites and place the whites in a grease-free bowl. Start beating the whites with an electric whisk and slowly add the sugar as you whisk until stiff peaks form (1).

Beat the yolks in a separate bowl until liquid, then add them to the whisked egg whites. Using a silicone spatula, gently fold the yolks into the egg whites with an upwards motion, taking care not to knock any air out of the mixture (2).

Sift all the flour directly into the bowl containing the egg mix (3) and gently fold the flour into the mixture using a silicone spatula until incorporated and the mixture is smooth (4).

Transfer the mix to a pastry (piping) bag fitted with a ½-inch/1-cm plain piping tip (nozzle) (5). Pipe the dough onto the lined baking sheet in the characteristic "finger" shape, each measuring 4 inches/10cm long (6).

Dust with half the confectioners' (icing) sugar and leave to rest for 20 minutes, until the sugar has been absorbed (7). Dust again with the remaining confectioners' sugar and bake in the preheated oven for 10 minutes or until lightly golden and set. Let the sponge fingers cool completely on the baking sheet.

These sponge fingers can be stored in an airtight container for up to 3 days.

TIPS AND TRICKS
The characteristic lightness of savoiardi sponge fingers is due to the fact that the egg whites are whisked separately from the yolks, then folded into the mixture. Another trick to make them even softer and more dimpled is to dust them with confectioners' (icing) sugar and cornstarch (cornflour) before baking.

VARIATIONS
To obtain a sponge finger with an even smoother and silkier texture, substitute one-third of the flour with potato starch or cornstarch (cornflour).

CHESTNUT MINI SPONGE CAKES

Pasticcini ai marroni

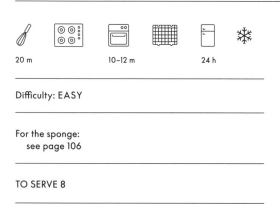

20 m   10–12 m   24 h

Difficulty: EASY

For the sponge:
   see page 106

TO SERVE 8

FOR THE SPONGE
Butter, for greasing
½ quantity of classic sponge mix prepared following
   the base recipe on page 106

FOR THE FILLING
3½ ounces/scant ½ cup/100 g chestnut spread or sweetened
   chestnut puree

FOR THE FROSTING
10 fl oz/1¼ cups/300 ml heavy (whipping) cream
1 ounce/¼ cup/30 g confectioners' (icing) sugar
8 marrons glacés (candied chestnuts)

EQUIPMENT NEEDED
12-cup muffin pan (tin), 1¾ inches/4 cm in diameter
Cooling rack
Small serrated knife
Bowl
Electric whisk
Small spatula or palette knife
Pastry (piping) bag fitted with 1/2-inch/1-cm star piping
   tip (nozzle)

Preheat the oven to 350°F/180°C/160°C Fan/Gas 4. Grease 8 cups of the muffin pan (tin) with a little butter.

Pour the sponge mix into the greased cups of the muffin pan to two-thirds full. Bake in the preheated oven for 10–12 minutes, or until golden and a skewer inserted into the center comes out clean.

Leave to cool slightly then remove from the pan by gently running a small knife around the edge of each sponge to ease it out of the pan. Leave to cool on a cooling rack.

Cut off the tops of the sponges using a small serrated knife, then use the knife to hollow out a small cavity in center of each sponge. Fill each cavity with the chestnut spread and replace the sponge top.

Whip the cream and confectioners' (icing) sugar together with an electric whisk. Place in the pastry (piping) bag fitted with a star piping tip (nozzle) and pipe over the sponge cakes. Place a marron glacé (candied chestnut) in the center of each cake and serve.

VARIATIONS
If you cannot find chestnut spread, combine 3½ ounces/scant 1 cup/100 g of unsweetened chestnut puree with 2 ounces/¼ cup/ 50 g of superfine (caster) sugar in a pan and gently warm over low heat. Cook, stirring continuously, for 4–5 minutes or until the sugar has dissolved and the puree has a smooth consistency. Cool before using.

FOREST FRUITS PUDDING
Pudding ai frutti di bosco

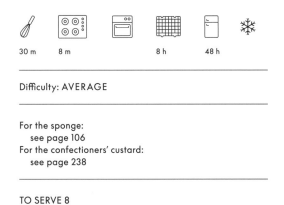

30 m   8 m   8 h   48 h

Difficulty: AVERAGE

For the sponge:
    see page 106
For the confectioners' custard:
    see page 238

TO SERVE 8

FOR THE PUDDING
¼ ounce/5 g platinum gelatin sheets
10½ ounces/3 cups/300 g strawberries
3½ ounces/1 cup/100 g red currants, plus extra
    for decorating
2 ounces/½ cup/50 g black currants
10½ ounces/3 cups/300 g raspberries
3½ ounces/1 cup/100 g alpine strawberries
3½ ounces/1 cup/100 g blackberries
4 ounces/½ cup/120 g superfine (caster) sugar
1 quantity of classic sponge mix prepared and baked in
    a 8-inch/20-cm square cake pan (tin) the day before,
    following the base recipe on page 106
7 ounces/¾ cup/200 g confectioners' custard prepared
    following the base recipe on page 238

EQUIPMENT NEEDED
Bowls
Paper towels
Saucepan
Fine-mesh strainer (sieve)
Large serrated knife
1–1½-quart/1–1.5-litre pudding basin or deep mixing bowl
Plastic wrap (cling film)
Small saucepan
Hand whisk
Heavy weight, such as cans of food

Soak the gelatin in cold water for 5 minutes. Wash and hull the strawberries and cut each one into quarters. Remove the currants from their stalks using the tines of a fork, reserving a few clusters for decoration. Delicately wash the remaining berries and pat dry with paper towels.

Place the sugar in a saucepan, add 4 tablespoons of water, and slowly bring to a boil over a low heat to dissolve the sugar and make a syrup. Let the syrup come to a boil.

Still over a low heat, add all the berries except the strawberries to the saucepan. Cook for 3–4 minutes until the fruit has softened, then add the strawberries and cook for a further 2 minutes. Turn off the heat and pour the fruit into a fine-mesh strainer (sieve) set over a bowl to collect the juice.

Line the pudding basin with two layers of plastic wrap (cling film). Using a large serrated knife, slice the sponge cake into layers that are ½ inch/1 cm thick and then completely cover the base and sides of the pudding basin with the sponge slices, making sure there are no gaps between the slices. Moisten the sponge with some of the fruit cooking syrup. Spoon half the cooked fruit into the pudding basin to cover the bottom sponge layer, then cover with another layer of sponge.

Squeeze the water from the gelatin. Put in a small saucepan with 2 tablespoons water and place over a low heat to dissolve, without letting it boil.

Pour the dissolved gelatin into the custard and stir with a hand whisk to combine, then pour over the uppermost layer of sponge in the pudding basin. Cover the custard mix with another layer of sponge, add a layer of the remaining cooked fruit then finish with the last few slices of sponge and moisten with a little more juice.

Bring the edges of the plastic wrap together and loosely seal to cover the sponge. Put a small plate over the top of the pudding basin and weight down. Let rest in the refrigerator for 8 hours.

When ready to serve, place a serving plate over the pudding basin, turn it upside down, and lift the basin off the pudding. Remove the plastic wrap from the pudding, drizzle over the remaining juice, and decorate with the reserved fruit.

VARIATIONS
Alpine strawberries are small, very sweet strawberries, sometimes called wild strawberries. If you cannot find alpine strawberries, replace them with extra blackberries, red currants, or black currants.

PISTACHIO AND PASSION FRUIT PUDDING

Dolce al pistacchio e frutti della passione

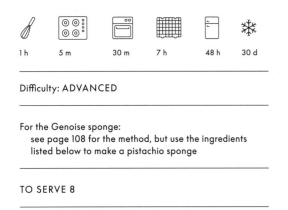

1 h   5 m   30 m   7 h   48 h   30 d

Difficulty: ADVANCED

For the Genoise sponge:
  see page 108 for the method, but use the ingredients
  listed below to make a pistachio sponge

TO SERVE 8

FOR THE SPONGE
2 ounces/⅓ cup/50 g shelled pistachios
2½ ounces/generous ½ cup/70 g type "00" flour or
  all-purpose (plain) flour
4 eggs
3½ ounces/½ cup/110 g superfine (caster) sugar
Pinch of salt
¾ ounce/2 tablespoons/25 g unsalted butter

FOR THE MOUSSE
½ ounce/15 g platinum gelatin sheets
2 ounces/¼ cup/50 g superfine (caster) sugar
1¾ fl oz/3 tablespoons/50 ml water
2 egg whites
8½ fl oz/1 cup/250 ml unsweetened passion fruit juice
11¾ fl oz/scant 1½ cups/350 ml heavy (whipping) cream

FOR THE GELÉE (JELLY)
½ ounce/10 g platinum gelatin sheets
7 fl oz/scant 1 cup/200 ml unsweetened passion fruit juice
2 ounces/¼ cup/50 g superfine (caster) sugar

TO DECORATE
Chopped pistachios
Edible flowers

EQUIPMENT NEEDED
10½ × 12½-inch/27 × 32-cm rectangular
  baking sheet
Parchment paper
Food processor
7-inch/18-cm ring mold or springform cake pan (tin)
Acetate sheet
Bowl
Small saucepan
Measuring cup or jug
Kitchen thermometer
Stand mixer fitted with whisk attachment or
  electric whisk and bowl
Saucepan
Silicone spatula
Metal spatula or palette knife

Preheat the oven to 350°F/180°C/160°C Fan/Gas 4 and line the baking sheet with parchment paper.

Blitz the pistachios and flour in the food processor until you have a fine, smooth powder. Using the ingredients quantities listed on this page, prepare the Genoise sponge following the instructions on page 108. Pour the sponge mix onto the lined baking sheet and bake in the preheated oven for 30 minutes. Leave to cool completely then cut the sponge to size, using the ring mold or springform cake pan (tin) as a template. Line the inner sides of the ring mold or pan with the acetate sheet and place the sponge disk inside the mold.

To make the mousse, soak the gelatin in cold water for 5 minutes. Place the sugar in a small saucepan with the water over low heat until the sugar has dissolved. Increase the heat to medium and bring to a boil to make a syrup. Heat the syrup to 250°F/121°C using a thermometer to check it reaches the correct temperature.

Meanwhile, place the egg whites in a grease-free bowl and whisk to soft peaks. When the syrup has reached the correct temperature, drizzle it into the whisked egg whites, continuing to whisk until the mixture has cooled and forms firm glossy peaks.

Pour the passion fruit juice into a saucepan and bring to a boil over low heat then remove from the heat. Squeeze the water from the gelatin. Add to the saucepan with the fruit juice and stir until it has dissolved. Leave to cool.

In a separate bowl, whip the cream to soft peaks. Use a silicone spatula to gently fold the cream and the cooled passion fruit mixture into the whisked egg whites, taking care not to deflate it. Pour the mousse onto the Genoise sponge base inside the lined ring mold, smoothing it with a spatula or palette knife to form an even layer and leave in the refrigerator for 2–3 hours.

To make the gelée (jelly), soak the gelatin in cold water for 5 minutes. Place the passion fruit juice and sugar in a saucepan and set over low heat until the sugar has dissolved. Squeeze the water from the gelatin. Add to the saucepan with the fruit juice and stir until it has dissolved. Leave to cool, stirring occasionally.

Pour the gelée mix onto the mousse to form an even layer and leave in the refrigerator for 1 hour or until the gelée has set. Remove the pudding from the mold, transfer to a serving plate, and carefully remove and discard the acetate. Decorate with chopped pistachios and edible flowers.

CANDIED ORANGE AND GINGER SYRUP CAKE

Cake con arancia candita e sciroppo allo zenzero

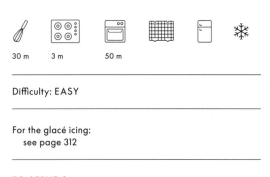

30 m   3 m   50 m

Difficulty: EASY

For the glacé icing:
    see page 312

TO SERVE 8

FOR THE SPONGE
10½ ounces/1¼ cups/300 g unsalted butter
5 ounces/⅔ cup/140 g superfine (caster) sugar
¾ ounce/1 tablespoon/20 g orange flower honey
11 ounces/2½ cups/320 g type "00" flour or all-purpose
    (plain) flour
¼ ounce/1 heaping teaspoon/6 g baking powder
4 eggs
2½ ounces/70 g candied orange peel, chopped

FOR THE SYRUP
¾ ounce/1-inch piece/20 g fresh ginger
¾ ounce/5 teaspoons/20 g sugar
1¾ fl oz/3 tablespoons/50 ml water

TO DECORATE
Candied orange peel
Thyme sprigs
Edible rose petals
1 quantity of glacé icing prepared following
    the base recipe on page 312

EQUIPMENT NEEDED
Stand mixer fitted with flat beater attachment
Bowls
Fine-mesh strainer (sieve)
10-inch/25.5-cm bundt pan (tin)
Small saucepan
Measuring cup or jug

Preheat the oven to 350°F/180°C/160°C Fan/Gas 4. Cut the butter into small cubes, place in a mixing bowl, and leave to soften. Grease the bundt pan (tin) with butter and dust lightly with a little flour.

Place the cubes of softened butter in the bowl of the stand mixer, add the sugar and honey, then mix on a medium speed using the flat beater attachment, until it looks pale and fluffy.

Sift the flour into a separate bowl along with the baking powder.

Add the eggs, one at a time, alternating them with a spoonful of flour, whisking continuously as you do so. Add the remainder of the flour and use a silicone spatula to fold in the ingredients to form a batter. Add the chopped candied peel and mix to incorporate.

Pour the cake batter into the prepared bundt pan. Bake the cake in the preheated oven for 50 minutes, or until risen and just firm to the touch—a skewer inserted into the center comes out clean. Leave the cake to cool in the pan for 10 minutes.

Meanwhile, make the syrup. Peel and thinly slice the ginger and place in a small saucepan with the sugar and water. Bring to a boil over medium heat and cook the syrup for 2 minutes. Leave to cool then strain into a bowl.

Remove the cake from the pan, place on a cooling rack, and drizzle over the syrup.

Just before serving, drizzle the glacé icing over the cake, letting it run down the channels in the sponge. Decorate with the strips of candied orange peel, thyme sprigs, and edible rose petals.

This cake can be stored in an airtight container for up to 2 days.

TIPS AND TRICKS
Bundt pans can be intricately shaped. Make sure that the pan is thoroughly greased and that the butter gets right into any corners or sharp edges, so that the cake can be turned out easily.

TEA CAKE WITH APRICOT COMPOTE AND CREAM

Torta al tè con composta di albicocche e panna

30 m   15 m   30 m   4 h   48 h   30 d

Difficulty: AVERAGE

For the Genoise sponge:
see page 108 for the method, but use the ingredients listed below to make an Earl Grey tea sponge

TO SERVE 8

FOR THE SPONGE
1¾ ounces/3 tablespoons/45 g unsalted butter, plus extra for greasing
4 Earl Grey tea bags
6 eggs
5 ounces/generous ⅔ cup/150 g superfine (caster) sugar
Pinch of salt
5 ounces/1¼ cups/150 g type "00" flour or all-purpose (plain) flour

FOR THE COMPOTE
10½ ounces/1½ cups/300 g dried apricots
7 fl oz/scant 1 cup/200 ml water
2 Sichuan peppercorns
1 orange

TO DECORATE
10 fl oz/1¼ cups/300 ml heavy (whipping) cream
1 ounce/¼ cup/30 g confectioners' (icing) sugar, plus extra for dusting
1 teaspoon dried rose petals

EQUIPMENT NEEDED
Bowls
8-inch/20-cm round springform pan (tin) with deep sides or 3 × 8-inch/20-cm layer cake pans (tins)
Bain-marie or double boiler
Cooling rack
Saucepan
Measuring cup or jug
Mortar and pestle
Juicer
Strainer
Immersion (stick) blender
Large serrated knife
Electric whisk
Pastry (piping) bag fitted with ¾-inch/1.5-cm plain piping tip (nozzle)
Small strainer (sieve) or dusting spoon

Cover 9 ounces/1⅓ cups/250 g of the dried apricots in boiling water, ensuring they are completely submerged, and leave to soak for 4 hours.

Preheat the oven to 350°F/180°C/160°C Fan/Gas 4 and butter the base and sides of the springform pan (tin) then lightly dust with flour.

To make the sponge, melt the butter in a bain-marie or double boiler over very low heat, add the tea bags and take off the heat. Leave to infuse for 5 minutes, then squeeze the tea bags and discard. Using the tea-infused butter and the remaining ingredients and quantities listed on this page, prepare the Genoise sponge following the instructions on page 108.

Pour the sponge mix into the springform pan and bake in the preheated oven for 30 minutes or until risen, firm to the touch, and a skewer inserted into the center comes out clean. Leave to cool in the pan for 10 minutes then remove and place on a cooling rack to cool completely.

To make the compote, drain the apricots, chop into small pieces, and place in a saucepan with the water. Crush the peppercorns using a mortar and pestle, and add these to the pan. Bring to a boil over medium heat, then lower the heat, cover, and cook over low heat for 15 minutes, until the apricots are very soft. Leave to cool then juice the orange and pour through a strainer into the pan. Use an immersion (stick) blender to blitz the compote to a smooth puree.

Slice the sponge cake into three even layers. Whisk the cream with the confectioners' (icing) sugar to soft peaks, and transfer it to the pastry (piping bag) fitted with the plain piping tip (nozzle). Pipe one-third of the cream onto the bottom layer of sponge then spread one-third of the apricot compote on top. Place the middle layer of sponge on the bottom layer and repeat, adding a layer of cream then a layer of compote. Top with the final layer of sponge and pipe the remaining cream over the cake, then spread the remaining compote in the centre. Decorate with the reserved dried apricots, a dusting of confectioners' sugar, and a sprinkle of dried rose petals.

TIPS AND TRICKS
For an extra tall cake, bake the cake batter in three separate, individual Genoise sponges and use these for the different layers.

CHOCOLATE CAKE WITH CHERRIES IN BAROLO CHINATO

Torta al cioccolato con ciliegie al Barolo Chinato

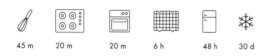

| 45 m | 20 m | 20 m | 6 h | 48 h | 30 d |

Difficulty: AVERAGE

For the roulade sponge:
see page 110 for the method, but use the ingredients listed below to make a chocolate sponge

TO SERVE 8

FOR THE CHOCOLATE SPONGE
4 eggs
4 ounces/generous ½ cup/120 g superfine (caster) sugar
Pinch of salt
3½ ounces/¾ cup/100 g type "00" flour or all-purpose (plain) flour
1 ounce/¼ cup/25 g unsweetened cocoa powder

FOR THE CHERRY SYRUP
14 ounces/3 cups/400 g cherries
2 fl oz/¼ cup/60 ml Barolo Chinato wine (or use Barolo or Barbaresco wine)
1¾ fl oz/3 tablespoons/50 ml water
2 ounces/¼ cup/50 g sugar

FOR THE MOUSSE
7 ounces/200 g bittersweet (dark) chocolate
1 ounce/2 tablespoons/30 g unsalted butter
3 ounces/generous ⅓ cup/80 g superfine (caster) sugar
1¾ fl oz/3 tablespoons/50 ml water
5 egg whites

EQUIPMENT NEEDED
10 × 12-inch/24 × 30-cm baking sheet
Parchment paper
Bowls
Pitting tool
Saucepan
Measuring cup or jug
Fine-mesh strainer (sieve)
7-inch/18-cm round loose bottom cake pan (tin) with deep sides or springform pan (tin)
Acetate sheet
Bain-marie or double boiler
Small saucepan
Kitchen thermometer
Electric whisk
Grater with medium holes
Spatula or palette knife

Preheat the oven to 350°F/180°C/160°C Fan/Gas 4 and line the baking sheet with parchment paper.

Reserve a few cherries for decoration then wash and stone (pit) the remaining cherries using the pitting tool. Place in a saucepan with the wine, water and sugar, bring to a boil over medium heat and cook for 5 minutes. Leave to cool then pour into a fine-mesh strainer (sieve) set over a bowl to collect the cooking liquid.

Using the ingredient quantities listed on this page, prepare the roulade sponge following the instructions on page 110 but adding the sifted flour and cocoa powder in several stages making sure it is fully incorporated between each addition. Pour the mix into the lined baking sheet, spread it evenly and bake in the preheated oven for 20 minutes or until risen and just firm to the touch—a skewer inserted into the center comes out clean. Leave to cool completely.

To make the mousse, finely chop 5 ounces/150 g of the bittersweet (dark) chocolate and melt in a bain-marie or double boiler with the butter, then set aside to cool.

Place the sugar in a small saucepan with the water and bring to a boil over low heat to make a syrup. Heat the syrup to 250°F/121°C using a thermometer to check it reaches the correct temperature.

Meanwhile, place the egg whites in a grease-free bowl and whisk to soft peaks. When the syrup has reached the correct temperature, drizzle it into the whisked egg whites, continuing to whisk until the mixture has cooled to room temperature and forms firm glossy peaks.

Grate 1 ounce/30 g of the bittersweet (dark) chocolate, add to the cooled melted chocolate and mix.

Using the cake pan as a cutter, cut two 7-inch/18-cm disks of sponge. Place one in the base of the cake pan (tin) and line the inner sides with an acetate sheet. Dampen the sponge base with some of the cherry cooking liquid, then pour two-thirds of the mousse over the sponge, and add the drained cooked cherries. Cover with the remaining layer of sponge, and finish with the remaining mousse, using a spatula or palette knife to spread it evenly over the top. Leave in the refrigerator for 5–6 hours.

To serve, remove the cake from the pan, transfer to a serving plate, and carefully remove and discard the acetate. Grate the remaining bittersweet (dark) chocolate over the top of the cake and decorate with the reserved cherries.

BANANA, MANGO, AND MINT CHARLOTTE

Charlotte alla banana, mango e menta

45 m	10 m	20 m	6 h 30 m	48 h	30 d

Difficulty: ADVANCED

For the roulade sponge:
    see page 110

TO SERVE 8

FOR THE SPONGE
1 quantity of roulade sponge mix prepared following
    the base recipe on page 110
7 ounces/⅔ cup/200 g red currant jelly

FOR THE BANANA BAVARIAN CREAM
¼ ounce/7 g platinum gelatin sheets
4 egg yolks
2 ounces/¼ cup/50 g superfine (caster) sugar
7 fl oz/scant 1 cup/200 ml heavy (whipping) cream
8½ fl oz/1 cup/250 ml whole (full-fat) milk
10 mint leaves
10½ ounces/300 g bananas

FOR THE MANGO MOUSSE
½ ounce/10 g platinum gelatin sheets
9 ounces/250 g mango flesh
2 ounces/¼ cup/50 g superfine (caster) sugar
7 fl oz/scant 1 cup/200 ml heavy (whipping) cream

TO DECORATE
3½ ounces/100 g mango
10 fl oz/1¼ cups/300 ml heavy (whipping) cream
2½ ounces/¾ cup/75 g confectioners' (icing) sugar
Edible flowers

EQUIPMENT NEEDED
9 × 16-inch/28 × 40-cm baking sheet
Parchment paper
Cooling rack
Plastic wrap (cling film)
Bowls
Electric whisk
Measuring cup or jug
Saucepans
Fine-mesh strainer (sieve)
Bain-marie or double boiler
Immersion (stick) blender
Large glass trifle bowl or other serving dish

Preheat the oven to 350°F/180°C/160°C Fan/Gas 4 and line the baking sheet with parchment paper, leaving some excess paper overhanging the edges of the tray.

Pour the prepared sponge mix into the lined baking sheet and bake in the preheated oven for 20 minutes, or until lightly golden, risen, and just firm to the touch—a skewer inserted into the center comes out clean. Leave in the tray to cool slightly for 10 minutes then lift out the sponge on the parchment paper and place on a cooling rack to cool completely.

When cool, spread the jam over the sponge and, starting from one long side, roll it into a cylinder as tightly as possible. Wrap in plastic wrap (cling film) and leave to rest for 30 minutes.

To make the banana Bavarian cream, soak the gelatin in cold water for 5 minutes (see page 40). Whisk the egg yolks with the sugar. Pour the cream and milk into a saucepan, add the mint leaves and warm over low heat. Pour through a fine-mesh strainer (sieve) into a bowl, then slowly pour into the egg yolk mix, whisking continuously as you do so. Transfer the mix to a bain-marie or double boiler and cook over boiling water until it forms a thin coat on the back of a spoon. Squeeze the water from the gelatin. Add to the custard and stir until it has dissolved. Leave to cool. Puree the peeled bananas with an immersion (stick) blender and add to the cooled custard, stirring to combine.

To make the mango mousse, soak the gelatin in cold water for 5 minutes, puree the mango flesh using an immersion blender then place in a saucepan with the sugar. Bring to a boil over low heat then cook for 2 minutes. Squeeze the water from the gelatin. Add to the saucepan and stir until it has dissolved. Leave to cool to room temperature, stirring occasionally. Whisk the cream, then fold it into the mango mixture until just combined.

Remove the plastic wrap from the roulade and cut into ¼-inch/½-cm slices. Line the sides of the glass trifle bowl with the roulade sponge slices. Arrange more sponge slices on the bottom of the bowl, pour in the banana Bavarian cream and place in the refrigerator for 1 hour. Once the banana Bavarian cream is set, pour in the mango mousse and return the bowl to the refrigerator for 4–5 hours.

Whip the cream with the confectioners' (icing) sugar. To serve, remove the trifle bowl from the refrigerator and cover the surface with the whipped cream. Decorate with thinly sliced fresh mango and edible flowers.

SUMMER TIRAMISÙ

Tiramisù d'estate

40 m   20 m   4 h   48 h

Difficulty: EASY

For the savoiardi sponge fingers:
  see page 112

TO SERVE 8

FOR THE TIRAMISÙ
1 pound 2 ounces/500 g peaches
3½ ounces/¾ cup/100 g raspberries
7 ounces/2 cups/200 g red currants or white currants
Juice of 1 lemon
7 fl oz/scant 1 cup/200 ml water
2 eggs
6 ounces/¾ cup/180 g superfine (caster) sugar
7 ounces/scant 1 cup/200 g mascarpone
3½ ounces/½ cup/100 g Greek yogurt
1¾ fl oz/3 tablespoons/50 ml water
1½–2 quantities of savoiardi sponge fingers prepared
  following the base recipe on page 112

TO DECORATE
A few strings of red currants or white currants

EQUIPMENT NEEDED
Saucepan with lid
Juicer
Fine-mesh strainer (sieve)
Measuring cup or jug
Bowls
Silicone spatula
Bain-marie or double boiler
Hand whisk
Kitchen thermometer
Stand mixer fitted with whisk attachment or
  electric whisk and bowl
Small saucepan
8 individual serving glasses or dishes
Plastic wrap (cling film)

Blanch 10½ ounces/300 g of the peaches in boiling water for 30 seconds, then drain and peel. Chop the peach flesh into small pieces and place in a saucepan with the raspberries. Remove the white currants from their stalks using the tines of a fork and add to the pan with the other fruit. Pour the lemon juice through a fine-mesh strainer (sieve) into the pan, add the 7 fl oz/scant 1 cup/200 ml water and bring to a boil over medium–high heat. Cook the fruit, covered, for 5 minutes. Tip the cooked fruit into a fine-mesh strainer set over a bowl to collect the juice. Leave to drain, then press with a silicone spatula to extract as much juice from the fruit as possible. Discard what is left in the strainer.

Separate the egg yolks from the whites, and place the yolks in a bain-marie or double boiler with 1½ ounces/¼ cup/40 g of the sugar. Beat the yolks with the sugar using a hand whisk, until the temperature reaches 110°F/45°C. Transfer to a bowl and beat with an electric whisk or stand mixer until cooled.

In a separate bowl, beat the mascarpone with the Greek yogurt until just combined. Add to the yolk mix a little at a time, folding it in gently with a silicone spatula.

Place the remaining sugar in a small saucepan with 1¾ fl oz/3 tablespoons/50 ml water and bring to a boil over low heat to make a syrup. Heat the syrup to 250°F/121°C using a thermometer to check it reaches the correct temperature.

Meanwhile, place the egg whites in a grease-free bowl and whisk to soft peaks. When the syrup has reached the correct temperature, drizzle it into the whisked egg whites, continuously whisking until the mixture cools and forms firm glossy peaks, then gently fold into the mascarpone mix.

Dip the sponge fingers in the reserved fruit juice and arrange a few over the bottom of each serving glass or dish. Cover the sponge fingers with half of the mascarpone cream. Slice the remaining peaches and chop them into small pieces, then arrange in an even layer on top of the mascarpone cream. Continue with another layer of soaked sponge fingers then finish with the rest of the mascarpone cream. Loosely cover the glasses or dishes with plastic wrap (cling film) and place in the refrigerator for at least 4 hours.

To serve, decorate each tiramisù with a small string of red currants.

CHOUX

Choux pastry
Impasto per bignè

25 m   5 m   37–42 m   48 h

Difficulty: AVERAGE

MAKES 1 QUANTITY
(APPROXIMATELY 1 POUND 2 OUNCES/500 G
CHOUX DOUGH OR ENOUGH TO MAKE
24–30 PROFITEROLES OR 12–15 CHOUX BUNS
OR ÉCLAIRS)

FOR THE CHOUX
8½ fl oz/1 cup/250 ml water
3 ounces/5 tablespoons/80 g unsalted butter
Pinch of salt
5 ounces/1¼ cups/150 g type "00" flour or all-purpose
(plain) flour
3 eggs

EQUIPMENT NEEDED
Measuring cup or jug
Saucepan
Wooden spoon or silicone spatula
Stand mixer fitted with flat beater attachment
Pastry (piping) bag with a ½-inch/1-cm plain piping
tip (nozzle)
2–3 baking sheets
Parchment paper

AS USED IN
– Craquelin Choux with Pear Chantilly Cream
(see page 136)
– Matcha Tea Cake with Craquelin Choux
(see page 138)
– Pont Neuf Tartlets with Red Currants
(see page 140)
– "Zeppole"—Italian Donuts
(see page 142)

Preheat the oven to 450°F/230°C/210°C Fan/Gas 8. Line the baking trays with parchment paper.

Put the water, butter, and salt in a large saucepan (1). Place over low heat until the butter has melted, then turn the heat up to high and bring the mixture to a full boil. Remove the saucepan from the heat and immediately add the flour (2). Stir with a wooden spoon to mix to a paste, then return to a low heat and cook, stirring continuously, for 1–2 minutes until the mixture forms a smooth dough that comes away from the sides of the pan (3).

Transfer the dough to a bowl and leave to cool to room temperature. Add one egg (4) and mix using a wooden spoon until it has been fully incorporated into the dough (5). Add the remaining two eggs in the same way, only adding the second egg when the first has been completely incorporated. When finished, place the dough in a pastry (piping) bag fitted with a plain piping tip (nozzle) (6).

Pipe the choux dough directly onto the lined baking trays to form the desired shape for profiteroles, éclairs, or choux buns (7). When piping, leave enough space between each shape to allow for the pastries to rise during baking. Wet your finger with cold water and gently level off the top of each choux dough shape (8).

Bake in the preheated oven for 12 minutes, then lower the oven temperature to 325°F/160°C/140°C Fan/Gas 3 and bake for a further 15 minutes for profiteroles and 20 minutes for éclairs or choux buns, until the pastries are puffed up, golden, crisp on the outside, and hollow in the center. Do not open the oven door until the end of the cooking time, then turn the oven off and open the oven door halfway. Leave the pastries to rest in the oven for 10 minutes. This lets some of the steam escape, so the pastries become light and crispy.

Any uncooked choux dough can be stored in an airtight container in the refrigerator for up to 3 days. Remove from the refrigerator an hour before using to let the dough come to room temperature.

Unfilled, baked choux can be stored in an airtight container for 3 days. The pastry will soften but can be re-crisped by putting the choux in an oven preheated to 350°F/180°C/160°C Fan/Gas 4 for 5 minutes and then cooling with the oven door ajar for 10 minutes. Leave to cool completely on a cooling rack before using.

TIPS AND TRICKS
If you do not have a fan oven, cook the choux pastries in batches on the center shelf of the oven.

VARIATIONS
Rather than using water, choux can also be prepared by replacing half the quantity of water with an equal quantity of milk, or by completely replacing the water with all milk. Choux made with water will bake up lighter in texture and paler in color, whereas the pastry made with milk will be slightly heavier and a darker shade. Before baking, brush the choux with an egg wash—this will help the pastry take on an attractive golden color when baked. To make an egg wash, whisk an egg yolk with a few drops of cold water.

Craquelin pastry
Pasta per bignè craquelin

20 m   40–50 m   30 m   24 h   30 d

Difficulty: AVERAGE

MAKES 1 QUANTITY
(APPROXIMATELY 5 OUNCES/140 G CRAQUELIN
DOUGH OR ENOUGH TO TOP 12 CHOUX BUNS)

FOR THE CRAQUELIN
1½ ounces/2 tablespoons/40 g unsalted butter
2 ounces/¼ cup/50 g soft light brown sugar
2 ounces/⅓ cup/50 g type "00" flour or all-purpose
(plain) flour

EQUIPMENT NEEDED
Bowl
Silicone spatula
Fine-mesh strainer (sieve)
Parchment paper
Rolling pin
Round pastry cutter (in the size to fit the pre-prepared
choux pastries)

AS USED IN
– Craquelin Choux with Pear Chantilly Cream
(see page 136)
– Matcha Tea Cake with Craquelin Choux
(see page 138)

Beat the butter in a bowl with a silicone spatula until soft and creamy (1).

Add the sugar and continue to beat until the sugar has almost fully dissolved (2).

Sift the flour, add it to the bowl and mix with the spatula to fully combine and form a dough (3).

Place the dough between two sheets of parchment paper (4) and roll it out using a rolling pin to a thickness of ⅛ inch/2 mm (5). Place the sheet of dough in the freezer for approximately 30 minutes, until it has hardened.

Discard the top sheet of parchment paper (6) and quickly cut out small rounds of craquelin dough using the pastry cutter (7). Immediately place the disks on the choux and bake in the oven following the instructions in your recipe.

VARIATIONS
You can prepare chocolate craquelin pastry by reducing the quantity of sugar to 1½ ounces/scant ¼ cup/40 g and adding ½ ounce/10 g of bittersweet (dark) chocolate, melted in a bain-marie or double boiler.

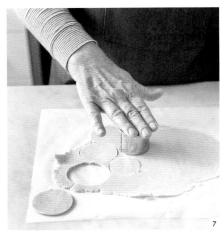

CRAQUELIN CHOUX WITH PEAR CHANTILLY CREAM

Bignè craquelin con chantilly alle pere

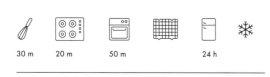

30 m   20 m   50 m   24 h

Difficulty: ADVANCED

For the choux pastry:
    see page 132
For the craquelin pastry:
    see page 134

TO SERVE 6–12 (MAKES 12 CRAQUELIN CHOUX)

FOR THE CRAQUELIN CHOUX
1 quantity (10½ ounces/300 g) of choux pastry prepared
    following the base recipe on page 132
1 quantity (5 ounces/140 g) of craquelin pastry prepared
    following the base recipe on page 134

FOR THE PEAR CHANTILLY CREAM
10½ ounces/300 g Williams pears
1½ ounces/scant ¼ cup/40 g superfine (caster) sugar
1½ tablespoons/20 ml water
1 star anise
7 fl oz/scant 1 cup/200 ml fresh heavy (whipping) cream
1½ ounces/⅓ cup/40 g confectioners' (icing) sugar

EQUIPMENT NEEDED
Pastry (piping) bag fitted with ½-inch/1-cm plain piping
    tip (nozzle)
Baking sheet
Parchment paper
2-inch/5-cm round pastry cutter
Saucepan
Measuring cup or jug
Paper towels
Food processor
Electric whisk
Large star piping tip (nozzle)

Preheat the oven to 450°F/230°C/210°C Fan/Gas 8. Line a baking sheet with parchment paper.

Place the choux dough in a pastry (piping) bag fitted with a plain piping tip (nozzle). Pipe the choux dough directly onto the lined baking sheet to form 12 regular mounds, that are 2 inches/5 cm in diameter. When piping, leave enough space between each mound to allow for the pastries to rise during baking. Wet your finger with cold water and gently level off the top of each mound. Cut out 12 disks from the frozen sheet of craquelin pastry using the pastry cutter and place them on the piped choux mounds.

Bake in the preheated oven for 10 minutes, then lower the oven temperature to 325°F/160°C/140°C Fan/Gas 3 and bake for a further 20–30 minutes, until the choux are puffed up, golden, crisp on the outside, and hollow in the center. Do not open the oven door until the end of the cooking time, then turn the oven off and open the oven door halfway. Leave the pastries to rest in the oven for 10 minutes before removing to cool completely. This lets some of the steam escape, so the pastries become light and crispy.

To make the pear cream, peel and chop the pears into small wedges, then place in a saucepan with the superfine (caster) sugar, water, and star anise. Cook over medium heat for 20 minutes, until the pears are soft, then drain the pears and pat them dry with paper towels. Puree the pear wedges in a food processor.

Whip the cream with the confectioners' (icing) sugar to soft peaks and mix it into the pear puree. Fill a pastry (piping) bag fitted with the large star piping tip (nozzle) with the pear cream.

Cut each choux bun in half, horizontally, just below the craquelin pastry cap. Pipe the pear cream into each choux bun to cover the bottom half of the pastry, then place the pastry cap on top. To serve, place one or two choux buns on individual plates.

TIPS AND TRICKS
Any unbaked choux dough can be stored in an airtight container in the refrigerator for up to 3 days. An hour before using, remove the dough from the refrigerator to let it come to room temperature. Unfilled, baked choux can be stored in an airtight container for up to 3 days. The choux pastry will soften but can be re-crisped by baking in an oven preheated to 350°F/180°C/160°C Fan/Gas 4 for 5 minutes and then cooling with the oven door ajar for 10 minutes. Leave to cool completely on a wire rack before serving.

MATCHA TEA CAKE WITH CRAQUELIN CHOUX

Torta al tè matcha con bignè craquelin

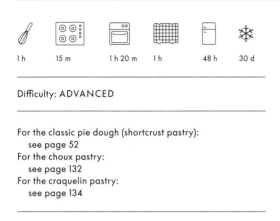

1 h   15 m   1 h 20 m   1 h   48 h   30 d

Difficulty: ADVANCED

For the classic pie dough (shortcrust pastry):
  see page 52
For the choux pastry:
  see page 132
For the craquelin pastry:
  see page 134

TO SERVE 10

FOR THE MATCHA BASE
½ quantity of classic pie dough (shortcrust pastry) prepared
  following the base recipe on page 52 with ½ ounce/
  5 teaspoons/10 g powdered matcha green tea

FOR THE CHESTNUT MOUSSE
1½ ounces/2 tablespoons/40 g unsalted butter
3 ounces/80 g bittersweet (dark) chocolate
13 ounces/2¾ cups/380 g cooked chestnuts
5 fl oz/scant ⅔ cup/150 ml whole (full-fat) milk
2 ounces/¼ cup/50 g superfine (caster) sugar
1 bay leaf

FOR THE CRAQUELIN CHOUX
½ quantity of choux pastry prepared following the base
  recipe on page 132
1 quantity of chocolate craquelin pastry prepared following
  the base recipe variation on page 134
7 fl oz/scant 1 cup/200 ml heavy (whipping) cream
1 ounce/¼ cup/30 g confectioners' (icing) sugar

TO DECORATE
Cocoa powder, for dusting
1 ounce/30 g bittersweet (dark) chocolate shavings

EQUIPMENT NEEDED
7-inch/18-cm round springform pan (tin)
Rolling pin
Parchment paper
Baking beans
Acetate sheet
Bain-marie or double boiler
Saucepan
Immersion (stick) blender
Pastry (piping) bags fitted with ½-inch/1-cm and
  ¾-inch/1.5-cm plain piping tips (nozzles)
Baking sheet
1½-inch/3-cm round pastry cutter
Bowl
Electric whisk
Grater with large holes
Spatula or palette knife
Small strainer (sieve) or dusting spoon

Preheat the oven to 350°F/180°C/160°C Fan/Gas 4.

On a lightly floured surface, roll out the pie dough (pastry) to ¼ inch/ ½ cm thick. Cut out a disk from the dough using the springform pan as a cutter. Assemble the springform pan by clipping the sides around the base that has been lined with parchment paper. Carefully transfer the dough disk to the pan to cover the base. Prick the dough with a fork, cover it with parchment paper, and fill with baking beans. Place in the lower part of the preheated oven for 25 minutes to blind bake. After 25 minutes, remove the baking beans and parchment paper and return to the oven for a further 10–15 minutes, or until the pastry base has dried out. Leave to cool in the pan, then line the inner sides of the pan with the acetate sheet.

To make the chestnut mousse, cut the butter into small cubes and melt with the chocolate in a bain-marie or double boiler. Crumble the cooked chestnuts into a saucepan, add the milk, sugar, and bay leaf, then cook over medium–low heat until the milk has been absorbed. Add the butter and melted chocolate, then puree with an immersion (stick) blender. Leave to cool, then pour into the pan over the base and place in the refrigerator for 1 hour.

Increase the oven temperature to 450°F/220°C/210°C Fan/Gas 8.

Line the baking sheet with parchment paper. Place the choux in a pastry (piping) bag fitted with a ½-inch/1-cm plain piping tip (nozzle). Pipe the choux onto the baking sheet to form 5 mounds, that are 1½ inch/3 cm wide. When piping, leave enough space to allow for the pastries to rise during baking. Wet your finger with cold water and gently level off the top of each mound. Using the pastry cutter, cut out 5 disks from the craquelin and place them on the piped choux mounds. Bake in the preheated oven for 10 minutes, then lower the oven temperature to 325°F/160°C/140°C Fan/Gas 3 and bake for a further 20–30 minutes, until the choux are puffed up, golden, crisp on the outside, and hollow in the center. Do not open the oven door until the end of the cooking time, then turn the oven off and open the oven door halfway. Leave the pastries to rest in the oven for 10 minutes before removing to cool completely. This lets some of the steam escape, so the pastries become light and crispy.

Using an electric whisk, whip the cream with the confectioners' (icing) sugar to soft peaks. Fill a pastry bag fitted with a ¾-inch/ 1.5-cm plain piping tip with the cream. Cut each choux bun in half, just below the craquelin pastry cap. Pipe the cream into each bun to cover the bottom half, then replace the cap. Carefully unmold the cake onto a serving plate. Remove and discard the acetate. Arrange the craquelin choux on the cake. To serve, decorate with a dusting of cocoa powder and bittersweet (dark) chocolate shavings.

PONT NEUF TARTLETS WITH RED CURRANTS

Tartellette Pont Neuf ai ribes

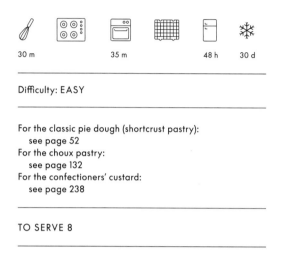

30 m   35 m   48 h   30 d

Difficulty: EASY

For the classic pie dough (shortcrust pastry):
    see page 52
For the choux pastry:
    see page 132
For the confectioners' custard:
    see page 238

TO SERVE 8

FOR THE TARTLETS
Butter, for greasing
½ quantity (7 ounces/200 g) of classic pie dough (shortcrust pastry) flavored with the grated zest of ½ unwaxed lemon prepared following the base recipe on page 52
⅓ quantity (4 ounces/125 g) of choux pastry prepared following the base recipe on page 132
¼ quantity (4 ounces/½ cup/125 g) of confectioners' custard prepared following the base recipe on page 238
2 ounces/3 tablespoons/50 g red currant jelly

TO DECORATE
4 ounces/¾ cup/125 g red currants
Confectioners' (icing) sugar, for dusting

EQUIPMENT NEEDED
4-inch/10-cm round loose-bottom tartlet pans (tins)
Parchment paper
Rolling pin
4½-inch/11-cm round pastry cutter
Baking beans
Bowl
Pastry (piping) bag fitted with ¾-inch/1.5-cm plain piping tip (nozzle)
Cooling rack
Small saucepan
Pastry brush
Small strainer (sieve) or dusting spoon

Preheat the oven to 350°F/180°C/160°C Fan/Gas 4. Grease the tartlet pans (tins) with a little butter.

On a lightly floured surface, roll out the pie dough (pastry) to ⅛ inch/3 mm thick. Using the pastry cutter, cut out 8 disks of dough. Place a pastry disk in each tartlet pan, pressing down on the base and sides and trimming off the excess dough with a small sharp knife.

Prick the dough with a fork, cover it with parchment paper, and cover with baking beans. Place in the lower part of the preheated oven for 15 minutes to blind bake. After 15 minutes, remove the baking beans and parchment paper and return to the oven for a further 5 minutes, or until the pastry cases have dried out and started to become golden.

Increase the oven temperature to 425°F/220°C/200°C Fan/Gas 7.

Place the choux pastry in a bowl, add the custard and mix to combine. Fill a pastry (piping) bag fitted with the plain piping tip (nozzle) with this mixture and pipe it into the cooked pastry cases. Bake in the preheated oven for 15 minutes. Leave to cool a little in the pans, then remove from the pans and leave to cool completely on a cooling rack.

In a small saucepan, heat the red currant jelly with ¼ cup/60 ml water over low heat until dissolved, then brush this syrup over the tartlets and leave to cool.

To serve, decorate the tartlets with the fresh red currants and a dusting of confectioners' (icing) sugar.

"ZEPPOLE"—ITALIAN DONUTS

Zeppole

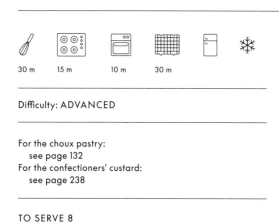

30 m   15 m   10 m   30 m

Difficulty: ADVANCED

For the choux pastry:
    see page 132
For the confectioners' custard:
    see page 238

TO SERVE 8

FOR THE DONUTS
9 ounces/2 cups/250 g type "00" flour or all-purpose
    (plain) flour
6 eggs
3½ ounces/7 tablespoons/100 g unsalted butter
8½ fl oz/1 cup/250 ml water
Vegetable oil for frying

TO DECORATE
Confectioners' (icing) sugar, for dusting
1 quantity of confectioners' custard prepared following
    the base recipe on page 238
Black cherries in syrup, halved

EQUIPMENT NEEDED
2 baking sheets
Parchment paper
Pastry (piping) bag fitted with star or zeppole piping
    tip (nozzle)
Deep saucepan with heavy base
Candy (sugar) thermometer
Skimmer
Paper towels
Small strainer (sieve) or dusting spoon
Pastry (piping) bag fitted with 1-inch/2.5-cm plain piping
    tip (nozzle)

Preheat the oven to 425°F/220°C/200°C Fan/Gas 7. Line the baking sheets with parchment paper.

Using the ingredients quantities listed on this page, prepare the choux pastry following the instructions on page 132. Leave to rest in the refrigerator for 30 minutes.

Place the choux dough in a pastry (piping) bag fitted with a zeppole piping tip (nozzle). Pipe the choux directly onto the lined baking sheets to form ring shapes, that are 3 inches/8 cm in diameter. When piping, leave enough space between each ring to allow for the zeppole to spread during baking.

Bake in the preheated oven for 10 minutes to slightly firm up the pastry.

Meanwhile, half-fill a deep saucepan with vegetable oil and heat to 350°F/180°C. Remove the zeppole from the oven and fry them in batches of 2 or 3 until they are fluffy and golden, turning them over with a skimmer.

Drain on paper towels and leave to cool a little then transfer to a serving plate and sprinkle with confectioners' (icing) sugar.

Place the confectioners' custard in a pastry (piping) bag fitted with a plain piping tip (nozzle). Pipe the custard into the middle of each zeppole to fill the hole. Place a few black cherry halves on the top of each zeppole to decorate.

TIPS AND TRICKS
The temperature of the oil for frying the zeppole must be kept constantly at 350°F/180°C, so that the zeppole cook through before they start to brown too much. Allow the oil to return to temperature in between frying the batches.

BATTER

Waffle batter

Pastella per gaufre

10 m   4–5 m   10 m

Difficulty: EASY

MAKES 1 QUANTITY
(2¾ CUPS/700 ML BATTER)

FOR THE BATTER
3 ounces/5 tablespoons/80 g unsalted butter,
   plus extra for greasing
4 eggs
11¾ fl oz/scant 1½ cups/350 ml whole (full-fat) milk
2 ounces/¼ cup/50 g superfine (caster) sugar
9 ounces/2 cups/250 g type "00" flour or all-purpose
   (plain) flour
½ ounce/2 teaspoons/10 g baking powder
Pinch of salt

EQUIPMENT NEEDED
Small saucepan
Bowls
Measuring cup or jug
Hand whisk
Fine-mesh strainer (sieve)
Waffle iron (manual or electric)
Ladle

AS USED IN
– Chocolate Belgian Waffles with Sour Cream
  (see page 150)
– Liège Waffles with Peaches and Ice Cream
  (see page 152)

Cut the butter into small cubes, melt in a small saucepan, and set aside to cool. Break the eggs into a bowl, add the milk and whisk gently (1).

When the melted butter has cooled, slowly pour it into the bowl with the beaten eggs, whisking continuously (2). If you add the butter when it is still warm the eggs will begin to scramble.

Add the sugar, whisking continuously, until incorporated. Sift the flour into a bowl with the baking powder and salt, then add to the egg mix, stirring continuously with the whisk to avoid any lumps forming (3). Leave the batter to rest for 10 minutes.

Meanwhile, heat the waffle iron over medium–low heat if using a manual one or to medium if using an electric one. Lightly grease the plates of the waffle iron with butter.

Using a ladle, spoon the batter onto the hot waffle iron (4) and close it immediately. The amount of batter required varies according to the size of the waffle iron, so check the instructions for your appliance (5).

If using a manual iron, cook for about 2 minutes per side or a little longer if you prefer the waffles to be more golden and crisp. If using an electric waffle maker, follow the manufacturer's instructions. Remove the waffles from the iron when golden and serve immediately with your preferred toppings.

MISTAKES TO AVOID
Electric waffle makers are thermostatically controlled, so maintain an even temperature. If using a manual waffle iron, you must check the iron does not become too hot. If necessary, let the waffle iron cool slightly before continuing to make the waffles. The waffle batter needs to cook evenly without burning.

 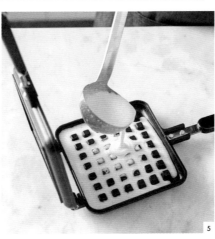

Crêpe batter

Pastella per crêpe

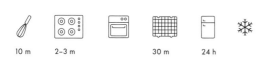

| 10 m | 2–3 m | | 30 m | 24 h | |

Difficulty: EASY

MAKES 1 QUANTITY
   (APPROXIMATELY 1½ CUPS/350 ML BATTER)

FOR THE BATTER
1 ounce/2 tablespoons/30 g unsalted butter
2½ ounces/⅔ cup/75 g type "00" flour or all-purpose
   (plain) flour
Pinch of salt
¾ ounce/5 teaspoons/20 g superfine (caster) sugar
4½ ounces/generous ½ cup/130 ml whole (full-fat) milk
2½ fl oz/5 tablespoons/70 ml water
2 eggs
Vegetable oil, for frying

EQUIPMENT NEEDED
Small saucepan
Bowl
Fine-mesh strainer (sieve)
Measuring cup or jug
Hand whisk
Crêpe pan or non-stick skillet (frying pan)
Ladle
Batter spreader (optional)
Spatula or palette knife

AS USED IN
– "Boûkètes"—Belgian Pancakes
   (see page 154)
– Chestnut Crêpes with Ricotta
   (see page 156)

Cut the butter into small cubes, melt in a small saucepan, and set aside to cool. Sift the flour into a bowl and add a pinch of salt and the sugar. Dilute the milk with the water, then slowly pour onto the dry ingredients, stirring continuously with a hand whisk to avoid any lumps forming (1).

When the melted butter has cooled, slowly pour it into the flour mix, whisking continuously until incorporated (2).

Break the eggs into a bowl and gently beat them with a hand whisk. Slowly add the beaten eggs to the mix, continuously stirring with the whisk until combined (3). Leave the batter to rest for 30 minutes.

Meanwhile, heat the crêpe pan over medium heat and lightly grease with a little vegetable oil.

Spoon a ladleful of batter onto the crêpe pan (4) and let it spread over the entire surface, working the pan with your wrist to evenly distribute the batter (5). Alternatively, use a batter spreader (see page 14). When the edges of the crêpe start to turn golden, lift it with a spatula or palette knife (6), flip it over and cook it on the other side (7). Repeat with the remaining batter, oiling the pan lightly between each crêpe.

Serve the crêpes immediately with your preferred toppings.

TIPS AND TRICKS
Alternatively, you can place all the ingredients in a food processor and blend to obtain a smooth and even batter. Different types of flour absorb more or less liquid and this may result in a batter that is too thick for making delicate, thin crêpes. If this happens, simply add a little water for a runnier batter that will spread uniformly across the pan. Once cooked, the crêpe should be thin with little holes, like lace.

VARIATIONS
You can also flavor the batter with 1 tablespoon of orange liqueur or Cognac, 1 teaspoon of orange flower water, the seeds from a vanilla bean (pod), or the grated zest of an unwaxed lemon, according to your taste.

CHOCOLATE BELGIAN WAFFLES WITH SOUR CREAM

Gaufre di Bruxelles al cacao con panna acida

15 m   5 m

Difficulty: EASY

TO SERVE 8

FOR THE WAFFLES
3 ounces/5 tablespoons/80 g unsalted butter,
    plus extra for greasing
3 eggs
1 vanilla bean (pod)
3 Cubeb peppercorns (or use a mixture of black pepper
    and allspice)
2 ounces/¼ cup/60 g superfine (caster) sugar
Pinch of salt
9 ounces/2 cups/250 g type "00" flour or all-purpose
    (plain) flour
2 ounces/½ cup/50 g unsweetened cocoa powder
¼ ounce/1½ teaspoons/8 g baking powder
13 fl oz/generous 1½ cups/400 ml whole (full-fat) milk

TO SERVE
5 ounces/⅔ cup/150 g crème fraîche
Ground cinnamon, for dusting

EQUIPMENT NEEDED
Small saucepan
Bowls
Mortar and pestle
Hand whisk
Fine-mesh strainer (sieve)
Measuring cup or jug
Electric whisk
Waffle iron (manual or electric)
Ladle
Small strainer (sieve) or dusting spoon

Place 2½ ounces/4½ tablespoons/70 g of the butter in a small saucepan and melt over a very low heat, then set aside to cool.

Separate the egg yolks from the whites, remove the seeds from the vanilla pod, and finely grind the peppercorns using a mortar and pestle. Place the egg yolks, sugar, vanilla seeds, pepper, and a pinch of salt in a bowl and beat with a hand whisk until light and frothy.

Sift the flour with the cocoa powder and the baking powder into a bowl. Add the cooled melted butter and the milk, stirring continuously with a whisk to prevent any lumps forming. Add the egg yolk mix, beating continuously until combined.

Using an electric whisk, beat the egg whites until they form soft peaks and then fold them into the batter mixture.

Meanwhile, heat the waffle iron over medium–low heat if using a manual one or to medium if using an electric one. Lightly grease the plates of the waffle iron with butter.

Using a ladle, spoon the batter onto the hot waffle iron into an oval shape and close it immediately. The amount of batter required varies according to the size of the waffle iron, so check the instructions for your appliance. Belgian waffle irons take more batter to fill than standard waffle irons.

If using a manual iron, cook for about 3–4 minutes per side, or a little longer if you prefer waffles to be more golden and crisp. If using an electric waffle maker, follow the manufacturer's instructions. Remove the waffles from the iron when crisp on the outside and cooked through. Continue until you have used all the batter.

Serve immediately, with the crème fraîche spooned on top and dusted with ground cinnamon.

LIÈGE WAFFLES WITH PEACHES AND ICE CREAM

Gaufre di Liegi con gelato e pesche bianche

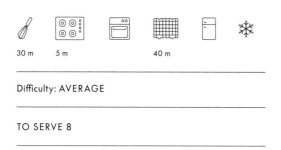

30 m 5 m 40 m

Difficulty: AVERAGE

TO SERVE 8

FOR THE WAFFLES
6 fl oz/¾ cup/180 ml whole (full-fat) milk
13 ounces/3 cups/380 g type "00" flour or all-purpose
   (plain) flour
½ teaspoon/2 g fast-action dried yeast (or use ¼ ounce/
   8 g fresh brewer's yeast)
1 vanilla bean (pod)
½ ounce/2 teaspoons/10 g superfine (caster) sugar
Pinch of salt
1 egg
1 egg yolk
7 ounces/½ cup plus 5 tablespoons/200 g unsalted butter,
   plus extra for greasing
9 ounces/1¼ cups/250 g pearl sugar crystals

TO SERVE
14 ounces/400 g mango ice cream
2 white peaches
Few sprigs of fresh mint
Confectioners' (icing) sugar, for dusting

EQUIPMENT NEEDED
Measuring cup or jug
Small saucepan
Fine-mesh strainer (sieve)
Stand mixer fitted with dough hook attachment
Plastic wrap (cling film)
Silicone spatula
Waffle iron (manual or electric)
Ladle

Pour the milk into a small saucepan and warm slightly over a very low heat. Sift the flour into the bowl of the stand mixer, stir in the yeast, add the tepid milk, the seeds from a vanilla bean (pod), and the sugar. Start to mix the ingredients at a low speed. When all of the ingredients have been incorporated, add a pinch of salt.

Add the egg and the additional yolk and mix for 10 minutes, until you obtain a dense, smooth mixture. Cover the bowl with plastic wrap (cling film) and leave to rise in a warm place for 40 minutes.

Cut the butter into small cubes and bring to room temperature to soften. Slightly deflate the mixture by pressing on it with the palms of your hands, put the bowl back on the stand mixer, then add the sugar crystals and mix to combine. Add the softened cubes of butter and mix for 3–4 minutes.

Meanwhile, heat the waffle iron over medium–low heat if using a manual one or to medium if using an electric one. Lightly grease the plates of the waffle iron with butter.

Using a ladle, spoon the batter onto the hot waffle iron into an oval shape and close it immediately. The amount of batter required varies according to the size of the waffle iron, so check the instructions for your appliance. Liège waffle irons take more batter to fill than standard waffle irons.

If using a manual iron, cook for about 3–4 minutes per side, or a little longer if you prefer waffles to be more golden and crisp. If using an electric waffle maker, follow the manufacturer's instructions. Remove the waffles from the iron when golden. Continue until you have used all the batter. Serve immediately, dusted with confectioners' (icing) sugar and with some peach slices, a sprig of fresh mint, and a scoop of mango ice cream on top.

"BOÛKÈTES"—BELGIAN PANCAKES

Bouquette

15 m	5 m		24 h	24 h	60 d

Difficulty: ADVANCED

TO SERVE 8

FOR THE PANCAKES
3½ ounces/¾ cup/100 g raisins
2 ounces/¼ cup/60 g unsalted butter, plus extra
    for greasing
9 ounces/generous 2 cups/250 g buckwheat flour
½ teaspoon/2 g fast-action dried yeast (or use ¼ ounce/
    8 g fresh brewer's yeast)
4 ounces/½ cup/120 g superfine (caster) sugar
7 fl oz/scant 1 cup/200 ml light beer
Pinch of salt
4 eggs

TO SERVE
Confectioners' (icing) sugar, for dusting

EQUIPMENT NEEDED
Small saucepan
Bowls
Fine-mesh strainer (sieve)
Paper towel
Stand mixer fitted with dough hook attachment
Measuring cup or jug
Plastic wrap (cling film)
Crêpe pan or non-stick skillet (frying pan)
Ladle
Spatula or palette knife
Small strainer (sieve) or dusting spoon

Soak the raisins in warm water for 15 minutes, then drain and pat dry using paper towels.

Melt 2 ounces/¼ cup/60 g of the butter in a small saucepan and set aside to cool.

Sift the flour into the bowl of the stand mixer, stir in the yeast, and add the sugar. Start to mix the ingredients on a low speed and slowly pour in the beer.

Continue to mix for 5 minutes, then add a pinch of salt. Add the eggs one at a time until you have a smooth batter, then add the melted butter and raisins. Mix for a further 2–3 minutes, then cover the bowl with plastic wrap (cling film) and leave the batter to rise in the refrigerator for 24 hours.

Remove the batter from the refrigerator and set aside for 30 minutes to bring to room temperature.

Meanwhile, heat the crêpe pan over medium heat and lightly grease with butter.

Spoon 4 small ladlefuls of batter onto the crêpe pan, spaced apart so they do not merge together.

Cook for 2 minutes, or until the bottom of the pancake is golden and the top looks set with a few bubbles on the surface. Lift with a spatula or palette knife, flip it over and cook it on the other side for about 1 minute, or until golden. Continue until you have used up all the batter. Serve immediately, dusted with confectioners' (icing) sugar.

CHESTNUT CRÊPES WITH RICOTTA

Crêpe di farina di castagne con ricotta

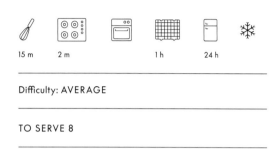

15 m 2 m 1 h 24 h

Difficulty: AVERAGE

TO SERVE 8

FOR THE CRÊPES
¾ ounce/2 tablespoons/20 g unsalted butter,
    plus extra for greasing
4 eggs
6½ ounces/1¾ cups/180 g chestnut flour
2 ounces/⅓ cup/50 g type "00" flour or all-purpose
    (plain) flour
2 ounces/¼ cup/50 g superfine (caster) sugar
20 fl oz/2½ cups/600 ml whole (full-fat) milk
Pinch of salt

FOR THE FILLING
10½ ounces/300 g sheep's ricotta
2 ounces/¼ cup/50 g superfine (caster) sugar
3½ ounces/100 g marrons glacés (candied chestnuts)
1½ ounces/40 g candied orange peel

TO SERVE
Confectioners' (icing) sugar, for dusting
Candied orange slices
Shredded orange peel

EQUIPMENT NEEDED
Small saucepan
Bowls
Hand whisk
Fine-mesh strainer (sieve)
Measuring cup or jug
Plastic wrap (cling film)
Crêpe pan or non-stick skillet (frying pan)
Ladle
Batter spreader (optional)
Spatula or palette knife
Small strainer (sieve) or dusting spoon

Cut the butter into small cubes, melt in a small saucepan and set aside to cool.

Beat the eggs together in a small bowl. Sift both the flours into a large bowl and add the sugar and beaten eggs, stirring continuously with a hand whisk to combine. Slowly pour the milk into the bowl, then the cooled melted butter and a pinch of salt, stirring continuously with the whisk to avoid any lumps forming. Cover the bowl with plastic wrap (cling film) and leave the batter to rest for 1 hour.

To make the filling, push the ricotta through the strainer (sieve) using the back of a spoon, directly into a bowl, add the sugar and mix until smooth and creamy.

Crumble the marrons glacés (candied chestnuts) and finely chop the candied orange peel and add to the filling mixture, stirring to combine.

Meanwhile, heat the crêpe pan over medium heat and lightly grease with butter.

Spoon a small ladleful of batter onto the crêpe pan and let it spread over the surface, working the pan with your wrist to evenly distribute the batter. Alternatively, use a batter spreader (see page 14).

When the edges of the crêpe start to turn golden, lift it with a spatula or palette knife, flip it over and cook it on the other side for a further 30 seconds or so, until golden. Repeat until all the batter has been used.

Place some ricotta cream in the middle of one half of the crêpe, then fold it in half and roll into a cone. Serve immediately dusted with confectioners' (icing) sugar and with candied orange slices and shredded orange peel.

ENRICHED DOUGH

Brioche dough
Pasta per brioche

30 m		20 m	14 h 30 m		60 d

Difficulty: AVERAGE

MAKES 1 QUANTITY
(2¾ POUNDS/1.25 KG DOUGH OR ENOUGH TO
MAKE 8 LARGE ROLLS OR 2 LARGE LOAVES)

FOR THE DOUGH
10½ ounces/1¼ cups/300 g unsalted butter
10½ ounces/2½ cups/300 g type "00" flour or all-purpose (plain) flour
7 ounces/1⅔ cups/200 g strong white bread flour
1 teaspoon/4 g fast-action dried yeast (or use ½ ounce/15 g fresh brewer's yeast)
1 vanilla bean (pod)
5 eggs
3 ounces/⅓ cup/80 g superfine (caster) sugar
Pinch of salt
7 fl oz/scant 1 cup/200 ml whole (full-fat) milk
1 egg yolk
Granulated white sugar, for sprinkling

EQUIPMENT NEEDED
Bowls
Fine-mesh strainer (sieve)
Stand mixer fitted with dough hook attachment
Measuring cup or jug
Plastic wrap (cling film)
Rolling pin
Baking sheet
Parchment paper
Kitchen foil
Pastry brush

AS USED IN
– Coffee and Chocolate Cream Bars
  (see page 172)
– Sugar and Vanilla Brioche
  (see page 174)
– Orange and Chocolate Braided Babka
  (see page 176)

Cut the butter into small cubes, place in a bowl, and bring to room temperature to soften. Sift the two types of flour into the bowl of the stand mixer. Stir in the yeast, add the seeds from the vanilla bean (pod), the eggs, sugar, salt, and milk, and mix until you obtain a smooth dough (1).

Add the cubes of softened butter and continue to mix until you obtain a soft, smooth dough, which easily comes away from the sides of the bowl (2).

Transfer the dough into a clean bowl and cover with plastic wrap (cling film) (3). Leave to rise in a warm place for about 2 hours or until it has doubled in volume.

After 2 hours, deflate the risen dough by pressing down on it with the palms of your hands (4). Cover again with plastic wrap and leave to rise in the refrigerator for 12 hours.

Again, press down on the dough with your palms to deflate (5) and roll it out with a rolling pin on a lightly floured surface (6).

Fold the dough onto itself (7–8) and shape into a cylinder, then slice into small blocks (9).

Shape each block of dough into a small ball (10) and place on a baking sheet lined with parchment paper. When all the dough balls have been rolled, loosely cover with a sheet of kitchen foil (11). If you plan to freeze any of the dough, do so now (see note below).

Leave to rise for 30 minutes before brushing with beaten egg yolk to glaze (12).

Preheat the oven to 350°F/180°C/160°C Fan/Gas 4.

Sprinkle with sugar and bake in the preheated oven for 20 minutes, or until the bottoms of the rolls sound hollow when tapped. When probed with a kitchen thermometer, the internal temperature of the rolls should be 200°F/95°C.

If you wish to freeze the brioche dough, do so after shaping the individual brioches and before they rise for the final time, without brushing them with the egg yolk. They will rise for the last time as they are defrosted before baking.

MISTAKES TO AVOID
For leavened dough made with dried or fresh brewer's yeast, which requires long rising periods, it is essential to maintain a constant room temperature and to ensure the dough is not left in a draft, which could cause it to deflate. In environments with a low temperature the rising time will be longer and, conversely, it will be shorter if the temperature is warmer.

TIPS AND TRICKS
Brioche dough is very rich and buttery, and so it must be made with a flour that has strong gluten strands to withstand the action of the butter. If you can find it, try using Manitoba flour, which is a strong wheat flour from Canada that is very high in gluten.

Croissant dough (pastry)
Pasta per cornetti

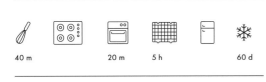

40 m   20 m   5 h   60 d

Difficulty: ADVANCED

MAKES 1 QUANTITY
(APPROXIMATELY 2½ POUNDS/1.2 KG DOUGH
OR ENOUGH TO MAKE 10 CROISSANTS)

FOR THE DOUGH
12 ounces/1½ cups/350 g unsalted butter
8½ fl oz/scant 1 cup/240 ml milk
10½ ounces/2½ cups/300 g type "0" flour
7 ounces/2 cups/200 g strong white bread flour
3 ounces/⅓ cup/80 g superfine (caster) sugar
1 teaspoon/4 g fast-action dried yeast (or use ½ ounce/
    15 g fresh brewer's yeast)
Pinch of salt
1 egg yolk

EQUIPMENT NEEDED
Small saucepan
Measuring cup or jug
Fine-mesh strainer (sieve)
Stand mixer fitted with dough hook attachment
Bowl
Plastic wrap (cling film)
Rolling pin
Baking sheet
Parchment paper
Pastry wheel or triangular pastry cutter for croissants
Pastry brush

AS USED IN
– Jam Croissant
  (see page 178)
– Candied Ginger Pinwheels
  (see page 180)

Cut 3½ ounces/¼ cup/100 g of the butter into cubes and bring to room temperature. Place the remaining butter in the refrigerator.

Pour the milk into a saucepan and warm it over low heat. Sift the flours into the bowl of the stand mixer, add the sugar then stir in the yeast. Start the mixer on low speed and gradually add the warmed milk, a pinch of salt, and the softened butter. Increase the speed to medium and mix for 10 minutes, until the dough begins to cling to the dough hook (1). Form the dough into a ball, place in a bowl, cover with plastic wrap (cling film), and leave to rise in a warm place for 1 hour. Leave the dough in the refrigerator overnight.

Place the dough on a lightly floured surface and gently press down on it with the palms of your hands to deflate, then roll it out into a large rectangle. Place the dough on a baking sheet lined with parchment paper (2) and cover it with plastic wrap. Place in the refrigerator for 20 minutes, then turn the dough over and return to the refrigerator for a further 25 minutes. Remove from the refrigerator. Roll the dough into 30 × 16-inch/70 × 40-cm rectangle that is ¼ inch/½ cm thick.

Remove the remaining butter from the refrigerator and place it between two sheets of parchment paper (3). Using a rolling pin, tap the butter to flatten it into a rectangle the same width as the sheet of dough and half the length (4). Place the butter in the center of the sheet of dough, and fold the edges of the dough so that the two short sides meet in the middle (5–6). Fold the dough in half to make a narrow rectangle (7). Wrap in plastic wrap and leave to rest in the refrigerator for 30 minutes.

Remove the dough from the plastic wrap and place on a lightly floured surface. Place the short side of the rectangle nearest to you, and roll out the dough (8) until you have a long rectangle about ¼ inch/½ cm thick. Taking the short edge nearest to you, fold the end third of the dough over the middle third, and repeat with the opposite short edge, folding it towards you, so that the three layers overlap (9). Wrap the dough in plastic wrap and leave to rest in the refrigerator for 30 minutes.

Remove the dough from the plastic wrap and place on a lightly floured surface. Place the short side of the rectangle nearest to you, and roll out the dough into a rectangle about 22 × 16 inches/ 56 × 40 cm, and ¼ inch/½ cm thick.

Cut the pastry lengthwise into two long rectangles. From each rectangle cut triangles lengthways with a 4½ inch/11 cm base. Gently stretch each triangle a further 1 inch/2–3 cm and make a ¾ inch/2 cm cut in the middle of the base with a small knife (10).

Starting from the base, roll the pastry triangles into compact crescent-shaped roll (11). Place on a baking sheet lined with parchment paper, with the narrow point of the rolled pastry facing downward. Loosely cover with foil and leave to rise in a warm place for 2 hours. Preheat the oven to 325°F/160°C/140°C Fan/ Gas 3 then brush the croissants with beaten egg yolk (12) and bake in the middle of the oven for 20 minutes depending on the size of the croissants, or until puffed up and golden.

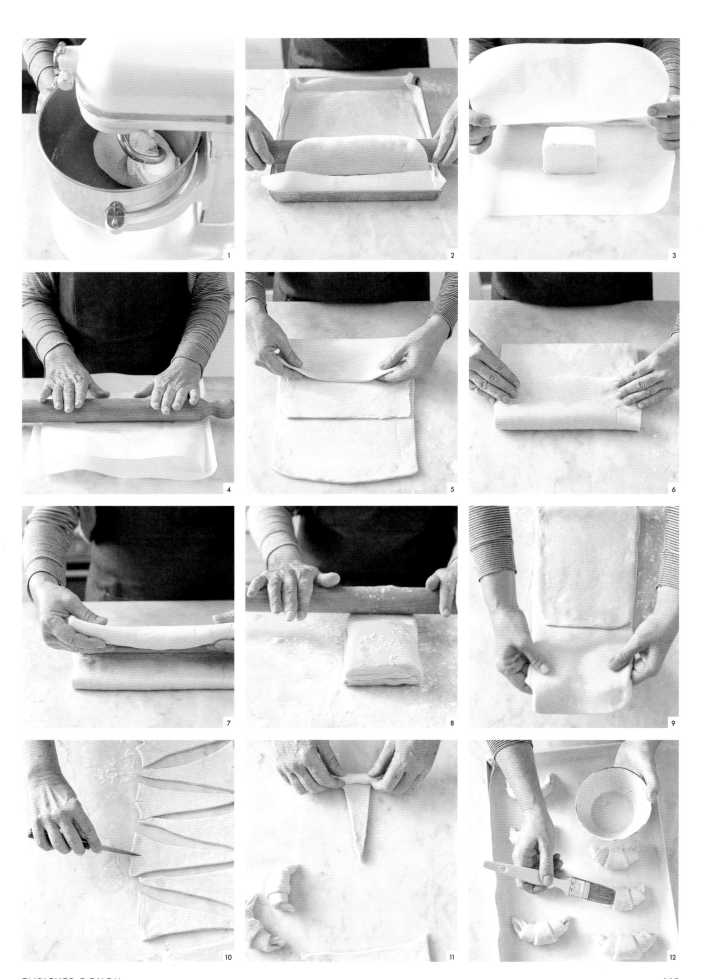

Baba dough
Pasta per babà

20 m   20–40 m   3 h

Difficulty: EASY

MAKES 1 QUANTITY
(7 OUNCES/200 G DOUGH OR ENOUGH TO
MAKE 4 MEDIUM BABAS OR 8 SMALL BABAS)

FOR THE DOUGH
6½ ounces/1½ cups/180 g type "00" flour or all-purpose
  (plain) flour, plus extra for dusting
½ teaspoon/2 g fast-action dried yeast (or use ¼ ounce/
  8 g fresh brewer's yeast)
¼ ounce/2 teaspoons/8 g superfine (caster) sugar
2 ounces/¼ cup/60 g unsalted butter
1 vanilla bean (pod)
4 eggs
Pinch of salt
Vegetable oil, for greasing
Butter, for greasing

FOR THE SYRUP
8½ fl oz/1 cup/250 ml water
3½ ounces/scant ½ cup/100 g superfine (caster) sugar
3½ fl oz/scant ½ cup/100 ml flavoring to taste (liqueur
  or citrus juice)

EQUIPMENT NEEDED
Fine-mesh strainer (sieve)
Stand mixer fitted with dough hook attachment
Bowl
Plastic wrap (cling film)
Savarin ring mold or individual rum baba molds
Kitchen foil

AS USED IN
– Limoncello Mini Baba
  (see page 182)
– Citrus Savarin with Cream and Fruit
  (see page 184)

Sift the flour into the bowl of the stand mixer. Stir in the yeast, then add the sugar, butter, the seeds from the vanilla bean (pod), eggs, and a pinch of salt (1).

Mix at a low speed until you obtain a smooth, shiny dough (2) and continue to mix until the dough comes away from the sides of the bowl.

Transfer the dough to a clean bowl that has been lightly oiled (3), cover with plastic wrap (cling film) and leave to rise for 30 minutes.

Grease the baba molds with butter and dust them with flour. Divide the baba dough into equal pieces to match the number of molds you are using. Shape the pieces of dough into smooth balls and place into the individual baba molds (4).

Loosely cover the babas with kitchen foil, placing all the molds in a larger dish if necessary (5). Leave to rise for 2 hours 30 minutes (6).

Preheat the oven to 350°F/180°C/160°C Fan/Gas 4. Remove the foil, place the molds on a baking sheet, and bake in the preheated oven for 20–40 minutes depending on the size and shape of the baba, or until risen and brown on top. When probed with a kitchen thermometer, the internal temperature of the baba should be 200°F/95°C.

Meanwhile, to prepare the syrup, place the sugar and water in a saucepan and warm it over low heat until the sugar has dissolved. Increase the heat to medium, add the flavoring, and boil the syrup for 2 minutes. Remove from the heat and set aside to cool.

Once baked, dip the babas in the cold syrup until they are soaked (7). Place the soaked babas on a cooling rack for 10 minutes to allow any excess syrup to drain before serving.

VARIATIONS
The savarin is a French cake very similar to the baba, which is typically baked in a ring-shaped pan (tin), then soaked with a flavored sugar syrup. After preparing the dough and letting it rise for the first time, it is placed into the pan and left to rise for about 1 hour before being baked. If you use a 9-inch/22-cm pan, bake in a preheated oven at 350°F/180°C/160°C Fan/Gas 4 for about 40 minutes or until it turns golden.

APRICOT AND VANILLA CAKE

Dolce di albicocche alla vaniglia

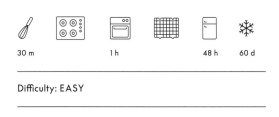

30 m   1 h   48 h   60 d

Difficulty: EASY

TO SERVE 8

FOR THE CAKE
3½ ounces/½ cup/110 g unsalted butter, plus extra
    for greasing
1 pound 5 ounces/2¾ cups/600 g apricots
½ lemon
10½ ounces/2½ cups/300 g type "00" flour or all-purpose
    (plain) flour
½ ounce/3 teaspoons/15 g baking powder
4 ounces/scant ⅔ cup/130 g superfine (caster) sugar
Pinch of salt
1 vanilla bean (pod)
4 eggs

TO SERVE
7 ounces/¾ cup/200 g Greek yogurt
14 ounces/1¾ cups/400 g apricots
3½ ounces/scant ½ cup/100 g superfine (caster) sugar
1 lemon

EQUIPMENT NEEDED
Bowls
Food processor
Juicer
Small strainer (sieve)
Fine-mesh strainer (sieve)
Electric whisk
Silicone spatula
10-inch/25.5-cm Bundt pan (tin)
Cooling rack

Preheat the oven to 350°F/180°C/160°C Fan/Gas 4. Cut the butter into small cubes, place in a mixing bowl, and leave to soften. Grease the bundt pan (tin) with butter and dust lightly with a little flour.

Wash and pit (stone) the apricots, place half in a food processor with the strained juice of ½ lemon and process to a puree. Chop the remaining apricots into small cubes.

Place the cubes of softened butter in the bowl of the stand mixer, add the sugar, a pinch of salt, and the seeds from the vanilla bean (pod), then mix on a medium speed using the flat beater attachment, until it looks pale and fluffy.

Sift the flour into a separate bowl along with the baking powder.

Add the eggs, one at a time, alternating them with a spoonful of flour, whisking continuously as you do so. Add the remainder of the flour and use a silicone spatula to fold in the ingredients to form a batter. Add the apricot puree and cubed apricots, then mix to combine.

Pour the cake batter into the prepared bundt pan. Bake the cake in the preheated oven for 1 hour, or until lightly golden, risen, and just firm to the touch—a skewer inserted into the center comes out clean. Leave the cake in the pan to cool a little, then remove and leave to cool completely on a cooling rack.

Wash and pit (stone) the remaining apricots, place in a food processor with the remaining sugar and the strained juice of a lemon, and process to a puree.

Serve the cake cold with the Greek yogurt and apricot puree.

The cake can be stored in an airtight container for up to 2 days.

TIPS AND TRICKS
Bundt pans can be intricately shaped. Make sure that the pan is thoroughly greased and that the butter gets right into any corners or sharp edges, so that the cake can be turned out easily.

POPPY SEED AND CARDAMOM CAKE

Cake ai semi di papavero e cardamomo

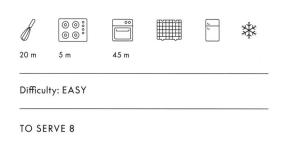

20 m   5 m   45 m

Difficulty: EASY

TO SERVE 8

FOR THE CAKE
6½ ounces/¾ cup/180 g unsalted butter, plus extra
    for greasing
11 ounces/2⅔ cups/330 g type "00" flour or all-purpose
    (plain) flour
¼ ounce/2 teaspoons/9 g baking powder
Grated zest and juice of 1 unwaxed orange
5 ounces/¾ cup/150 g superfine (caster) sugar
5 eggs
2 ounces/6 tablespoons/50 g poppy seeds
Pinch of salt
2½ fl oz/5 tablespoons/75 ml whole (full-fat) milk
1¾ fl oz/3 tablespoons/50 ml orange juice
Confectioners' (icing) sugar, for dusting

FOR THE SYRUP
2 ounces/¼ cup/50 g superfine (caster) sugar
1¾ fl oz/3 tablespoons/50 ml water
2 cardamom pods

EQUIPMENT NEEDED
Bowls
Fine-mesh strainer (sieve)
Zester
Electric whisk
Measuring cup or jug
10-inch/25-cm bundt pan (tin)
Small saucepan
Pastry brush
Small strainer (sieve) or dusting spoon

Preheat the oven to 350°F/180°C/160°C Fan/Gas 4. Cut the butter into cubes, place in a mixing bowl, and leave to soften. Grease the bundt pan (tin) with butter and lightly dust with a little flour.

Sift the flour and the baking powder into a bowl and set aside. Take the bowl containing the cubes of softened butter and add the orange zest and sugar. Using an electric whisk, beat until pale and fluffy.

Add the eggs, one at a time, alternating them with a spoonful of the flour mix, whisking continuously as you do so. Add the remainder of the flour, poppy seeds, pinch of salt, milk and orange juice, and mix to form a batter, then pour into the bundt pan.

Bake the cake in the preheated oven for 45 minutes, or until lightly golden, risen, and just firm to the touch—a skewer inserted into the center comes out clean. Leave the cake in the pan to cool a little, then remove and leave to cool completely on a cooling rack.

To make the syrup, heat the sugar with the water in a small saucepan over low heat. Crush the cardamom pods to open them and add to the pan. Cook, stirring regularly, until the sugar has dissolved then set aside to cool a little. When cooled, pour through a fine-mesh strainer (sieve) into a bowl. Brush the cake with the syrup. Dust with confectioners' (icing) sugar before serving.

This cake can be stored in an airtight container for up to 2 days.

RHUBARB, CHOCOLATE, AND CINNAMON MUFFINS

Muffin con rabarbaro, cioccolato e cannella

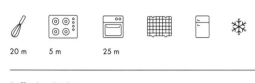

20 m   5 m   25 m

Difficulty: EASY

TO SERVE 12 (MAKES 12 MUFFINS)

FOR THE MUFFINS
2½ ounces/5 tablespoons/70 g unsalted butter
3½ ounces/½ cup/100 g rhubarb
2 tablespoons superfine (caster) sugar
10½ ounces/2½ cups/300 g type "00" flour or all-purpose
   (plain) flour
¾ ounce/4 teaspoons/18 g baking powder
3½ ounces/scant ½ cup/100 g superfine (caster) sugar
1 teaspoon ground cinnamon
3 ounces/80 g bittersweet (dark) chocolate, finely chopped
2 eggs
8½ fl oz/1 cup/250 ml whole (full-fat) milk
Confectioners' (icing) sugar, for dusting

EQUIPMENT NEEDED
2 × 6-cup muffin pans (tins)
Paper muffin cases
Small saucepan
Fine-mesh strainer (sieve)
Bowls
Measuring cup or jug
Electric whisk
Silicone spatula
Small strainer (sieve) or dusting spoon

Preheat the oven to 350°F/180°C/160°C Fan/Gas 4 and place paper muffin cases into the muffin pans (tin).

Cut the butter into small cubes, place in a small saucepan and melt, then set aside to cool.

Slice the rhubarb stalks into ½-inch/1-cm pieces and toss them in 2 tablespoons of the superfine (caster) sugar until evenly coated.

Sift the flour and baking powder into a bowl. Add 3 ounces/scant ½ cup/100 g of the superfine (caster) sugar, cinnamon, chopped chocolate, and sugar-coated rhubarb pieces to the bowl, then gently mix to combine.

Break the eggs into a separate bowl. Add the milk and cooled melted butter to the eggs, then whisk until just combined.

Pour the egg mixture onto the dry ingredients and, using a silicone spatula, mix just long enough for the flour to be incorporated.

Divide the mixture between the paper cases in the two muffin pans (tins), half filling each case.

Bake the muffins in the preheated oven for 25 minutes, or until lightly golden, risen, and just firm to the touch—a skewer inserted into the center comes out clean. Leave the muffins in the pans to cool a little, then remove from the pans and serve dusted with confectioners' (icing) sugar.

These muffins can be stored in an airtight container for up to 2 days.

TIPS AND TRICKS
To ensure that the muffins are soft, gently mix the liquid ingredients into the dry ones just long enough to combine them. Stirring too much will result in heavy, dense muffins.

To ensure the muffins are all the same size, use a large ice-cream scoop to fill the cups of the muffin pans.

COFFEE AND CHOCOLATE CREAM BARS

Barrette alla crema con caffè e cioccolato

30 m   20 m   1 h 45 m

Difficulty: ADVANCED

For the brioche dough:
   see page 160
For the confectioners' custard:
   see page 238

MAKES 24 SMALL BARS

FOR THE BARS
½ quantity (1 pound 5 ounces/600 g) of brioche dough
   prepared following the base recipe on page 160
½ quantity (10½ ounces/1¼ cups/300 g) of confectioners'
   custard prepared following the base recipe on page 238
3 ounces/80 g bittersweet (dark) chocolate
1 tablespoon roasted coffee beans
1 egg
2 tablespoons turbinado (demerara) sugar

EQUIPMENT NEEDED
Baking sheet
Parchment paper
Rolling pin
Silicone spatula
Chocolate grater or sharp knife
Mortar and pestle
Metal spatula or palette knife
Kitchen foil
Pastry brush
Cooling rack

Line the baking sheet with parchment paper.

On a lightly floured surface, roll out the brioche dough into a 18 × 12-inch/45 × 30-cm rectangle, that is ¼ inch/½ cm thick. Spread the confectioners' custard over the dough using a spatula.

Shred (grate) or finely chop the chocolate and sprinkle evenly over the custard. Using a mortar and pestle, crush the coffee beans as finely as possible and then that sprinkle over the custard too.

Fold the two short sides of the dough towards the center so that they come together but do not overlap and cut the pastry along the center line, where they join. Transfer the dough rectangles to the refrigerator for 15 minutes.

Cut each rectangle into 12 bars using the metal spatula or palette knife, and press the pastry to seal the sides. Transfer the bars to the lined baking sheet, spacing them 2 inches/5 cm apart. Loosely cover the baking sheet with a sheet of kitchen foil and leave to rise for 1 hour 30 minutes.

Preheat the oven to 375°F/190°C/170°C Fan/Gas 5. Beat the egg to make a glaze and brush the surface and sides of the brioches. Sprinkle the turbinado (demerara) sugar over the brioche then bake in the preheated oven for 20 minutes, or until golden brown and risen. Leave to cool on a cooling rack before serving.

These bars can be stored in an airtight container for 1 day.

TIPS AND TRICKS
To prevent the filling from leaking out during baking, it is important to carefully seal the sides of the bars after they have been cut. Use a little of the egg glaze to stick them together, if necessary.

SUGAR AND VANILLA BRIOCHE

Brioche allo zucchero e vaniglia

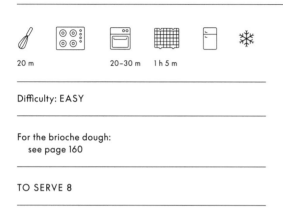

20 m   20–30 m   1 h 5 m

Difficulty: EASY

For the brioche dough:
    see page 160

TO SERVE 8

FOR THE BRIOCHE
Butter, for greasing
1 vanilla bean (pod)
3½ fl oz/scant ½ cup/100 ml heavy (whipping) cream
½ quantity (1 pound 5 ounces/600 g) of brioche dough
    prepared following the base recipe on page 160 up
    to the end of the first two-hour rise
1 egg yolk
1 tablespoon soft light brown sugar
2 tablespoons pearl sugar

EQUIPMENT NEEDED
Baking sheet
1-lb/450-g loaf pan (tin) or 6 fluted brioche
    à tête molds
Small sharp knife
Bowl
Measuring cup or jug
Rolling pin
Parchment paper
Pastry brush
Cooling rack

Line the baking sheet with parchment paper and grease the loaf pan (tin) or molds with butter.

Slice the vanilla bean (pod) lengthways and remove the seeds, scraping them with the blade of a small sharp knife. Pour the cream into a bowl and add both the bean and the seeds, and mix.

After the brioche dough has had it's first two-hour rise, on a lightly floured surface, roll out the brioche dough (pastry) to ⅛ inch/3 mm thick. Transfer to the lined baking sheet and leave in the refrigerator to rest for 20 minutes.

For the brioche loaf, divide the dough equally into three pieces. Roll each piece into a ball and place them side by side in the loaf pan. Leave to rise for 45 minutes. For the brioches à tête, divide the dough equally into six pieces. Using the palms of your hands, roll each piece into a tight ball and place in the molds.

Beat the egg yolk with a few drops of cold water to make a glaze and brush over the brioche dough then sprinkle with the sugar. Leave to rise for 45 minutes.

Preheat the oven to 325°F/160°C/140°C Fan/Gas 3 then bake in the preheated oven for 25–30 minutes for the brioche loaf or 20 minutes for the brioches à tête or until golden, risen, and sounds slightly hollow when tapped on the bottom. When probed with a kitchen thermometer, the internal temperature of the brioche should be 200°F/95°C.

As soon as they are taken out of the oven, glaze the brioche with the vanilla-infused cream and scatter over the pearl sugar. Leave to cool on a cooling rack before serving.

These brioche can be stored in an airtight container for 1 day.

ORANGE AND CHOCOLATE BRAIDED BABKA

Babka intrecciato arancia e cioccolato

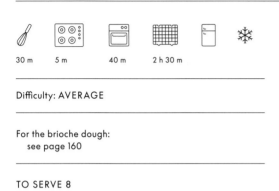

30 m   5 m   40 m   2 h 30 m

Difficulty: AVERAGE

For the brioche dough:
  see page 160

TO SERVE 8

FOR THE BABKA
½ quantity (1 pound 5 ounces/600 g) of brioche dough
  flavored with the grated zest of 1 unwaxed orange
  and prepared following the base recipe on page 160 up
  to the end of the first two-hour rise

FOR THE CHOCOLATE CREAM
4 ounces/120 g bittersweet (dark) chocolate
4 ounces/½ cup/120 g unsalted butter
1 ounce/scant ⅓ cup/30 g unsweetened cocoa powder
2 ounces/¼ cup/60 g superfine (caster) sugar

FOR THE SYRUP
1 orange
3 ounces/⅓ cup/80 g superfine (caster) sugar

EQUIPMENT NEEDED
Chocolate grater or sharp knife
Bain-marie or double boiler
Fine-mesh strainer (sieve)
Juicer
Small saucepan
Rolling pin
Silicone spatula
Plastic wrap (cling film)
2-lb/900-g loaf pan (tin)
Parchment paper
Kitchen foil
Kitchen thermometer
Pastry brush

To make the chocolate cream, shred (grate) or finely chop the chocolate and cut the butter into small cubes. Place the chocolate and butter in a bain-marie or double boiler and melt, stirring until smooth. Remove from the heat, sift the cocoa powder into the bowl and add the sugar. Mix until the ingredients are combined and leave to cool in the refrigerator for 30 minutes, until the cream thickens.

To make the syrup, juice the orange and strain it into a small saucepan then add the sugar. Bring to a boil over low heat, then turn off the heat and leave to cool.

After the brioche dough has had it's first two-hour rise, on a lightly floured surface, roll out the orange-flavored brioche dough into a rectangular sheet that is ⅛ inch/3 mm thick.

Using a silicone spatula, spread the chocolate cream over the dough, leaving a small clear border all around the edges. Starting from one long side of the rectangle, roll the dough tightly into a log. Wrap the log in plastic wrap (cling film) and place in the freezer for 30 minutes.

Line the loaf pan (tin) with parchment paper. Remove the log from freezer, unwrap it, and cut it in half lengthwise. Twist the two halves around each other to form a rope that is the same length as the loaf pan. Place the dough rope in the loaf pan, cover loosely with kitchen foil, and leave to rise in a warm place for 30 minutes to 1 hour, or until doubled in size.

Preheat the oven to 350°F/180°C/160°C Fan/Gas 4 and bake the babka for 40 minutes or until golden, risen, and sounds slightly hollow when tapped on the bottom. When probed with a kitchen thermometer, the internal temperature of the babka should be 200°F/95°C.

Remove from the oven and brush the top of the babka with the orange syrup while still in the pan. Leave to cool before serving.

The babka can be stored, covered, at room temperature for 2 days.

JAM CROISSANT

Croissant alla marmellata

30 m   20 m   2 h

Difficulty: AVERAGE

For the croissant dough:
  see page 162

TO SERVE 8 (MAKES 32 SMALL CROISSANTS)

FOR THE CROISSANTS
1 quantity (2½ pounds/1.2 kg) of croissant dough prepared
  following the base recipe on page 162
9 ounces/1 cup/250 g preserves (jam) in the flavor of
  your choice
1 egg yolk

EQUIPMENT NEEDED
Rolling pin
Pastry wheel or triangular pastry cutter for croissants
Long-bladed knife
Baking sheet
Parchment paper
Pastry brush
Kitchen foil

Prepare the dough following the instructions on pages 162–3 to the end of step 9, then rest in the refrigerator for 30 minutes. Roll out the dough to a 22 × 16-inch/56 × 40-cm rectangle. Cut the rectangle lengthways into four equal strips, each strip measuring 22 × 4 inches/56 × 10 cm. Next, cut each strip into 8 triangles with a base of 2¾ inches/7 cm. Stretch the triangles slightly and make a small cut at the base of each triangle.

Line the baking sheet with parchment paper. Place a teaspoonful of jam over the cut at the base of the triangle and, starting from the base, roll the dough to enclose the filling, right to the point of the triangle. Repeat with all the other triangles of dough. Put the croissants on the lined baking sheet, with the narrow point of the rolled pastry facing down.

Brush the croissants with egg glaze, made by beating the egg yolk with a few drops of water, cover loosely with kitchen foil, and leave to rise in a warm place for 2 hours.

Preheat the oven to 325°F/160°C/140°C Fan/Gas 3, brush the croissants with the egg wash again and bake for 20 minutes or until puffed up and golden. If you are not using a fan-assisted oven, increase the cooking time by 5–10 minutes.

The croissants can be stored, covered, at room temperature for 2 days.

TIPS AND TRICKS
If you want to prepare croissants in advance and freeze them to cook at a later date, place them in the freezer after the first brushing with the egg wash. Defrost overnight in the refrigerator and then leave to rise slowly in a warm place for 1 hour before brushing with more egg wash and baking.

CANDIED GINGER PINWHEELS

Rotelle allo zenzero candito

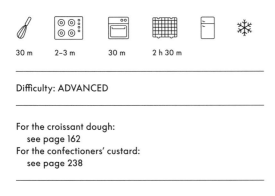

30 m	2–3 m	30 m	2 h 30 m		

Difficulty: ADVANCED

For the croissant dough:
  see page 162
For the confectioners' custard:
  see page 238

MAKES 16 PINWHEELS

FOR THE PINWHEELS
1 quantity (2½ pounds/1.2 kg) of croissant dough prepared
  following the base recipe on page 162
⅔ quantity (14 ounces/1⅔ cups/400 g) of confectioners'
  custard prepared following the base recipe on page 238
3 ounces/⅜ cup/80 g candied (crystallized) ginger
Butter, for greasing

FOR THE SYRUP
7 ounces/scant 1 cup/200 g superfine (caster) sugar
7 fl oz/scant 1 cup/200 ml water

EQUIPMENT NEEDED
Rolling pin
Immersion (stick) blender
Silicone spatula
Plastic wrap (cling film)
Pastry brush
2 × 6-cup muffin pans (tins), measuring 3-inches/8-cm
Measuring cup or jug
Small saucepan

Prepare the dough following the instructions on page 162 to the end of step 9, then rest in the refrigerator for 30 minutes.

On a lightly floured surface, roll out the dough into a 31 × 12-inch/80 × 30-cm rectangle, that is ¾ inch/2 cm thick.

Using an immersion (stick) blender, blitz the custard until soft. Spread the custard over the surface of the dough with a silicone spatula. Chop the candied (crystallized) ginger into very small cubes and scatter over the custard, distributing them evenly.

Starting from one long side, roll the dough over the filling to form a compact log. Cut the log in half, loosely wrap both pieces in plastic wrap (cling film), and place them in the refrigerator for 30 minutes.

Grease the muffin pans (tins) with a little butter. Cut each log into 8 slices to give 16 pinwheels. Pull the outer edge of each pinwheel towards its base and pinch it with the dough of the base to seal. Transfer the pinwheels to the buttered muffin pans, cover loosely with kitchen foil, and leave to rise in a draft- (draught-) free place for 2 hours.

Preheat the oven to 350°F/180°C/160°C Fan/Gas 4 and bake the pinwheels in the preheated oven for 30 minutes, or until golden and risen. Leave to cool slightly in the pans for 10 minutes.

Meanwhile, to prepare the syrup place the sugar and water in a saucepan and warm it over low heat until the sugar has dissolved, then increase the heat to medium and boil the syrup for 1 minute.

Transfer the pinwheels to a cooling rack. While they are still warm, brush the pinwheels with the syrup and leave to cool before serving.

These pinwheels can be stored in an airtight container for 1 day.

LIMONCELLO MINI BABA

Mini babà al limoncello

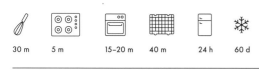

30 m	5 m	15–20 m	40 m	24 h	60 d

Difficulty: AVERAGE

TO SERVE 8 (MAKES 24 SMALL BABAS)

FOR THE BABA
6½ ounces/¾ cup/180 g unsalted butter
7 eggs
10½ ounces/2½ cups/300 g strong white bread flour
7 ounces/1⅔ cups/200 g type "00" flour or all-purpose (plain) flour
¼ ounce/7 g fast-action dried yeast (or use 1 ounce/ 25 g fresh brewer's yeast)
1½ ounces/¼ cup/40 g superfine (caster) sugar
½ ounce/1½ teaspoons/10 g salt
Vegetable oil, for greasing

FOR THE SYRUP
17 fl oz/2 cups/500 ml water
7 ounces/scant 1 cup/200 g superfine (caster) sugar
7 fl oz/scant 1 cup/200 ml limoncello

TO SERVE
10 fl oz/1¼ cups/300 ml heavy (whipping) cream
3 ounces/scant ½ cup/80 g candied lemon slices

EQUIPMENT NEEDED
Bowl
Fine-mesh strainer (sieve)
Stand mixer fitted with dough hook attachment
Hand whisk
Small individual baba molds, 3-inch/7-cm
Baking sheet
Kitchen foil
Cooling rack
Saucepan
Measuring cup or jug
Electric whisk
Pastry (piping) bag
Large star piping tip (nozzle)

Cut the butter into small cubes, place in a bowl, and leave to soften.

Beat the eggs together in a bowl. Sift the two types of flour into the bowl of the stand mixer, stir in the yeast and sugar and then start to mix. Add the salt and beaten eggs to the flour and continue to mix until incorporated. Add 5 ounces/½ cup plus 2 tablespoons/150 g of the softened butter, a few cubes at a time, and continue to mix on low speed until the dough is elastic that comes away easily from the sides of the bowl.

Lightly oil a clean bowl with vegetable oil. Transfer the dough to the oiled bowl, cover with plastic wrap (cling film), and leave to rise for 1 hour or until doubled in size.

Use the remaining butter to grease the individual baba pans (tins), then lightly dust with flour and place on a baking sheet. Deflate the dough then divide it equally into 24 balls. Put one ball of dough into each mold—the molds should be approximately half full. Loosely cover with kitchen foil, and leave to rise in a warm place for about 20 minutes or until they have doubled in volume.

Preheat the oven to 475°F/240°C/220°C Fan/Gas 9, remove the foil and bake the babas in the preheated oven for 15–20 minutes or until golden, risen, and springy to the touch. Leave to cool a little then remove from the pans and place on a cooling rack to cool completely.

Meanwhile, to prepare the syrup, place the sugar in a small saucepan and pour in the water. Set the pan over low heat. Let the sugar dissolve, gently swirling the pan from time to time. Once the sugar has dissolved completely, increase the heat to medium, add the limoncello, and bring to a boil for 2 minutes. Remove from the heat and set aside to cool.

Dip the babas into the syrup until they are soaked, then place on a cooling rack to drain for 10 minutes. Whip the cream using an electric whisk and transfer to a pastry (piping) bag fitted with a star piping tip (nozzle). Make a vertical cut in each baba, but do not cut all the way through, and insert a candied lemon slice into each cut. Place the baba on serving plates, add a spoonful of syrup to each and then pipe the cream on top.

TIPS AND TRICKS
If you have time, leave the cooked babas to stand for 12 hours on the cooling rack before soaking with the syrup. They will dry out a little when exposed to the air, then they will absorb the syrup better and will retain their shape more easily.

CITRUS SAVARIN WITH CREAM AND FRUIT

Savarin agli agrumi con panna e frutta

30 m · 5 m · 40 m · 2 h 20 m · 24 h · 60 d

Difficulty: AVERAGE

For the baba dough:
see page 164

TO SERVE 8

FOR THE DOUGH
2½ ounces/5 tablespoons/70 g unsalted butter
3½ ounces/generous ¾ cup/100 g type "00" flour or
all-purpose (plain) flour
3½ ounces/generous ¾ cup/100 g strong white bread flour
½ teaspoon/2 g fast-action dried yeast (or use ¼ ounce/
7 g fresh brewer's yeast)
Pinch of salt
¼ ounce/2 teaspoons/8 g superfine (caster) sugar
4 eggs
Vegetable oil, for greasing

FOR THE SYRUP
34 fl oz/4 cups/1 litre water
1 pound/2¼ cups/450 g superfine (caster) sugar
Grated zest of 1 unwaxed orange
Grated zest of 1 unwaxed lemon
1 teaspoon fennel seeds

TO SERVE
3½ ounces/scant ½ cup/100 g red currant jelly
10 fl oz/1¼ cups/300 ml heavy (whipping) cream
1½ ounces/⅓ cup/40 g confectioners' (icing) sugar
1 papaya
1 mango
1½ ounces/¼ cup/40 g pomegranate seeds

EQUIPMENT NEEDED
Bowls
Fine-mesh strainer (sieve)
Stand mixer fitted with dough hook attachment
Plastic wrap (cling film)
7-inch/18-cm ring-shaped or savarin pan (tin)
Kitchen foil
Cooling rack
Saucepans
Measuring cup or jug
Peeler
Electric whisk
Pastry (piping) bag
Star piping tip (nozzle)

Cut the butter into small cubes, place in a bowl, and bring to room temperature to soften.

Sift the two types of flour into the bowl of the stand mixer. Stir in the yeast, add 2 ounces/¼ cup/60 g of the softened butter, a pinch of salt and the sugar, and start to mix at low speed. After a few minutes, add the eggs, one at a time, and continue to mix for 10 minutes until you obtain a smooth, elastic dough that easily comes away from the sides of the bowl.

Transfer the dough to a clean bowl that has been lightly oiled, cover with plastic wrap (cling film), and leave to rise for 20 minutes.

Grease the pan (tin) with butter and lightly dust with flour, then place the dough in the pan, loosely cover with kitchen foil, and leave to rise for 2 hours.

Preheat the oven to 325°F/160°C/140°C Fan/Gas 3, remove the foil and bake the savarin in the preheated oven for 40 minutes, or until golden, risen, and springy to the touch. Leave in the pan to cool a little then remove and place on a cooling rack to cool completely.

Meanwhile, to prepare the syrup place the water in a saucepan with the sugar, orange and lemon zests, and fennel seeds. Warm it over low heat until the sugar has dissolved. Increase the heat to medium and, stirring continuously, boil the syrup for 2 minutes. Remove from the heat and set aside to cool. Pour through a fine-mesh strainer (sieve) set over a large bowl.

Dip the savarin into the syrup until it is soaked, turning it over, and then leave to drain on a cooling rack.

Meanwhile, warm the red currant jelly in a saucepan with a tablespoon of water and set aside to cool. Whip the cream with the confectioners' (icing) sugar using an electric whisk and transfer to a pastry (piping) bag fitted with a star piping tip (nozzle). Peel and chop the papaya and mango into small pieces.

Transfer the savarin to a serving plate and drizzle the jelly over the top. Fill the center of the savarin with the whipped cream and top with the chopped fruit and the pomegranate seeds.

CHOCOLATE

Tempered chocolate
Temperare il cioccolato

30 m   3 m

Difficulty: AVERAGE

MAKES 1 QUANTITY
(9 OUNCES/250 G CHOCOLATE)

FOR THE CHOCOLATE
9 ounces/250 g good-quality bittersweet (dark), milk,
or white chocolate

EQUIPMENT NEEDED
Bain-marie or double boiler
Kitchen thermometer
Marble board or work surface
Metal spatula or palette knife
Silicone spatula

AS USED IN
– Milk Chocolates with Hazelnut Cream
(see page 194)
– Fennel-Infused Dark Chocolates
(see page 196)
– Chocolate and Strawberry Cake
(see page 198)
– Peanut, Caramel, and Chocolate Squares
(see page 200)
– White Chocolates with Chai Tea Ganache
(see page 204)
– Gianduja Chocolate and Coffee Cake
(see page 208)
– White Chocolate and Thyme Cupcakes
(see page 212)
– Steamed Chocolate Raspberry Sponge Pudding
(see page 214)

Using a sharp knife, finely chop the chocolate, then place in a bain-marie or double boiler (1). Melt until you obtain a smooth and even consistency, ensuring the water doesn't boil or have any contact with the bottom of the bain-marie or double boiler. Stir gently as soon as the chocolate starts to melt (2).

Continuously monitoring the temperature with a kitchen thermometer (3), continue to heat the chocolate in the bain-marie until it reaches 122°F/50°C for bittersweet (dark) chocolate, 113°F/45°C for milk chocolate, and 113°F/45°C for white chocolate. In particular, white chocolate is extremely temperature sensitive.

Pour three-quarters of the melted chocolate onto a marble work surface (4), leaving the rest in the bain-marie, and work it with a metal spatula or palette knife (5) until the temperature drops to 81°F/27°C for bittersweet (dark) chocolate and milk chocolate, and 77°F/25°C for white chocolate (6).

Scrape the remaining chocolate from the bain-marie and set aside in a bowl. Wash and dry the bain-marie, then place the semi-tempered chocolate into it (7).

Add the reserved warm chocolate a little at a time until you reach a temperature of 89.5°F/32°C for bittersweet (dark) chocolate and 86°F/30°C for milk and white chocolate.

When this temperature is reached, stop adding the reserved chocolate (8). Use the tempered chocolate immediately at this final temperature (not at the higher initial melting temperature).
If the tempered chocolate is not being used immediately, maintain it at between 1°F/1–2°C of the lower temperature until use. If the chocolate does cool down, bring it back up to this temperature again in the bain-marie.

TIPS AND TRICKS
Tempering chocolate makes it shiny and break with a "snap." Tempered chocolate is used for chocolate making, for making decorations, and for dipping cookies or fruit.

The greater the quantity of chocolate being tempered, the easier it will be to control its temperature. A quantity of 9 ounces/250 g is easy to manage. Any leftovers can be stored and used at a later date. Pour any remaining chocolate into an ice cube tray, let it solidify, then store the cubes in a food-grade plastic bag in the butter compartment of the refrigerator. Tempered chocolate stored in the refrigerator will need to be re-tempered before use in order to regain its shine.

MISTAKES TO AVOID
The bottom of the heatproof bowl must not touch the hot water; the chocolate must melt using only the heat of the steam. If the temperature of the water is too high then the chocolate tends to burn, making it grainy and unusable. Also make sure that no droplets of water get into the chocolate. This can cause it to seize and become unworkable.

Chocolate decorations

Decorazioni con il cioccolato

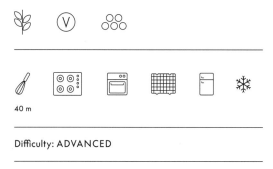

40 m

Difficulty: ADVANCED

MAKES 1 QUANTITY
(9 OUNCES/250 G CHOCOLATE)

FOR THE CHOCOLATE
9 ounces/250 g bittersweet (dark), milk, or white chocolate

EQUIPMENT NEEDED
Marble board or work surface
Metal spatula or palette knife
Acetate sheet
Metal or plastic cylinder
Paper cone

AS USED IN
– Chocolate and Strawberry Cake
  (see page 198)
– White Chocolate and Thyme Cupcakes
  (see page 212)
– Steamed Chocolate Raspberry Sponge Pudding
  (see page 214)

Temper the chocolate following the instructions on page 188. Spread the tempered chocolate out on a marble work surface with a metal spatula or palette knife to achieve a uniform thickness (1).

Leave to solidify and, using the same spatula inclined at an angle, scrape away several chocolate curls (2).

Depending on the angle (3) of the spatula, you can vary the size of the curls (4).

Alternatively, spread the chocolate directly onto a narrow acetate sheet (5), then roll the acetate into a cylinder (6–7), and leave the chocolate to cool and harden. When the chocolate has set, unroll the sheet. As it comes away from the acetate, the chocolate will form thin, irregular flakes, which can be used for decoration.

It is possible to create unique chocolate decorations using a pastry (piping) bag or paper cone to pipe tempered chocolate over an acetate sheet and various shaped objects (8).

TIPS AND TRICKS
You can store chocolate decorations, in any shape and size, at room temperature, in an airtight container. In the summer months, however, store them in the refrigerator.

Simple ganache
Ganache semplice

10 m   3 m   48 h

Difficulty: EASY

MAKES 1 QUANTITY
(15 OUNCES/430 G GANACHE)

FOR THE GANACHE
1 ounce/2 tablespoons/30 g unsalted butter
7 ounces/200 g bittersweet (dark), milk, or white chocolate
7 fl oz/scant 1 cup/200 ml heavy (whipping) cream

EQUIPMENT NEEDED
Bowl
Small saucepan
Silicone spatula

AS USED IN
– Almond Milk and Sea Salt Truffles
  (see page 202)
– Chocolate Truffle Cake with Raspberry Glaze
  (see page 330)
– Chocolate Torte
  (see page 332)

Bring the butter to room temperature and finely chop the chocolate with a large, sharp knife (1). It will be easier to chop the chocolate if you a start from a corner, rotating the chocolate as necessary. Transfer the chopped chocolate to a bowl (2).

Heat the cream in a saucepan over low heat until just below boiling point and pour it onto the finely chopped chocolate, a little at a time (3), stirring continuously with a silicone spatula.

Continue to mix until the chocolate has evenly melted and the mixture becomes smooth and creamy (4).

Add the very soft butter in small pieces and mix until this has completely melted and has been fully incorporated (5).

TIPS AND TRICKS
When pouring the chocolate ganache over a cake, any ganache that drips onto the baking sheet below the cake can be stored in the refrigerator for up to 2 days. Gently warm the leftover chocolate ganache and use it as a sauce to serve with ice cream.

VARIATIONS
This simple ganache is the base for making a whipped ganache for filling cakes, for decorations or for making chocolates using a pastry (piping) bag. After preparing the ganache, leave to cool in the refrigerator until it starts to thicken, then whip with an electric whisk until fluffy. Use immediately. If it becomes too hard, heat it gently in a bain-marie.

CHOCOLATE

MILK CHOCOLATES WITH HAZELNUT CREAM

Cioccolatini al latte con crema di nocciole

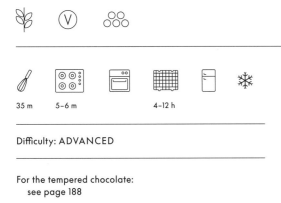

35 m   5–6 m   4–12 h

Difficulty: ADVANCED

For the tempered chocolate:
see page 188

TO SERVE 8 (MAKES 30–40 TRUFFLES)

FOR THE CHOCOLATES
2 quantities (1 pound 2 ounces/500 g) of tempered
milk chocolate prepared following the base recipe
on page 188
3½ ounces/¾ cup/100 g toasted and skinned hazelnuts
½ ounce/2 teaspoons/10 g unsalted butter
3 ounces/80 g milk chocolate
3 tablespoons/40 ml heavy (whipping) cream

EQUIPMENT NEEDED
Silicone chocolate molds
Baking sheet
Metal spatula or palette knife
Food processor
Bowl
Small saucepan
Silicone spatula
Pastry (piping) bag

Fill each chocolate mold with the tempered milk chocolate. Tilt and rotate to ensure the chocolate evenly coats each mold. Turn the molds upside down over a clean baking sheet to drain any excess chocolate. Keep the excess chocolate at 86°F/30°C.

When the chocolate in the molds starts to set, scrape the top surface of the molds with a metal spatula or palette knife to clean up any spilled chocolate, reserving it for later use. Set aside the molds to let the chocolate shells harden completely.

Blitz the hazelnuts in the food processor until they are reduced to a paste and transfer to a bowl. Bring the butter to room temperature and finely chop the non-tempered milk chocolate with a large, sharp knife. Transfer the chocolate into a bowl. Heat the cream in a saucepan over low heat until just below boiling point and pour it onto the finely chopped chocolate, a little at a time, stirring continuously with a silicone spatula. Continue to mix until the chocolate has evenly melted and the mixture becomes smooth and creamy.

Add the very soft butter, in small pieces, and the hazelnut paste and mix until the butter has completely melted and has been fully incorporated.

Transfer the hazelnut cream to a pastry (piping) bag without a piping tip (nozzle) and cut away the tip. Pipe the hazelnut cream into the chocolate shells until each is two-thirds full. Chill in the refrigerator for 4 hours or leave to cool at room temperature for 12 hours.

Pour the reserved tempered chocolate over the chocolates to seal them. Remove any excess chocolate with a metal spatula or palette knife, then place the molds in the refrigerator for 15 minutes. Tap the upturned molds on a clean work surface until the chocolates drop out of the molds. The chocolates can be stored in a cool place for up to 7 days.

TIPS AND TRICKS
Do not discard the chocolate you scrape away from the surface of the mold. Store it in a clean container to be reused at a later date.

FENNEL-INFUSED DARK CHOCOLATES

Cioccolatini fondenti infusi al finocchio

35 m   5–6 m   4–12 h

Difficulty: ADVANCED

For the tempered chocolate:
    see page 188

TO SERVE 8 (MAKES 30–40 TRUFFLES)

FOR THE CHOCOLATES
2 quantities (1 pound 2 ounces/500 g) of tempered
    bittersweet (dark) chocolate prepared following the
    base recipe on page 188
¼ fennel bulb
1¾ fl oz/3 tablespoons/50 ml heavy (whipping) cream
3 ounces/90 g milk chocolate
1½ teaspoons/7 g unsalted butter

EQUIPMENT NEEDED
Silicone chocolate molds
Baking sheet
Metal spatula or palette knife
Bowl
Small saucepan
Fine-mesh strainer (sieve)
Silicone spatula
Pastry (piping) bag

Fill each chocolate mold with the tempered bittersweet (dark) chocolate. Tilt and rotate to ensure the chocolate evenly coats each mold. Turn the molds upside down over a clean baking sheet to drain any excess chocolate. Keep the excess chocolate at 89.5°F/32°C.

When the chocolate in the molds starts to set, scrape the top surface of the molds with a metal spatula or palette knife to clean up any spilled chocolate, reserving it for later use. Set aside the molds to let the chocolate shells harden completely.

To make the ganache, finely chop the fennel, place it in a small saucepan with the cream and bring to a boil over low heat. Leave to infuse for 30 minutes. Pour the cream through a fine-mesh strainer (sieve), pressing the fennel with the back of a spoon to squeeze out all the cream.

Bring the butter to room temperature and finely chop the non-tempered milk chocolate with a large, sharp knife. Transfer the chopped chocolate to a bowl.

Warm the cream again and pour it onto the finely chopped chocolate, a little at a time, stirring continuously with a silicone spatula. Continue to mix until this has completely melted and has been fully incorporated. Add the softened butter in small pieces and mix until this has completely melted and has been fully incorporated.

Transfer the ganache to a pastry (piping) bag without a piping tip (nozzle) and cut away the tip. Pipe the ganache into the chocolate shells until each is three-quarters full. Chill in the refrigerator for 4 hours or leave to cool at room temperature for 12 hours.

Pour the reserved tempered chocolate over the chocolates to seal them. Remove any excess chocolate with the metal spatula or palette knife, then place the molds in the refrigerator for 15 minutes. Tap the upturned molds on a clean work surface until the chocolates drop out of the molds. The chocolates can be stored in a cool place for up to 7 days.

CHOCOLATE AND STRAWBERRY CAKE

Torta di cioccolato e fragole

---

40 m   5–6 m   45 m   15 m   48 h

Difficulty: ADVANCED

For the tempered chocolate:
    see page 188
For the buttercream:
    see page 322
For the chocolate decorations:
    see page 190

TO SERVE 8

FOR THE CAKE
8 ounces/1 cup/220 g unsalted butter, plus extra
    for greasing
8½ fl oz/1 cup/240 ml freshly brewed coffee
2½ ounces/scant ⅔ cup/75 g unsweetened cocoa powder
9 ounces/2 cups/240 g type "00" flour or all-purpose
    (plain) flour
Scant teaspoon/3 g baking powder
¼ teaspoon/1 g baking soda (bicarbonate of soda)
4 ounces/scant ⅔ cup/130 g superfine (caster) sugar
Pinch of salt
1 vanilla bean (pod)
2 eggs
4 ounces/scant ½ cup/120 g Greek yogurt
14 ounces/1⅓ cups/400 g strawberry compote

FOR THE BUTTERCREAM
1 quantity (1 pound 2 ounces/500 g) of buttercream
    prepared following the base recipe on page 322

TO DECORATE
½ quantity (3½ ounces/125 g) of tempered bittersweet
    (dark) chocolate prepared following the base recipe
    on page 188
7 ounces/1 cup/200 g strawberries
Bittersweet (dark) chocolate, finely chopped

EQUIPMENT NEEDED
7-inch/18-cm round springform pan (tin)
    with deep sides
Saucepan
Measuring cup or jug
Fine-mesh strainer (sieve)
Bowls
Stand mixer fitted with whisk attachment
    or electric whisk and bowl
Cooling rack
Metal spatula or palette knife
Acetate sheet
Paper cone
Small sharp knife

Preheat the oven to 350°F/180°C/160°C Fan/Gas 4. Grease the springform pan (tin) with a little butter then lightly dust with flour. Cut the butter into small cubes and leave to soften.

Place the butter in a saucepan with the coffee. Sift the cocoa powder into the saucepan and cook over low heat, stirring, until the butter has melted. Transfer to a bowl and set aside to cool for 10 minutes. Sift the flour with the baking powder and baking soda (bicarbonate of soda) into a separate bowl, add the sugar and a pinch of salt. Pour the cocoa mixture into the dry ingredients, continuously mixing with a whisk as you do so.

Slice the vanilla bean (pod) and remove the seeds, place in a bowl with the eggs and yogurt, and beat together to combine. Pour into the cocoa mixture, stirring with a whisk to combine. Pour into the prepared springform pan and bake in the preheated oven for 45 minutes, or until risen and firm to the touch—a skewer inserted into the center comes out clean. Leave the cake in the pan to cool slightly for 5 minutes, then remove from the pan and place on a cooling rack to cool completely.

Cut the cake horizontally into three layers, then spread half the strawberry compote over the top of the base layer. Place the middle layer over the compote and spread with the remaining half of the compote. Cover with the top layer of cake and spread the buttercream over the top and sides using a metal spatula or palette knife to obtain a smooth, even finish.

To make the decoration, cut the acetate sheet to the same length as the circumference of the cake and 4 inches/10 cm taller than its sides. Transfer the tempered bittersweet (dark) chocolate to a paper cone made from parchment paper and let it fall in lines or "squiggles" onto the acetate. When the chocolate starts to set but is still malleable, wrap the acetate around the cake with the chocolate side facing the cake. Secure the acetate with sticky tape and place the cake in the refrigerator for 15 minutes. When the chocolate has set, carefully remove and discard the acetate, decorate the top of the cake with strawberries arranged in a crescent shape. Before serving, decorate with a little extra finely chopped bittersweet (dark) chocolate.

TIPS AND TRICKS
When you apply the chocolate decorations to the sides of the cake, lightly press them onto the buttercream so the chocolate flakes adhere perfectly.

PEANUT, CARAMEL, AND CHOCOLATE SQUARES

Quadrotti alle arachidi, caramello e cioccolato

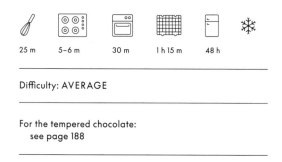

25 m   5–6 m   30 m   1 h 15 m   48 h

Difficulty: AVERAGE

For the tempered chocolate:
   see page 188

TO SERVE 8 (MAKES 8 BARS OR 16 SMALL SQUARES)

FOR THE BASE
8 ounces/1½ cups/230 g toasted unsalted peanuts,
   plus 1 ounce/¼ cup/30 g for decoration
3 eggs
Pinch of salt
1½ teaspoons/7 g baking soda (bicarbonate of soda)
3½ ounces/½ cup/110 g superfine (caster) sugar

FOR THE CARAMEL
7¾ ounces/generous 1 cup/220 g soft light brown sugar
14-ounce/397-g can of sweetened condensed milk
3½ ounces/7 tablespoons/100 g salted butter

FOR THE TOPPING
1 quantity (9 ounces/250 g) of tempered bittersweet
   (dark) chocolate prepared following the base recipe
   on page 188

EQUIPMENT NEEDED
8-inch/20-cm square cake pan (tin)
Parchment paper
Food processor
Spatula
Saucepans
Measuring cup or jug
Hand whisk
Metal spatula or palette knife

Preheat the oven to 350°F/180°C/160°C Fan/Gas 4 and line the cake pan (tin) with parchment paper.

Blitz the peanuts in a food processor until they are fine and evenly ground. Add the eggs, a pinch of salt, the baking soda (bicarbonate of soda) and the sugar, and process until evenly mixed. Scrape into the prepared cake pan, level the surface and bake in the preheated oven for 30 minutes, or until lightly golden and dry on top. When it is still very hot, press down on the base using a wide spatula to compress it, then leave to cool.

To make the caramel, place the sugar, condensed milk, and butter in a small saucepan. Cook over low heat, stirring continuously, until the sugar dissolves. Turn the heat up to medium and cook for a further 5 minutes or until the caramel has thickened slightly. Pour the caramel over the peanut base and spread it evenly using a metal spatula or palette knife. Place in the refrigerator for 1 hour or until set.

Pour the tempered chocolate onto the caramel cream, using a metal spatula or palette knife to spread it in an even layer. Place in the refrigerator for 15 minutes, or until the chocolate has set but is still soft. Roughly chop the remaining peanuts. Remove the cake from the pan and decorate with the chopped peanuts. To serve, cut the cake into 8 bars or 16 small squares.

ALMOND MILK AND SEA SALT TRUFFLES

Tartufi al latte di mandorla e sale

25 m   5 m   2 h 30 m   7 d

Difficulty: AVERAGE

TO SERVE 8 (MAKES 40–50 TRUFFLES)

FOR THE TRUFFLES
10½ ounces/300 g bittersweet (dark) chocolate
3½ fl oz/scant ½ cup/100 ml almond milk
1 teaspoon extra-virgin olive oil
2 ounces/scant ½ cup/50 g unsweetened cocoa powder
Coarse sea salt flakes or black sea salt flakes

EQUIPMENT NEEDED
Bowls
Measuring cup or jug
Small saucepan
Silicone spatula
Plastic wrap (cling film)
Electric whisk
Baking sheet

To make a chocolate ganache, finely chop the chocolate and place in a bowl. Pour the almond milk into a small saucepan and bring almost to boiling point over low heat.

Slowly pour the almond milk onto the chopped chocolate, stirring continuously with a silicone spatula as you do so, then add the olive oil. Continue to mix until you have a smooth, even cream. Let cool a little and then cover with plastic wrap (cling film). Leave in the refrigerator for at least 2 hours, or until thick and starting to become firm. Using an electric whisk, whisk until it becomes light and fluffy.

Use a teaspoon to scoop a small quantity of ganache and use a second teaspoon to shape into an irregular ball. Transfer to the refrigerator and leave the balls to cool for 30 minutes. Sprinkle the cocoa powder onto a baking sheet, then place the ganache balls onto the tray and shake the tray until the balls are covered in cocoa. Decorate each truffle with sea salt flakes or black sea salt flakes. Store in the refrigerator until you are ready to serve.

TIPS AND TRICKS
If you want to prepare the almond milk at home, coarsely chop 7 ounces/1⅓ cup/200 g of organic almonds still in their skins, cover with cold water and leave to soak for 2–3 hours. Drain, but keep the soaking liquid and add more cold water to make up to 4 cups/ 1 litre. Blitz the almonds in a food processor, adding the liquid a little at a time. Transfer to a fine-mesh strainer (sieve) lined with a large piece of damp cheesecloth or muslin, set over a bowl, and let it run through. Gather the muslin around the nut pulp and twist it tightly closed. Squeeze and press with your hands to extract as much liquid as possible. Store the milk in the refrigerator for a maximum of 4 days.

WHITE CHOCOLATES WITH CHAI TEA GANACHE

Barrette di cioccolato bianco al tè chai

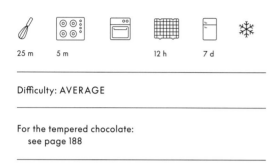

25 m   5 m   12 h   7 d

Difficulty: AVERAGE

For the tempered chocolate:
see page 188

TO SERVE 8 (MAKES 30–40 CHOCOLATES)

FOR THE CHOCOLATES
2 quantities of tempered white chocolate prepared
following the base recipe on page 188

FOR THE GANACHE
1 ounce/2 tablespoons/30 g cocoa butter
6½ ounces/180 g white chocolate
1¾ fl oz/3 tablespoons/50 ml heavy (whipping) cream

FOR THE CHAI TEA
6 fl oz/¾ cup/180 ml water
3 black tea bags
4 green cardamom pods
2 teaspoons/4 g garam masala
1-inch/3-cm cinnamon stick
2 teaspoons/3 g ground ginger

TO DECORATE
10 Timut peppercorns (or use Szechuan peppercorns)
Edible flowers

EQUIPMENT NEEDED
Silicone chocolate mold with multiple bar cavities
Baking sheet
Metal spatula or palette knife
Measuring cup or jug
Saucepan
Fine-mesh strainer (sieve)
Bowls
Small saucepan
Silicone spatula
Bain-marie or double boiler
Mortar and pestle
Pastry (piping) bag

Fill each chocolate mold with the tempered white chocolate. Tilt and rotate to ensure the chocolate evenly coats each mold. Turn the molds upside down over a clean baking sheet to drain any excess chocolate. Keep the excess chocolate at 86°F/30°C.

When the chocolate in the molds starts to set, scrape the top surface of the molds with a metal spatula or palette knife to clean up any spilled chocolate, reserving it for later use. Set aside the molds to let the chocolate shells harden completely.

To make the chai tea, pour the water into a saucepan and add the tea bags, lightly crushed cardamom pods, and the remaining spices. Bring to a boil then simmer over low heat for 5 minutes. Remove from the heat, leave to infuse for 15 minutes and strain into a bowl. Measure out 3½ fl oz/scant ½ cup/90 ml of the tea and freeze the remainder to use on another occasion.

To make the ganache, bring the cocoa butter to room temperature and finely chop the non-tempered white chocolate with a large, sharp knife and place in a bowl. Pour the concentrated chai tea into a small saucepan with the cream and bring to a boil over low heat. Slowly pour the tea mixture onto the chopped white chocolate, continuously stirring with a silicone spatula as you do so, until the chocolate has melted. Add the softened cocoa butter in small cubes and mix thoroughly until smooth and even.

Transfer the ganache to a pastry (piping) bag without a piping tip (nozzle) and cut away the tip. Pipe the ganache into the chocolate shells until each is three-quarters full. Chill in the refrigerator for 4 hours or leave to cool at room temperature for 12 hours.

Pour the reserved tempered chocolate over the chocolates to seal them. Remove any excess chocolate with a metal spatula or palette knife, then place the molds in the refrigerator for 15 minutes.

Tap the upturned molds on a clean work surface until the chocolates drop out of the molds. Crush the peppercorns with the mortar and pestle, then sprinkle over the chocolates. Decorate each chocolate with edible flowers.

The chocolates can be stored in a cool place for up to 7 days.

CHEESECAKE WITH MINT CHOCOLATE GANACHE

Cheesecake con ganache acqua e menta

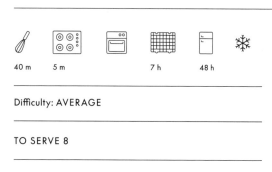

40 m 5 m 7 h 48 h

Difficulty: AVERAGE

TO SERVE 8

FOR THE BASE
3½ ounces/7 tablespoons/100 g unsalted butter
7 ounces/200 g chocolate-coated graham crackers or
   digestive biscuits

FOR THE CHEESECAKE
1 pound 2 ounces/2 cups/500 g fresh cream cheese
3½ ounces/scant ½ cup/100 g superfine (caster) sugar
Grated zest of 2 unwaxed lemons
10 fl oz/1¼ cups/300 ml heavy (whipping) cream

FOR THE MINT CHOCOLATE GANACHE
7 ounces/200 g bittersweet (dark) chocolate (minimum
   70% cocoa solids)
5 fl oz/scant ⅔ cup/150 ml water
½ ounce/15 g mint leaves

TO DECORATE
Sprig of mint leaves

EQUIPMENT NEEDED
Small saucepan
Food processor
8-inch/20-cm springform cake pan (tin)
Bowls
Zester
Electric whisk
Measuring cup or jug
Silicone spatula
Acetate sheet
Metal spatula or palette knife
Plastic wrap (cling film)
Small saucepan

Line the inner sides of the springform pan (tin) with an acetate sheet.

To make the base, melt the butter in a small saucepan. Roughly crush the graham crackers or digestive biscuits, place in a food processor, and blitz to crumbs. While the processor is running, drizzle in the melted butter until you obtain a fine and even mix. Place the mixture into the pan and press down on it with the back of a spoon to compress it.

To make the cheesecake, place the cream cheese, sugar, and lemon zest in a bowl and, using an electric whisk, beat to soft peaks. In a separate bowl, whip the fresh cream and gently fold into the cream cheese with a silicone spatula. Transfer the mix to the pan. Level the surface with a metal spatula or palette knife, cover with plastic wrap (cling film) and leave to set in the refrigerator for 6 hours.

To make the ganache, finely chop the bittersweet (dark) chocolate and place in a bowl. Place the water in a small saucepan with the mint leaves and bring to a boil over medium heat. Simmer for 3 minutes, turn the heat off and leave to cool. Strain, discard the mint, reheat the infusion then drizzle onto the chopped chocolate, stirring continuously with a silicone spatula as you do so, until the chocolate has melted and you have a smooth and shiny ganache. Set aside to cool to room temperature then spread over the cheesecake and place in the refrigerator for 1 hour.

Remove the cheesecake from the pan, peel away the acetate sheet, and place on a serving plate. Decorate with mint leaves.

TIPS AND TRICKS
If you cannot find chocolate-coated graham crackers or digestive biscuits, use 7 ounces/200 g of plain graham crackers (13 sheets of graham crackers, where each sheet has 4 crackers).

GIANDUJA CHOCOLATE AND COFFEE CAKE

Torta al cioccolato gianduia e caffè

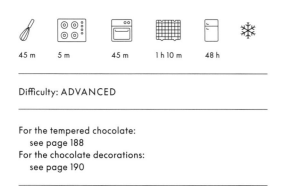

45 m   5 m   45 m   1 h 10 m   48 h

Difficulty: ADVANCED

For the tempered chocolate:
   see page 188
For the chocolate decorations:
   see page 190

TO SERVE 8

FOR THE CHOCOLATE GANACHE
3½ ounces/100 g gianduja chocolate
3½ fl oz/scant ½ cup/100 ml whole (full-fat) milk
1 heaping teaspoon instant coffee granules

FOR THE BASE
4 eggs
9 ounces/2 cups/250 g type "00" flour or all-purpose
   (plain) flour
2 teaspoons/8 g baking powder
6½ ounces/¾ cup/180 g unsalted butter, plus extra
   for greasing
5 ounces/⅔ cup/150 g superfine (caster) sugar
Pinch of salt

FOR THE CHOCOLATE GLAZE
5 ounces/150 g gianduja chocolate
10½ ounces/1¼ cups/300 g mascarpone cheese
2 ounces/½ cup/60 g confectioners' (icing) sugar

TO DECORATE
½ quantity (3½ ounces/125 g) of tempered gianduja
   chocolate prepared following the base recipe and
   temperatures for milk chocolate on page 188
1 ounce/¼ cup/30 g toasted hazelnuts, roughly chopped
Caramel-dipped hazelnuts (see page 324)

EQUIPMENT NEEDED
9-inch/22-cm round springform pan (tin)
Bowls
Measuring cup or jug
Small saucepan
Silicone spatula
Fine-mesh strainer (sieve)
Stand mixer fitted with flat beater attachment
Electric whisk
Cooling rack
Bain-marie or double boiler
Metal spatula or palette knife
Acetate sheet
Parchment paper

Preheat the oven to 350°F/180°C/160°C Fan/Gas 4. Grease the springform pan (tin) with butter then lightly dust with flour. Cut the butter into cubes, place in a bowl, and leave to soften.

To make the chocolate ganache, finely chop the gianduja chocolate and place in a bowl. Pour the milk into a small saucepan and bring almost to boiling point over low heat then add the instant coffee granules and mix.

Slowly pour the coffee milk onto the chopped chocolate, stirring continuously with a silicone spatula as you do so until you obtain a smooth, even cream.

To make the base, separate the egg yolks from the whites. Sift the flour with the baking powder into a separate bowl. Place the butter, sugar and a pinch of salt into the bowl of the stand mixer and beat until you obtain a fluffy cream. Add one egg yolk and a tablespoon of the dry ingredients and mix. Add the remaining yolks in the same way, then the chocolate ganache, continuously mixing as you do so. Add the remaining flour and mix with a silicone spatula until incorporated.

Using an electric whisk, whisk the egg whites to soft peaks then gently fold into the base mixture. Pour the mixture into the prepared pan and bake in the preheated oven for 45 minutes, or until risen and firm to the touch—a skewer inserted into the center should come out clean or with just a few damp cake crumbs attached. Leave to rest for 10 minutes, then remove from the pan and place on a cooling rack to cool completely.

To make the glaze, melt the chocolate in a bain-marie or double boiler, then set aside to return to room temperature. Stir together the mascarpone and sugar to combine, add the melted chocolate and mix. Spread on the top and sides of the cake, using a metal spatula or palette knife to obtain a smooth, even finish.

To make the decoration, cut the acetate sheet to the same length as the circumference of the cake and 4 inches/10 cm taller than its sides. Return the gianduja chocolate to tempering temperature, transfer it to a paper cone made from parchment paper and let it fall in "squiggles" onto the acetate. When the chocolate starts to set but is still malleable, wrap the acetate around the cake with the chocolate side facing the cake. Secure the acetate with sticky tape and place the cake in the refrigerator for 15 minutes. When the chocolate has set, carefully remove and discard the acetate, sprinkle the top of the cake with chopped hazelnuts and leave in the refrigerator for 1 hour. Before serving, decorate with the caramel-dipped hazelnuts.

AMARETTI MARQUISE

Marquise agli amaretti

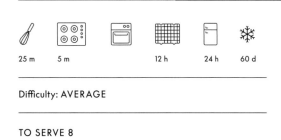

25 m	5 m		12 h	24 h	60 d

Difficulty: AVERAGE

TO SERVE 8

FOR THE BASE
4 ounces/130 g crisp amaretti cookies (biscuits)
2 ounces/¼ cup/60 g unsalted butter

FOR THE CHOCOLATE PARFAIT
10½ ounces/300 g bittersweet (dark) chocolate
4 eggs
6½ ounces/¾ cup/180 g unsalted butter
2 ounces/scant ½ cup/50 g confectioners' (icing) sugar

TO DECORATE
¾ ounce/1 heaping tablespoon/20 g unsweetened
   cocoa powder
¾ ounce/20 g crisp amaretti cookies
1½ ounces/40 g pink chocolate pralines (or use pink
   Jordan almonds/sugared almonds)

EQUIPMENT NEEDED
8 × 3-inch/8-cm round cake pans (tins) or ring molds
Acetate sheet
Small saucepan
Food processor
Bain-marie or double boiler
Bowls
Stand mixer fitted with whisk attachment or
   electric whisk and bowl
Silicone spatula
Small strainer (sieve) or dusting spoon

Line the inner sides of each cake pan (tin) or ring mold with an acetate sheet, cut to fit. If using ring molds, place them on a lined baking sheet.

Melt the butter in a small saucepan and set aside to cool slightly. Place the amaretti cookies (biscuits) in the food processor, add the melted butter, and process until you obtain a fine, even mix. Divide between the individual pans or molds and press down on the base with the back of a spoon to compress.

To make the chocolate parfait, cut the butter into small cubes, place in a bowl, and bring to room temperature. Finely chop the chocolate and melt in a bain-marie or double boiler, then take off the heat and set aside to return to room temperature. Separate the egg yolks from the whites. Beat the softened butter with the confectioners' (icing) sugar in a stand mixer or with an electric whisk until pale and fluffy. Add the egg yolks and stir with a silicone spatula, then add the melted chocolate and mix well. Whisk the egg whites into soft peaks and gently fold into the chocolate mix using a spatula and taking care not to deflate it. Divide the mixture between the prepared pans or molds, level the surface and leave to set in the refrigerator for 12 hours.

Remove the marquise from the pans or molds, remove the acetate sheets, and place on individual serving plates. Dust each marquise with cocoa powder, sprinkle over some crushed amaretti cookies and a few pink chocolate pralines.

WHITE CHOCOLATE AND THYME CUPCAKES

Cupcake al cioccolato bianco e timo

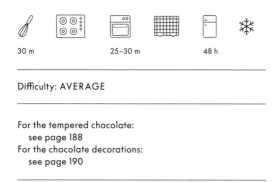

30 m   25–30 m   48 h

Difficulty: AVERAGE

For the tempered chocolate:
  see page 188
For the chocolate decorations:
  see page 190

TO SERVE 6–12 (MAKES 12 CUPCAKES)

FOR THE CUPCAKES
Butter, for greasing
2 eggs
3½ ounces/scant ½ cup/100 g superfine (caster) sugar
4 thyme springs
4 fl oz/½ cup/120 ml sunflower oil
8½ fl oz/1 cup/250 ml whole (full-fat) milk
1 teaspoon vanilla extract
Pinch of salt
14 ounces/3¼ cups/400 g type "00" flour or all-purpose (plain) flour
2 teaspoons/10 g baking powder
3½ ounces/scant ¾ cup/100 g white chocolate chips

TO DECORATE
7 fl oz/scant 1 cup/200 ml heavy (whipping) cream
¾ ounce/scant ¼ cup/20 g confectioners' (icing) sugar
White chocolate
Thyme leaves

EQUIPMENT NEEDED
3-inch/7-cm muffin pans (tins)
Paper cake cases
Bowl
Electric whisk
Measuring cup or jug
Fine-mesh strainer (sieve)
Silicone spatula
Cooling rack
Electric whisk
Pastry (piping) bag fitted with a ½-inch/1-cm plain piping tip (nozzle)

Preheat the oven to 400°F/200°C/180°C Fan/Gas 6. Grease the muffin pans (tins) with a little butter then lightly dust with flour or line with paper cake cases.

Break the eggs into a bowl and beat with an electric whisk. Add the sugar, finely chopped thyme leaves, oil, milk, vanilla extract, and a pinch of salt, and mix to combine.

Sift the flour with the baking powder into the bowl, add the chocolate chips and mix using a silicone spatula until incorporated. Divide the mixture equally between the prepared muffin pans but making sure they are no more than two-thirds full.

Bake the cupcakes in the preheated oven for 25–30 minutes, or until risen, firm to the touch, and a skewer inserted into the center comes out clean. Transfer to a cooling rack and leave to cool completely.

Whip the cream with the confectioners' (icing) sugar to soft peaks. Place the whipped cream in a pastry (piping) bag fitted with a plain piping tip (nozzle) and pipe onto the cakes. Decorate the cupcakes with a little finely chopped or shredded (grated) white chocolate and a few thyme leaves.

TIPS AND TRICKS
During the warmer summer months, white chocolate stored at room temperature becomes soft. In this case you can directly scrape the bar with a flat blade to make the curls more quickly. These will, however, be delicate and soft and must therefore be handled as little as possible to avoid them melting immediately.

STEAMED CHOCOLATE RASPBERRY SPONGE PUDDING

Dolce al vapore con cioccolato e lamponi

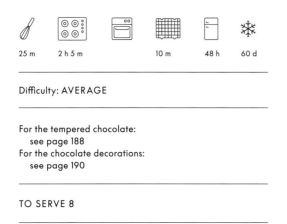

25 m   2 h 5 m   10 m   48 h   60 d

Difficulty: AVERAGE

For the tempered chocolate:
    see page 188
For the chocolate decorations:
    see page 190

TO SERVE 8

FOR THE PUDDING
4 ounces/½ cup plus 1 tablespoon/130 g unsalted butter,
    plus extra for greasing
5 ounces/140 g bittersweet (dark) chocolate
4 ounces/½ cup/120 g superfine (caster) sugar
2 eggs
Pinch of salt
2 tablespoons/30 ml whole (full-fat) milk
6½ ounces/1½ cups/180 g all-purpose (plain) flour
1 teaspoon/4 g baking powder
1 ounce/2 tablespoons/30 g unsweetened cocoa powder
6 ounces/1¼ cups/150 g raspberries

TO DECORATE
7 ounces/generous ¾ cup/200 g mascarpone
1½ ounces/⅓ cup/40 g confectioners' (icing) sugar
Bittersweet (dark) chocolate
Raspberries

EQUIPMENT NEEDED
40-fl oz/5-cup/1.2-litre pudding mold or heatproof bowl
Parchment paper
Bowls
Bain-marie or double boiler
Silicone spatula
Measuring cup or jug
Plastic wrap (cling film)
Kitchen foil
Hand whisk
Fine-mesh strainer (sieve)
Steamer (or steaming basket)
Cooling rack
Metal spatula or palette knife

Grease the pudding mold with a little butter then lightly dust with flour. Cut a circle of parchment paper the same size as the top of the pudding mold and grease one side with butter.

To make the chocolate sponge batter, cut the butter into small cubes, place in a bowl, and bring to room temperature. Finely chop the bittersweet (dark) chocolate and melt in a bain-marie or double boiler, then take off the heat and set aside to cool slightly.

Beat the softened butter with the sugar, using a silicone spatula, until light and fluffy. In a separate bowl, beat the eggs with a pinch of salt, and the milk. Drizzle the melted chocolate into the butter and mix to combine.

Sift the flour with the baking powder and cocoa powder into a bowl. Mix one-third of the flour into the chocolate mixture followed by half of the milk mixture. Mix in another one-third of the flour, followed by the remaining milk and then add the remaining flour. Gently fold through the raspberries. Pour the batter into the prepared pudding mold and level the top. Place the circle of buttered parchment paper, with the buttered side downwards, on top of the pudding batter. Wrap the mold tightly in a double layer of plastic wrap (cling film) followed by a double layer of kitchen foil, making sure that the edges of the wrapping overlap each other to form a water-tight seal.

Steam the pudding for 2 hours, adding more boiling water to the steamer if necessary. Remove the mold from the steamer, leave to rest for 10 minutes.

Meanwhile, beat the mascarpone with the confectioners' (icing) sugar until smooth, using a silicone spatula.

When ready to serve, remove the circle of parchment paper, place a plate over the pudding mold, turn it upside down, and lift the mold off the sponge pudding. Using a metal spatula or palette knife, spread the mascarpone over the top of the sponge pudding. Decorate the pudding with a little finely chopped or shredded (grated) bittersweet (dark) chocolate curls and a handful of fresh raspberries.

MERINGUE

Swiss meringue
Meringa svizzera

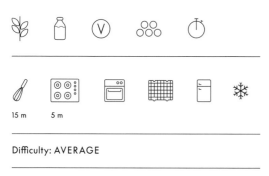

15 m   5 m

Difficulty: AVERAGE

MAKES 1 QUANTITY
  (11 OUNCES/300 G MERINGUE OR 8 LARGE
  OR 16 MEDIUM MERINGUES)

FOR THE MERINGUE
4 egg whites
7 ounces/scant 1 cup/200 g superfine (caster) sugar

EQUIPMENT NEEDED
Bain-marie or double boiler
Hand whisk
Kitchen thermometer
Stand mixer fitted with whisk attachment
Pastry (piping) bag fitted with ½-inch/1-cm plain or
  star piping tip (nozzle) or palette knife
Baking sheet
Parchment paper

AS USED IN
– Chai Tea Pavlova with Raspberries
  (see page 226)
– Chocolate and Pink Peppercorn Meringues
  (see page 228)

Place the egg whites in a bain-marie or double boiler with the sugar (1). It is important that the bain-marie or double boiler is grease-free and that the egg whites are at room temperature and do not contain any trace of the egg yolks.

Heat over a little gently simmering water and beat with a hand whisk, until the sugar has completely dissolved (2).

Using a kitchen thermometer to check the temperature, continue to beat until the mixture reaches 110°F/45°C (3).

Transfer the mixture to the grease-free bowl of a stand mixer and continue to whisk for 5–10 minutes at a medium speed until cooled and forms stiff, glossy peaks (4–5).

Using a pastry (piping) bag, pipe the meringue mix into the desired shape on a baking sheet lined with parchment paper, or simply spoon the meringue onto a baking sheet or on top of a dessert and spread it with a palette knife.

The oven temperature and baking time will vary depending on the size of the meringues.

MISTAKES TO AVOID
Do not exceed a temperature of 140°F/60°C while whisking the meringue mixture, otherwise the egg whites will start to cook—you only need to make sure the sugar dissolves completely. This type of mixture is used for the preparation of meringues and pavlovas or for meringues which are baked as part of a pudding or cake.

TIPS AND TRICKS
To make sure that your equipment is grease-free before whisking egg whites, wipe the clean bowl and whisk with a paper towel that has been dipped in a little lemon juice.

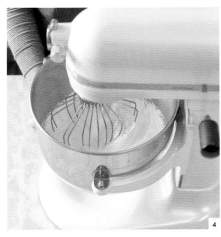 

Italian meringue
Meringa italiana

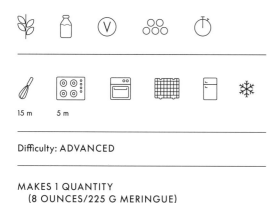

15 m   5 m

Difficulty: ADVANCED

MAKES 1 QUANTITY
(8 OUNCES/225 G MERINGUE)

FOR THE MERINGUE
9 ounces/1¼ cups/240 g superfine (caster) sugar
1¾ fl oz/3 tablespoons/50 ml water
3 egg whites

EQUIPMENT NEEDED
Small saucepan
Hand whisk
Kitchen thermometer
Stand mixer fitted with whisk attachment
Pastry (piping) bag fitted with ½-inch/1-cm plain or
    star piping tip (nozzle) or palette knife
Baking sheet
Parchment paper

AS USED IN
– Coconut Cake with Saffron Meringue
   (see page 230)
– Citron and Saffron Semifreddo
   (see page 304)
– Semifreddo with Pine Nuts and Peach Sauce
   (see page 308)

Place 7 ounces/1 cup/200 g of the sugar in a small saucepan and pour in the water. Set the pan over low heat (1). Let the sugar dissolve, gently swirling the pan from time to time. Once the sugar has dissolved completely, increase the heat to medium and bring the syrup to a boil. Using a kitchen thermometer, continuously monitor the temperature (2).

When the syrup reaches 230°F/110°C, start to whisk the egg whites. Place the egg whites in the bowl of the stand mixer with the remaining sugar (3). It is important that the bowl is grease-free and that the egg whites are at room temperature and do not contain any trace of the egg yolks. Whisk the egg whites on a medium speed to soft peaks.

As soon as the syrup reaches 250°F/121°C, remove from the heat and very slowly drizzle the hot syrup into the whisked egg whites, beating continuously as you do so. Continue to whisk the mixture until the meringue has cooled down (4). Do not pour the syrup onto the whisks as the it will set into sugar strands, instead pour the syrup down the side of the bowl.

Increase the speed of the mixer to incorporate more air into the meringue and whisk for about 10 minutes (5), until it is cold and forms stiff, glossy peaks (6).

Using a pastry (piping) bag, pipe the meringue mix into the desired shape on a baking sheet lined with parchment paper, or simply spoon the meringue onto a baking sheet or on top of a dessert and spread it with a palette knife.

The oven temperature and baking time will vary depending on the size of the meringues.

HOW TO USE
This type of meringue can be used for meringues that are to be browned with a cook's blowtorch, in the preparation of creams that require no further cooking, or as a base for buttercream. It adds the correct amount of sweetness and airiness in the preparation of semifreddos or fruit mousses.

TIPS AND TRICKS
To make sure that your equipment is grease-free before whisking egg whites, wipe the clean bowl and whisk with a paper towel that has been dipped in a little lemon juice.

French meringue
Meringa francese

15 m

Difficulty: ADVANCED

MAKES 1 QUANTITY
(14 OUNCES/400 G MERINGUE OR 10 LARGE
OR 20 MEDIUM MERINGUES)

FOR THE MERINGUE
4 ounces/generous ½ cup/125 g superfine (caster) sugar
4 ounces/1 cup/125 g confectioners' (icing) sugar
5 egg whites

EQUIPMENT NEEDED
Bowl
Stand mixer fitted with whisk attachment
Pastry (piping) bag fitted with ½-inch/1-cm plain or
    star piping tip (nozzle) or palette knife
Baking sheet
Parchment paper

AS USED IN
– Angel Cake with Cherries
  (see page 232)

Mix the superfine (caster) sugar with the confectioners' (icing) sugar in a bowl (1).

Place the egg whites in the bowl of the stand mixer (2). It is important that the bowl is grease-free and that the egg whites are at room temperature and do not contain any trace of the egg yolks.

Add half the sugar mix to the egg whites (3) and start to whisk them on a medium speed, until the whisk starts to form a trace on the surface.

Add the remaining sugar a spoonful at a time, whisking continuously as you do so (4). Continue to whisk for about 10 minutes at maximum speed, until you obtain a very firm and glossy meringue (5).

Using a pastry (piping) bag, pipe the meringue mix into the desired shape on a baking sheet lined with parchment paper, or simply spoon the meringue onto a baking sheet or on top of a dessert and spread it with a palette knife.

The oven temperature and baking time will vary depending on the size of the meringues.

HOW TO USE
This recipe for French meringue can used to make classic meringues and pavlova meringues. To make a pavlova meringue whisk in 1 teaspoon of lemon juice and ¾ ounce/3 heaping tablespoons/25 g of cornstarch (cornflour) once the meringue is firm and glossy.

Dacquoise (nut) meringue
Meringa dacquoise

15 m   30 m

Difficulty: AVERAGE

MAKES 1 QUANTITY
(13 OUNCES/350 G MERINGUE OR MAKES
TWO 8-INCH/20-CM ROUND MERINGUES)

FOR THE MERINGUE
4 egg whites
1 ounces/3 tablespoons/35 g superfine (caster) sugar
3½ ounces/1 cup/100 g dry nuts, such as almonds,
   pistachios, toasted hazelnuts, etc.
3½ ounces/scant 1 cup/110 g confectioners' (icing) sugar

EQUIPMENT NEEDED
2 baking sheets
Parchment paper
Stand mixer fitted with whisk attachment
Food processor
Bowls
Silicone spatula
Metal spatula or palette knife

AS USED IN
– Hazelnut and Salted Sesame Cream Dessert
   (see page 234)

Preheat the oven to 325°F/160°C/140°C Fan/Gas 3. Line the baking sheets with parchment paper.

Place the egg whites in the bowl of the stand mixer, add the superfine (caster) sugar and whisk at medium speed to form a stiff, glossy meringue (1). It is important that the bowl is grease-free and that the egg whites are at room temperature and do not contain any trace of the egg yolks.

Blitz the nuts in a food processor until finely ground, and combine them in a bowl with the confectioners' (icing) sugar (2).

Put the whisked egg whites in a large bowl and add the nut mixture (3).

Using a silicone spatula, gently fold to combine, taking care not to deflate the whisked egg whites (4).

Pile the meringue mix onto the lined baking sheets (5).

Spread the meringue out thinly and evenly using a metal spatula or palette knife (6). Bake the meringue in the preheated oven for 30 minutes or until the meringue is crisp on the outside and releases easily from the parchment paper. Turn off the oven and leave the meringue to cool in the turned-off oven with the door left ajar.

HOW TO USE
As well as being used in the preparation of the French dessert of the same name, this meringue can be used as the crunchy base for semifreddos or desserts made with whipped creams.

TIPS AND TRICKS
Be careful not to grind the nuts too much in the food processor as they can become oily. To reduce the risk of this happening, blitz the nuts with half of the confectioners' sugar.

CHAI TEA PAVLOVA WITH RASPBERRIES

Pavlova al tè chai e lamponi

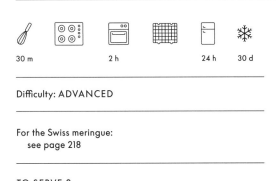

30 m 2 h 24 h 30 d

Difficulty: ADVANCED

For the Swiss meringue:
    see page 218

TO SERVE 8

FOR THE PAVLOVA
1 quantity (11 ounces/300 g) of Swiss meringue prepared
    following the base recipe on page 218 and flavored with
    chai tea spices
½ teaspoon ground chai tea spices
10 fl oz/1¼ cups/300 ml heavy (whipping) cream

FOR THE RASPBERRY COULIS
7 ounces/1 cup/200 g superfine (caster) sugar
7 fl oz/scant 1 cup/200 ml water
7 ounces/1⅔ cups/200 g raspberries
1 lemon

TO DECORATE
9 ounces/2 cups/250 g raspberries
Confectioners' (icing) sugar, for dusting

EQUIPMENT NEEDED
Parchment paper
Baking sheet
Metal spatula or palette knife
Small saucepan
Measuring cup or jug
Hand whisk
Bowls
Juicer
Immersion (stick) blender
Fine-mesh strainer (sieve)
Electric whisk
Small strainer (sieve) or dusting spoon

Preheat the oven to 210°F/100°C/80°C Fan/Gas ¼.

Prepare the Swiss meringue following the instructions on page 218, adding the ground chai tea spices after the egg whites and sugar have been whisked to soft peaks.

Draw a 7-inch/18-cm circle on a sheet of parchment paper. Turn the paper over so the pencil line is on the underside and place it on the baking sheet. Pile the meringue onto the lined baking sheet in the center of the circle.

Using the back of a large spoon or palette knife, spread out the meringue to the edges of the pencil guide line, to form an even circle with a large dip in the center. Smooth out the edges with a metal spatula or palette knife, using an upward movement. Bake the meringue in the preheated oven for 2 hours, or until crisp on the outside. Turn off the oven and leave the meringue to cool inside the turned-off oven.

To make the raspberry coulis, place the sugar in a small saucepan with the water. Bring to a boil over medium heat and stir with a hand whisk until the sugar has completely dissolved. Continue to cook for 3 minutes, then leave the syrup to cool. Place the raspberries in a bowl with 1 tablespoon lemon juice and puree using an immersion (stick) blender until you have a very smooth puree. Add the syrup, blitz again for a few more seconds then strain the coulis through a fine-mesh strainer (sieve) into a bowl.

Transfer the meringue to a serving plate. Whip the cream to soft peaks. Fill the center of the pavlova with the whipped cream, then top with the raspberries, drizzle over the raspberry coulis, and finish with a dusting of confectioners' (icing) sugar.

VARIATIONS
You can also prepare the pavlova using a different method. Whisk 4 egg whites to stiff peaks, then slowly add 7 ounces/1 cup/200 g superfine (caster) sugar and continue to whisk until glossy, stiff peaks form. Add ½ ounce/3 teaspoons/9 g cornstarch (cornflour) and 1 teaspoon white wine vinegar or lemon juice, fold in with a silicone spatula and continue as indicated in the recipe.

CHOCOLATE AND PINK PEPPERCORN MERINGUES

Meringhe al cioccolato e pepe rosa

20 m 5 m 2 h 24 h

Difficulty: AVERAGE

For the Swiss meringue:
   see page 218

TO SERVE 8 (MAKES 8 SANDWICHED MERINGUES)

FOR THE MERINGUE
3 egg whites
6½ ounces/generous ¾ cup/180 g superfine (caster) sugar

TO SERVE
3 ounces/80 g bittersweet (dark) chocolate
1 heaping teaspoon pink peppercorns
5 fl oz/⅔ cup/150 ml heavy (whipping) cream

EQUIPMENT NEEDED
Bain-marie or double boiler
Bowl
Baking sheet
Parchment paper
Mortar and pestle
Measuring cup or jug
Electric whisk
Metal spatula or palette knife
Pastry (piping) bag fitted with a ⅜-inch/1-cm plain piping
   tip (nozzle)

Preheat the oven to 210°F/100°C/80°C Fan/Gas ¼. Line a baking sheet with parchment paper.

Using the ingredient quantities listed on this page, prepare the Swiss meringue following the instructions on page 218.

Finely chop half of the chocolate and melt it in a bain-marie or double boiler. Transfer to a bowl and leave to cool. Drizzle the melted chocolate over the meringue, and use a spoon to stir it once to swirl the chocolate through the meringue without incorporating it.

Place 16 heaping teaspoonfuls of the meringue mixture onto the lined baking sheet. Alternatively, pipe 16 small meringues onto the baking sheet using a pastry (piping) bag fitted with a ⅜-inch/1-cm plain piping tip (nozzle). Crush the pink peppercorns using a mortar and pestle and sprinkle over the top of the meringues. Leave for 30 minutes to set.

Bake the meringues in the preheated oven for 2 hours. Turn the oven off and leave the meringues to cool in the turned-off oven with the door left ajar.

Melt the remaining chocolate in a bain-marie over low heat. Dip the flat base of each meringue into the melted chocolate and then sprinkle over a little crushed pink peppercorns.

Whip the cream to soft peaks using the electric whisk. Using a metal spatula or palette knife, spread the whipped cream on the flat side of half of the meringues. Top with the flat side of the remaining meringues. Serve the meringues immediately as they will start to soften once sandwiched with the cream.

Any leftover meringues that have not been sandwiched with cream can be stored in an airtight container in a cool, dry place for up to 3 days.

COCONUT CAKE WITH SAFFRON MERINGUE

Torta al cocco meringata allo zafferano

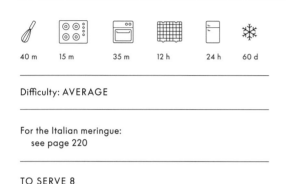

40 m   15 m   35 m   12 h   24 h   60 d

Difficulty: AVERAGE

For the Italian meringue:
    see page 220

TO SERVE 8

FOR THE BASE
Butter for greasing
3¼ ounces/¾ cup/90 g type "00" flour or all-purpose
    (plain) flour
1 teaspoon/3 g baking powder
1 teaspoon/3 g baking soda (bicarbonate of soda)
3½ ounces/scant ½ cup/100 g superfine (caster) sugar
Pinch of salt
4 fl oz/½ cup/120 ml coconut milk
1¾ fl oz/3 tablespoons/50 ml sunflower oil
2 eggs
½ teaspoon apple cider vinegar

FOR THE MOUSSE
½ ounce/10 g platinum gelatin sheets
15 fl oz/1¾ cups/450 ml coconut milk
⅞ ounce/4 tablespoons/25 g unsweetened shredded
    (desiccated) coconut
3½ ounces/scant ½ cup/100 g superfine (caster) sugar
15 fl oz/1¾ cups/450 ml heavy (whipping) cream

FOR THE MERINGUE
5 ounces/¾ cup/150 g superfine (caster) sugar
Large pinch of saffron threads
3 tablespoons/40 ml water
3 egg whites

EQUIPMENT NEEDED
7-inch/18-cm round springform pan (tin)
Fine-mesh strainer (sieve)
Bowls
Measuring cup or jug
Stand mixer fitted with flat beater
Small saucepans
Electric whisk
Silicone spatula
8-inch/20-cm round cake pan (tin)
Acetate sheet
Plastic wrap (cling film)
Metal spatula or palette knife
Cook's blowtorch

Preheat the oven to 350°F/180°C/160°C Fan/Gas 4. Grease the 7-inch/18-cm springform pan (tin) with a little butter and line with parchment paper.

Sift the flour, baking powder, and baking soda (bicarbonate of soda) into a bowl, add the sugar and a pinch of salt and mix to combine. Pour the coconut milk into the bowl of a stand mixer, add the oil, eggs, and vinegar, and mix on a medium speed until combined. Add the dry ingredients and continue to mix until the mixture is smooth. Pour into a springform pan and bake in the preheated oven for 35 minutes, or until golden, risen, and firm to the touch—a skewer inserted into the center of the cake should come out clean. Leave to cool a little, then remove from the pan and leave to cool completely.

To make the mousse, soak the gelatin in cold water for 5 minutes. Heat the coconut milk, unsweetened shredded (desiccated) coconut, and sugar in a small saucepan over low heat and stir until the sugar has dissolved. Squeeze the water from the gelatin. Add to the pan and stir until it has dissolved. Leave the coconut mixture to cool to room temperature, stirring occasionally.

Whip the cream to soft peaks and fold it into the coconut milk mix with a silicone spatula. Line the inner sides of the 8-inch/20-cm round cake pan (tin) with an acetate sheet and the base of the pan with plastic wrap (cling film) then transfer the coconut cake to the center of the pan. Pour the coconut mousse over the cake, covering the top and sides, then place in the refrigerator to set for 12 hours.

To make the meringue, place the sugar in a small saucepan, add the saffron and water, and put over low heat until the sugar has dissolved, then increase the heat to medium and bring to a boil. Whisk the egg whites and continue, following the instructions for the Italian meringue base recipe on page 220.

Remove the mousse-covered cake from the pan, carefully peel away the acetate, and cover it with the meringue, using a metal spatula or palette knife to spread it evenly around the sides and top. Brown the meringue using a cooks' blowtorch and serve immediately or within 2 hours.

ANGEL CAKE WITH CHERRIES

Angel cake con ciliegie

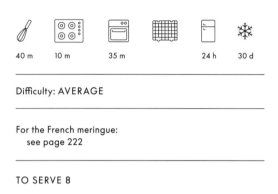

40 m	10 m	35 m		24 h	30 d

Difficulty: AVERAGE

For the French meringue:
see page 222

TO SERVE 8

FOR THE BASE
5 egg whites at room temperature
1 heaping teaspoon/4 g cream of tartar
1 vanilla bean (pod)
1 teaspoon lemon juice
5 ounces/⅔ cup/140 g superfine (caster) sugar
2½ ounces/scant ⅔ cup/75 g type "00" flour or all-purpose
   (plain) flour
Pinch of salt

FOR THE CHERRY SYRUP
1 pound 2 ounces/2¼ cups/500 g cherries
3½ ounces/scant ½ cup/100 g sugar
1½ tablespoons/20 ml water
1-inch/3-cm cinnamon stick
1 unwaxed lemon

TO DECORATE
7 fl oz/scant 1 cup/200 ml heavy (whipping) cream
1 ounce/4 tablespoons/30 g confectioners' (icing) sugar

EQUIPMENT NEEDED
Stand mixer fitted with whisk attachment
Small strainer (sieve)
Bowls
Fine-mesh strainer (sieve)
Silicone spatula
7-inch/18-cm non-stick angel cake pan (tin)
Cooling rack
Pitting tool
Saucepan
Measuring cup or jug
Peeler
Juicer
Electric whisk

Preheat the oven to 350°F/180°C/160°C Fan/Gas 4.

Place the egg whites in the bowl of the stand mixer, add the cream of tartar, seeds from the vanilla bean (pod), and the lemon juice, poured through a strainer (sieve). Start to whisk on a medium speed until the whisk starts to form a trace on the surface. Increase the speed and add the sugar, a teaspoonful at a time, whisking continuously as you do so. Continue to whisk for about 10 minutes at maximum speed, until you obtain a very firm, glossy meringue.

Sift the flour with a pinch of salt into the bowl and gently fold it into the meringue with a silicone spatula, taking care not to deflate the mixture. Pour into the cake pan (tin), level the surface, and bake in the preheated oven for about 35 minutes, or until golden, risen, and firm to the touch. Do not insert a skewer into the cake to test it, as it can deflate the cake. Remove the cake from the oven, immediately invert it onto a cooling rack, and leave to cool without removing the pan.

To make the cherry syrup, wash and pit (stone) the cherries using the pitting tool, remove the stalks, and place in a saucepan with the sugar, water, cinnamon stick, pared zest from the lemon, and strained juice of half the lemon. Put over low heat until the sugar has dissolved, then increase the heat to medium and cook for 6–7 minutes. Pour into a fine-mesh strainer (sieve) set over a bowl to collect the juice. Return the juice to the saucepan and cook for a further 2–3 minutes until it becomes syrupy. Leave to cool.

Remove the cake by running the blade of a small knife between the edges of the cake and the pan. Whip the cream to soft peaks with the confectioners' (icing) sugar and spoon or pipe it over the top of the cake. Decorate with half of the cherries and drizzle over some of the syrup. Serve with the remaining cherries and syrup.

MISTAKES TO AVOID
An angel cake pan should preferably not be non-stick and should never be greased. This is because the cake needs to "climb" the sides of the pan by sticking to it a little bit—if the pan is greased the cake will not rise as much.

HAZELNUT AND SALTED SESAME CREAM DESSERT

Dolce alle nocciole con crema al sesamo salato

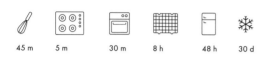

45 m   5 m   30 m   8 h   48 h   30 d

Difficulty: ADVANCED

For the Italian meringue:
   see page 220
For the Dacquoise meringue:
   see page 224

TO SERVE 8

FOR THE DACQUOISE MERINGUE
4 egg whites
1 ounces/3 tablespoons/35 g superfine (caster) sugar
3½ ounces/1 cup/100 g toasted hazelnuts
3½ ounces/scant 1 cup/110 g confectioners' (icing) sugar

FOR THE ITALIAN MERINGUE BUTTERCREAM
8 ounces/1 cup/220 g superfine (caster) sugar
1 vanilla bean (pod)
2 fl oz/¼ cup/60 ml water
4 egg whites
6 ounces/¾ cup/170 g unsalted butter
3½ ounces/100 g gomasio (sesame salt)

TO DECORATE
1½ ounces/40 g sesame brittle or sesame snaps

EQUIPMENT NEEDED
Rectangular baking sheet
Parchment paper
Metal spatula or palette knife
Small saucepan
Measuring cup or jug
Kitchen thermometer
Stand mixer fitted with whisk attachment
   and paddle attachment
2-lb/900-g loaf pan (tin)
Acetate sheet
Silicone spatula

Preheat the oven to 325°F/160°C/140°C Fan/Gas 3 and line the baking sheet with parchment paper. Cut the butter into small cubes and bring to room temperature.

Using the ingredient quantities listed on this page, prepare the Dacquoise meringue following the instructions on page 224. Pour onto the prepared baking sheet, using a metal spatula or palette knife to spread it into an even layer ½ inch/1 cm thick. Bake in the preheated oven for 30 minutes, opening the oven door for a few seconds halfway through the cooking time. Turn off the oven, leave the meringue to cool in the turned-off oven with the door ajar.

To make the cream, place the sugar in a small saucepan, add the seeds from the vanilla bean (pod), and the water, then warm over a low until the sugar has dissolved. Increase the heat to medium and boil to make a syrup. Heat the syrup to 250°F/121°C using a kitchen thermometer to check it has reached the correct temperature.

Meanwhile, place the egg whites in the bowl of the stand mixer fitted with the whisk attachment and start to whisk on a medium speed. When the syrup reaches 250°F/121°C, drizzle it into the egg whites, continuing to whisk for 15 minutes, until the meringue is cold. Remove the whisk attachment and mount the paddle attachment then continue to whisk on a low speed, adding the soft butter in small cubes. When the butter is incorporated, add the gomasio (sesame salt) and mix to combine.

Place an acetate sheet, cut to fit, into the base of the loaf pan (tin), then line the sides. Trim the edges of the meringue and cut it into two equal rectangles the same size as the loaf pan. Cover the base of the pan with a meringue rectangle. Spread the buttercream over it evenly. Cover with the second rectangle of meringue and place in the refrigerator for 8 hours. Remove from the cake pan to a serving plate, remove and discard the acetate, and decorate with broken shards of sesame brittle.

TIPS AND TRICKS
Opening the oven halfway through the cooking time allows condensation to escape, so that the meringue is dry at the end of the cooking time.

When adding the butter to the Italian meringue, the mixture may curdle slightly. If this happens, keep beating and adding butter and the mixture should come back together again.

CREAMS AND MOUSSES

Confectioners' custard
Crema pasticciera

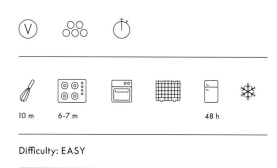

10 m   6–7 m   48 h

Difficulty: EASY

MAKES 1 QUANTITY
(1 POUND 5 OUNCES/2½ CUPS/600 G CUSTARD)

FOR THE CUSTARD
17 fl oz/2 cups/500 ml whole (full-fat) milk
Pared zest of 1 unwaxed lemon or 1 vanilla bean (pod)
6 egg yolks
3½ ounces/½ cup/100 g superfine (caster) sugar
3 ounces/⅔ cup/80 g type "00" flour or all-purpose
 (plain) flour

EQUIPMENT NEEDED
Measuring cup or jug
Saucepan
Peeler (optional)
Bowls
Hand whisk
Fine-mesh strainer (sieve)
Pitcher (jug)
Silicone spatula
Plastic wrap (cling film)

AS USED IN
– Almond and Chocolate Sfogliata
 (see page 96)
– Forest Fruits Pudding
 (see page 116)
– Pont Neuf Tartlets with Red Currants
 (see page 140)
– "Zeppole"—Italian Donuts
 (see page 142)
– Coffee and Chocolate Cream Bars
 (see page 172)
– Candied Ginger Pinwheels
 (see page 180)
– Chantilly Cream
 (see page 246)
– Chiboust Cream
 (see page 248)
– Mousseline Cream
 (see page 250)
– Frangipane Cream
 (see page 256)
– Tartlets with Pine Nuts and Chocolate Cream
 (see page 260)

Pour the milk into a saucepan and add the pared lemon zest or the vanilla bean (pod), split lengthwise (1). Set the pan over low heat and bring the milk almost to boiling point, then turn off the heat and set aside to cool.

Place the egg yolks and sugar in a bowl (2). Using a hand whisk, beat the egg yolks with the sugar until they are light and foamy (3). Add the flour and mix it into the yolk mixture (4).

Strain the warm milk through a fine-mesh strainer (sieve) into a clean saucepan or pitcher (jug). Slowly pour the milk into the bowl with the egg yolk mixture. Whisk continuously as you add the milk to avoid any lumps forming (5).

Strain the custard mixture through a fine-mesh strainer into a clean saucepan and bring to a simmer, then continue cooking over low heat for a further 5 minutes (6). Stir the custard continuously with a silicone spatula until it becomes quite thick (7).

Pour the custard into a bowl and set it in an ice bain-marie to cool. Cover it with plastic wrap (cling film), ensuring the wrap touches the surface of the custard, and leave to cool.

HOW TO USE
Confectioners' custard can be used to fill cakes, brioches, and pastries. It can be stored in the refrigerator for up to 3 days, stir before use if chilled.

TIPS AND TRICKS
Confectioners' custard is one of the most used base creams in pâtisserie. As well as flour, it can be made with potato starch or cornstarch (cornflour), which imparts a more delicate flavor. Rice starch or rice flour can be used for those who are gluten intolerant. Depending on the type of recipe, the custard can be flavored with spices, citrus fruits, or grated chocolate.

If you are worried about the warm milk potentially scrambling the egg yolks, you can "temper" the eggs first by adding a little of the milk to the yolks and whisking, before adding the remaining milk.

Crème anglaise
Crema inglese

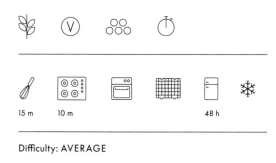

15 m   10 m   48 h

Difficulty: AVERAGE

MAKES 1 QUANTITY
(1 POUND 9 OUNCES/SCANT 3 CUPS/700 G
CRÈME ANGLAISE)

FOR THE CRÈME ANGLAISE
17 fl oz/2 cups/500 ml whole (full-fat) milk
1 vanilla bean (pod)
6 egg yolks
5 ounces/¾ cup/150 g superfine (caster) sugar

EQUIPMENT NEEDED
Saucepan
Measuring cup or jug
Bain-marie or double boiler
Hand whisk
Bowls
Fine-mesh strainer (sieve)
Silicone spatula
Kitchen thermometer

AS USED IN
– Banana, Mango, and Mint Charlotte
  (see page 126)
– Chocolate and Lemon Balm Bavarian Cream
  (see page 264)

Pour the milk into a saucepan and add the vanilla bean (pod), split lengthwise (1). Set the pan over low heat and bring the milk almost to boiling point, then turn off the heat and set aside to cool.

Place the egg yolks and sugar in a bain-marie or double boiler (2). Using a hand whisk, beat the egg yolks with the sugar until they are light and foamy (3).

Strain the warm milk through a fine-mesh strainer (sieve) into a clean saucepan or pitcher (jug). Slowly pour the milk into the bowl with the egg yolk mix. Whisk continuously as you add the milk to make a smooth custard (4).

Heat the custard in a bain-marie or double boiler. Stir the custard continuously with a silicone spatula until it starts to thicken (5). Constantly monitoring the temperature with a kitchen thermometer, continue to cook the custard until it lightly coats the back of a spoon and do not let the temperature exceed 185°F/85°C (6).

Strain the custard into a bowl and set it in an ice bain-marie to cool. Cover it with plastic wrap (cling film), ensuring the wrap touches the surface of the custard, and leave to cool.

HOW TO USE
Crème anglaise is the classic custard served with many desserts and can be used as a base in the preparation of ice cream, or mixed with whipped cream and gelatin in the preparation of Bavarian cream. Crème anglaise can also be served warm, in which case strain it straight into a pitcher (jug) after it has reached the correct thickness. Crème anglaise can be reheated, but do this very gently in a bain marie and do not reheated above 185°F/85°C.

MISTAKES TO AVOID
Crème anglaise is a very delicate custard that needs extreme care during cooking. In fact, its temperature must not exceed 185°F/85°C, because at higher temperatures the egg yolks solidify and the cream curdles, forming small clots. If you are experienced, you can cook it directly on the heat using a kitchen thermometer to monitor the temperature. Alternatively, you can cook it in a bain-marie or double boiler, ensuring that the bottom of the bowl does not touch the water and heats by steam only.

VARIATIONS
Crème anglaise can be flavored to taste with spices, citrus peel, coffee, or finely chopped chocolate added at the end of the cooking time, when it is still warm.

Chocolate cremoso

Cremoso

15 m   10 m   12 h   48 h

Difficulty: AVERAGE

MAKES 1 QUANTITY
(1 POUND 11 OUNCES/3 CUPS/750 G CREMOSO)

FOR THE CREMOSO
⅛ ounce/2.5 g platinum gelatin sheets
4 egg yolks
1½ ounces/scant ¼ cup/40 g superfine (caster) sugar
7 fl oz/scant 1 cup/200 ml heavy (whipping) cream
7 fl oz/scant 1 cup/200 ml whole (full-fat) milk
1 vanilla bean (pod)
10 ounces/280 g bittersweet (dark), milk, or white chocolate

EQUIPMENT NEEDED
Bowls
Bain-marie or double boiler
Hand whisk
Saucepan
Measuring cup or jug
Fine-mesh strainer (sieve)
Silicone spatula
Immersion (stick) blender
Plastic wrap (cling film)

AS USED IN
– White Chocolate Cremoso with Grapefruit
  (see page 266)

Soak the gelatin in cold water for 5 minutes.

Meanwhile, pour the cream and milk into a saucepan and add the vanilla bean (pod) split lengthwise. Set the pan over low heat and bring almost to boiling point, then turn off the heat and set aside to cool.

Place the egg yolks and sugar in a bain-marie or double boiler. Using a hand whisk, beat the egg yolks with the sugar until they are light and foamy.

Strain the cream and milk mixture through a fine-mesh strainer (sieve) into a clean saucepan or pitcher (jug). Slowly pour into the bowl with the egg yolk mix. Whisk continuously as you add the cream and milk mixture to make a smooth custard.

Heat the custard in a bain-marie or double boiler. Stir the custard continuously with a silicone spatula until it starts to thicken. Constantly monitoring the temperature with a kitchen thermometer, continue to cook the custard until it lightly coats the back of a spoon and do not let the temperature exceed 185°F/85°C.

Once the custard has cooked, squeeze the water from the gelatin, add to the cream mixture and stir until it has dissolved (1).

Finely chop the chocolate using a large knife (2) and add it to the warm custard, stirring with a silicone spatula to combine (3).

Blitz with an immersion (stick) blender until you have a smooth, even mixture (4) and then transfer to a bowl (5).

Cover with plastic wrap (cling film), ensuring the wrap touches the surface of the chocolate cremoso (6), and leave to cool in the refrigerator for 12 hours.

HOW TO USE
Cremoso can be used on its own as a dessert or to fill tartlets, pastries, and cakes.

TIPS AND TRICKS
The cremoso needs to be left in the refrigerator for 6–8 hours before using, so it has time to chill and thicken to the correct consistency.

Lemon curd

Lemon curd

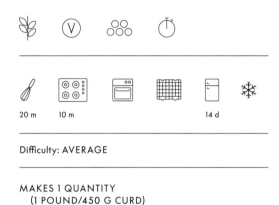

20 m   10 m   14 d

Difficulty: AVERAGE

MAKES 1 QUANTITY
   (1 POUND/450 G CURD)

FOR THE CURD
7 ounces/1 cup/200 g superfine (caster) sugar
4 unwaxed lemons
3½ ounces/7 tablespoons/100 g unsalted butter
3 eggs
1 egg yolk

EQUIPMENT NEEDED
Zester
Juicer
Bain-marie or double boiler
Strainer (sieve)
Bowl
Silicone spatula

AS USED IN
– Frozen Yogurt Ice Pops with Lemon Curd
  (see page 268)

Grate the zest of the lemons, then juice them. Place the zest in a bain-marie or double boiler. Pour the juice through a strainer (sieve) into the bain-marie, add the sugar, then stir to combine (1). Cut the cold butter into small cubes and add to the bowl (2).

In a separate bowl, beat the eggs and the additional yolk with a fork (3). Gently heat the butter, sugar and lemon mix in the bain-marie or double boiler until the butter has just melted then add the beaten eggs (4).

Cook for 10–12 minutes, stirring with a silicone spatula until the mixture thickens and coats the spatula. A line drawn with a finger through the mixture on the spatula should remain visible for several seconds (5).

Pour the lemon curd into a storage container and leave to cool in the refrigerator (6).

It is possible to store the curd in sterilized jars in the refrigerator for up to 14 days. To sterilize the jars, boil them in a saucepan and avoid touching them by using a clean dish towel (tea towel). Alternatively, wash in boiling water then place in the oven at 325°F/160°C for 15 minutes. Pour the lemon curd into the jars while they are still hot.

HOW TO USE
Combine the lemon curd with Greek yogurt or whipped cream and serve it as a last-minute dessert, or use it to fill cakes, biscuits, and pastries.

TIPS AND TRICKS
Lemon curd can also be cooked directly on a stove top. This way, the cooking time is reduced, but you must be very careful to keep the temperature low, without ever letting the mixture boil, to prevent the eggs curdling. Another method requires the juice and zest of the lemon, the eggs and sugar to be warmed together before adding the butter in small cubes, mixing until it has melted and the curd has thickened.

Chantilly cream
Crema Chantilly

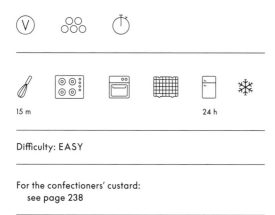

15 m

24 h

Difficulty: EASY

For the confectioners' custard:
  see page 238

MAKES 1 QUANTITY
  (2 POUNDS 2 OUNCES/1 KG CHANTILLY CREAM)

FOR THE CHANTILLY CREAM
10 fl oz/1¼ cups/300 ml heavy (double) cream
1 quantity (1 pound 9 ounces/700 g) of confectioners'
  custard prepared following the base recipe on page 238

EQUIPMENT NEEDED
Measuring cup or jug
Bowl
Electric whisk
Silicone spatula

AS USED IN
– Classic Cannoncini with Chantilly Cream
  (see page 98)
– Craquelin Choux with Pear Chantilly Cream
  (see page 136)
– Fruit au Gratin with Chantilly Cream
  (see page 270)

Pour the cream into a bowl. Using an electric whisk, whip the cream to soft peaks (1).

Add one-third of the whipped cream to the cooled custard and fold it in gently, using a silicone spatula (2).

Add the remaining cream and fold it in again until you obtain a soft, even mixture (3).

Chantilly cream is used to fill cakes and choux, but it can also be served with chocolate cakes and lightly sweetened fruit puddings.

MISTAKES TO AVOID
In Italian pâtisserie, Chantilly cream is a mix of whipped cream and custard. However, in French pâtisserie it simply means whipped cream to which confectioners' (icing) sugar has been added, and it is often flavored with vanilla. For that reason, this version of Chantilly cream may be referred to as Italian Chantilly cream or Diplomat cream.

TIPS AND TRICKS
Heavy (whipping) cream can be whipped with a hand whisk, an electric whisk, or a stand mixer fitted with a whisk attachment. Regardless of the tool used, cream must be whipped to a slightly firmer consistency if it is to be served as an accompaniment on the side, or softer if it is to be incorporated into other mixtures. Cream should not be whipped at room temperature—it must be stored in the refrigerator until the last moment and, preferably, the bowl and beaters used for whipping the cream should also be cold or you could even use an ice bain-marie. The cream must be fresh and not long-life or UHT.

Chiboust cream
Crema chiboust

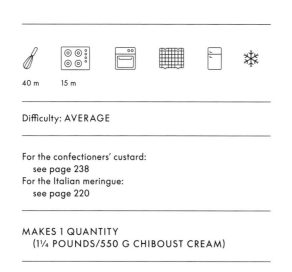

40 m   15 m

Difficulty: AVERAGE

For the confectioners' custard:
  see page 238
For the Italian meringue:
  see page 220

MAKES 1 QUANTITY
  (1¼ POUNDS/550 G CHIBOUST CREAM)

FOR THE CONFECTIONERS' CUSTARD
¼ ounce/7.5 g platinum gelatin sheets
4 egg yolks
1 ounce/2 tablespoons/25 g superfine (caster) sugar
¾ ounce/8 teaspoons/20 g cornstarch (cornflour)
8½ fl oz/1 cup/260 ml whole (full-fat) milk
1 vanilla bean (pod)

FOR THE ITALIAN MERINGUE
4 egg whites
2¼ ounces/scant ⅓ cup/65 g superfine (caster) sugar
2 tablespoons water

EQUIPMENT NEEDED
Measuring cup or jug
Bowls
Saucepan
Silicone spatula

AS USED IN
– Tart with Chiboust Cream, Walnuts, and Apples
  (see page 272)

Soak the gelatin in cold water for 5 minutes (1).

Using 4 egg yolks, 1 ounce/2 tablespoons/25 g of sugar, the cornflour, milk, and vanilla bean (pod), prepare the confectioners' custard following the instructions on page 238.

While the custard is still warm and in the saucepan, squeeze the water from the gelatin, and add to the custard (2).

Stir the custard until the gelatin has dissolved (3) then transfer to a large bowl and leave to cool to room temperature.

Prepare an Italian meringue with the egg whites, sugar and water, following the instructions on page 220 then carefully fold it into the custard using a silicone spatula (4–5).

HOW TO USE
This cream has a velvety and elastic consistency, ideal for serving on its own, perhaps with a forest fruit compote, or as a filling for a classic sponge.

MISTAKES TO AVOID
Chiboust cream must be used immediately because, as it contains gelatin, it solidifies as it cools.

Mousseline cream

Crema mousseline

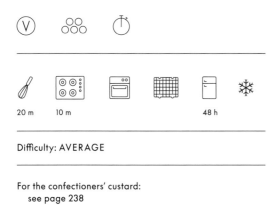

20 m   10 m   48 h

Difficulty: AVERAGE

For the confectioners' custard:
  see page 238

MAKES 1 QUANTITY
  (1 POUND 13 OUNCES/3 CUPS/800 G CREAM)

FOR THE CREAM
1 quantity (1 pound 12 ounces/800 g) of confectioners'
  custard prepared following the base recipe on page
  238 but replacing the flour with a mix of 2 ounces/
  ½ cup/50 g potato starch or cornstarch (cornflour)
  and ¾ ounce/20 g flour
7 ounces/½ cup plus 5 tablespoons/200 g unsalted butter

EQUIPMENT NEEDED
Saucepan
Hand whisk
Bowl
Plastic wrap (cling film)
Stand mixer fitted with whisk attachment

AS USED IN
– Fraisier
  (see page 274)

Prepare the confectioners' custard following the instructions on page 238 up to step 7.

Meanwhile, cut the butter into small cubes and set aside in a warm place until very soft. While the custard is still warm, add 2 ounces/ 4 tablespoons/50 g of the softened cubes of butter (1) and stir into the custard using a hand whisk until the butter has completely melted (2).

Transfer the mixture to a bowl and cover it with plastic wrap (cling film), ensuring the film touches the surface of the cream. Set aside to cool.

When the mixture has cooled to room temperature, transfer to the bowl of the stand mixer and start to mix at medium speed, adding the remaining softened butter a little at a time (3).

Continue to mix for 10 minutes, to obtain a very light, smooth cream (4).

HOW TO USE
The cream can be used immediately or can be stored in the refrigerator for a maximum of 48 hours. It can be used to fill cakes and pastries.

TIPS AND TRICKS
To ensure the butter blends perfectly with the custard, both the bowl of the stand mixer and the custard must be at room temperature.

Sabayon

Zabaione

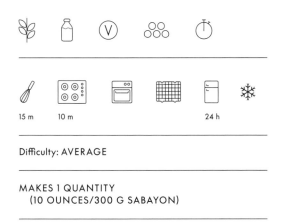

15 m   10 m   24 h

Difficulty: AVERAGE

MAKES 1 QUANTITY
(10 OUNCES/300 G SABAYON)

FOR THE SABAYON
4 eggs
3 ounces/⅓ cup/80 g superfine (caster) sugar
2½ fl oz/5 tablespoons/80 ml Marsala wine

EQUIPMENT NEEDED
Bain-marie or double boiler
Hand whisk
Measuring cup or jug
Saucepans
Kitchen thermometer

AS USED IN
– Frozen Sabayon with Limoncello
  (see page 276)

Separate the egg yolks from the whites, and place the yolks in a bain-marie or double boiler (1) with the sugar.

Beat with a hand whisk until the mixture is light and fluffy, then remove from the heat and set aside (2).

Pour the Marsala wine into a small saucepan and warm over low heat (3–4).

Slowly pour the wine over the whipped egg yolks (5), return the mixture to the bain-marie and whisk (6).

Constantly monitoring the temperature with a kitchen thermometer, continue to whisk and heat the mixture until it reaches 183°F/84°C (7), or until the mix is firm and airy and the mixture falls in ribbons from the whisk and leaves a trace on the surface.

HOW TO USE
The sabayon can be served immediately in individual serving glasses with crisp cookies alongside. Alternatively, spoon the sabayon over soft, fresh fruit and quickly gratinate (brown) the top under a hot broiler (grill), or use a cook's blowtorch.

TIPS AND TRICKS
If you want to store the sabayon, leave it to cool in an ice bain-marie, cover the bowl with plastic wrap (cling film) and keep in the refrigerator for 24 hours.

Chocolate mousse

Mousse al cioccolato

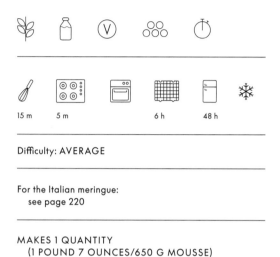

15 m   5 m   6 h   48 h

Difficulty: AVERAGE

For the Italian meringue:
  see page 220

MAKES 1 QUANTITY
  (1 POUND 7 OUNCES/650 G MOUSSE)

FOR THE MOUSSE
12 ounces/340 g bittersweet (dark) chocolate (minimum
  70% cocoa solids, dairy-free)
5 eggs
2½ ounces/scant ⅓ cup/70 g superfine (caster) sugar
2 fl oz/¼ cup/60 ml water

EQUIPMENT NEEDED
Bain-marie or double boiler
Silicone spatula
Bowls
Individual glasses or ramekins

Finely chop the chocolate (1), place in a bain-marie or double boiler and melt over a gentle heat, stirring with a silicone spatula (2).

When the chocolate has melted, transfer to a bowl and set aside to cool to room temperature (3).

Separate the egg yolks from the whites, and place the yolks in the bowl with the chocolate, mixing with a spatula to combine (4).

Prepare an Italian meringue with the egg whites, sugar, and water, following the instructions on page 220, then carefully fold it into the chocolate mixture using a silicone spatula (5–6).

Pour into individual glasses or ramekins, level the top, and leave to set in the refrigerator for at least 6 hours.

MISTAKES TO AVOID
When you mix the yolks and the melted chocolate, it is important that the two ingredients are the same temperature. This is to prevent the chocolate hardening, if the yolks are too cold. It is best, therefore, to use eggs at room temperature.

TIPS AND TRICKS
When melting chocolate for other uses, remove the heatproof bowl from the saucepan of hot water while there are still a few small pieces of unmelted chocolate left in the bowl. The residual heat means that the chocolate will continue to melt but prevent the chocolate from overheating.

Frangipane cream
Crema frangipane

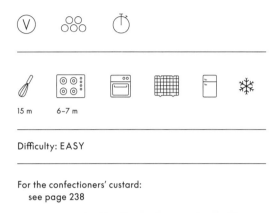

15 m   6–7 m

Difficulty: EASY

For the confectioners' custard:
 see page 238

MAKES 1 QUANTITY
 (2 POUNDS 2 OUNCES/950 G FRANGIPANE OR
 ENOUGH TO FILL A 8–10-INCH TART)

FOR THE FRANGIPANE
7 ounces/½ cup plus 5 tablespoons/200 g unsalted butter
7 ounces/1⅔ cups/200 g confectioners' (icing) sugar
2 eggs
7 ounces/scant 1 cup/200 g almond flour (ground almonds)
½ quantity of confectioners' custard prepared following the
 base recipe on page 238

EQUIPMENT NEEDED
Hand whisk
Bowls
Silicone spatula
Saucepan

AS USED IN
– Chocolate Frangipane Tart with Spiced Pears
 (see page 286)

Cut the butter into small cubes, place in a bowl, and leave to soften. Using a hand whisk, beat the softened butter with the confectioners' (icing) sugar until you obtain a smooth, velvety consistency (1–2).

Add one egg and a tablespoon of almond flour (ground almonds) and continue beating (3–4).

Add the remaining egg and 2 tablespoons of almond flour, stir together with a silicone spatula, then add the remaining almonds and stir to incorporate.

Allow the confectioners' custard to cool, then add to the bowl and mix carefully (5).

Transfer the mixture to a saucepan and cook over low heat until the frangipane cream has thickened (it should have a consistency similar to that of custard, only slightly grainier). As soon as you see small bubbles forming around the edge of the pan, remove from the heat.

HOW TO USE
Frangipane cream is used to fill cakes, brioches, and crêpes, and it must be cooked before using. If you use frangipane cream to fill a tart, you can add the uncooked cream to the pie dough (shortcrust pastry) shell and bake directly in the oven.

VARIATIONS
Omitting the custard will give an almond cream that can be flavored with vanilla, a little rum, or other flavors to taste and then baked in a tart or pie.

Fruit mousse
Mousse di frutta

20 m   5 m   6 h   48 h   60 d

Difficulty: AVERAGE

MAKES 1 QUANTITY
(1½ POUNDS/700 G MOUSSE)

FOR THE MOUSSE
½ ounce/8 g platinum gelatin sheets
10½ ounces/300 g soft fruit of your choice
2 egg whites
3 ounces/⅓ cup/80 g superfine (caster) sugar
3 tablespoons water
7 fl oz/scant 1 cup/200 ml heavy (whipping) cream

EQUIPMENT NEEDED
Bowls
Immersion (stick) blender
Fine-mesh strainer (sieve)
Saucepans
Silicone spatula
Electric whisk
Individual glasses or ramekins

AS USED IN
– Strawberry Mousse on Pistachio Sponge
  (see page 292)

Soak the gelatin in cold water for 5 minutes.

Wash and dry the fruit, if necessary, peel, pit (stone) and chop into small pieces.

Place the fruit in a bowl and puree it with an immersion (stick) blender (1). If the fruit has small seeds, such as blackberries, raspberries, or passion fruit, pour the puree through a fine-mesh strainer (sieve).

Heat half the puree in a saucepan over low heat without letting it reach boiling point (2). Squeeze the water from the gelatin, and add to the hot puree (3). Remove from the heat and stir until the gelatin has dissolved. Add this mix to the reserved cold fruit puree (4).

Prepare an Italian meringue with the egg whites, sugar, and water, following the instructions on page 220, then carefully fold into the fruit puree mixture using a silicone spatula.

Using an electric whisk, whip the cream to soft peaks (5) and fold it into the fruit mixture using a spatula (6–7).

Pour into individual glasses or ramekins, level the top, and leave it to set in the refrigerator for at least 6 hours.

TIPS AND TRICKS
Some types of fruit, such as kiwis, papayas, and pineapples, contain particular enzymes that prevent gelatin from setting. When using this type of fruit, these enzymes need to be de-activated—cook all of the fruit puree to boiling point after it has been puréed, then allow to cool slightly before adding the gelatin.

TARTLETS WITH PINE NUTS AND CHOCOLATE CREAM

Tartellette con pinoli e crema al cioccolato

30 m	5 m	28–30 m		48 h	60 d

Difficulty: EASY

For the classic pie dough (shortcrust pastry):
    see page 52
For the confectioners' custard:
    see page 238

TO SERVE 8

FOR THE TARTLETS
Butter, for greasing
4 ounces/120 g bittersweet (dark) chocolate
1 quantity (1 pound 5 ounces/600 g) of confectioners'
    custard prepared with cornstarch (cornflour) and
    following the base recipe on page 238
1 quantity (1 pound /450 g) of classic pie dough (shortcrust
    pastry) prepared following the base recipe on page 52
2 ounces/scant ½ cup/50 g pine nuts

TO DECORATE
9 ounces/1 cup/250 g mascarpone
1½ fl oz/3 tablespoons/50 ml heavy (whipping) cream
2½ ounces/¾ cup/75 g confectioners' (icing) sugar
Bittersweet (dark) chocolate

EQUIPMENT NEEDED
8 × 4-inch/10-cm tartlet pans (tins)
Rolling pin
Plastic wrap (cling film)
Small sharp knife
Bain-marie or double boiler
Silicone spatula
Bowls
Immersion (stick) blender
Grater with large holes
Oven rack
Cooling rack

Preheat the oven to 350°F/180°C/160°C Fan/Gas 4. Grease the tartlet pans (tins) with a little butter.

On a lightly floured surface, roll out the pie dough (pastry) to ⅛ inch/3 mm thick. Using a tartlet pan as a guide, cut out pastry disks slightly larger than the prepared tartlet pans. If necessary, re-roll any scraps to give enough disks. Press down firmly on the base and sides, then prick the base of the dough with a fork. Using a sharp knife, trim away any excess dough that is overhanging the sides of the tart pan to neaten. Make a ball from the excess dough, cover in plastic wrap (cling film) and freeze it until firm.

Meanwhile, coarsely chop the chocolate, place it in a bain-marie or double boiler, and melt over very low heat, stirring with a silicone spatula. Combine the melted chocolate with the confectioners' custard in a large bowl and blitz with an immersion (stick) blender to a smooth, runny cream.

When the pastry is firm, remove from the freezer and grate it on the large holes of a grater. Add the pine nuts and quickly mix with your fingertips until the mixture resembles large breadcrumbs.

Fill the tartlet pastry cases with the chocolate cream, then sprinkle on the pine nut and dough crumble. Place the tartlet pans on an oven rack and bake in the lower part of the preheated oven for 20 minutes, or until the pastry is golden at the edges and the filling is set. Move the rack to the middle part of the oven and continue to bake for 8–10 minutes. If using a fan oven, lower the oven temperature to 135°C Fan for the last 8–10 minutes of the cooking time. Leave to cool, then remove the tartlets from the pans and place on a cooling rack to cool completely.

Place the mascarpone, cream, and confectioners' (icing) sugar in a bowl and whisk until smooth. To serve, make a quenelle of the whipped cream using two soup spoons (dessertspoons) and place on top of each tart. Decorate the tarts with a little finely chopped or shredded (grated) chocolate.

ALMOND MILK TARTLETS WITH EGG-FREE CUSTARD

Crostata con crema senza uova e latte

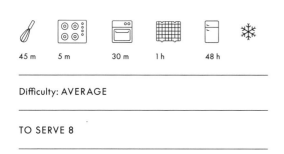

45 m   5 m   30 m   1 h   48 h

Difficulty: AVERAGE

TO SERVE 8

FOR THE BASE
Butter for greasing
9 ounces/2 cups/250 g type "2" flour (or use whole wheat
   (wholemeal) pastry flour or an equal mix of all-purpose
   (plain) flour and whole wheat (wholemeal) pastry flour)
3 ounces/⅓ cup/80 g superfine (caster) sugar
2 fl oz/¼ cup/60 ml sunflower oil
Grated zest of 1 unwaxed lemon
Pinch of salt
2 fl oz/¼ cup/60 ml ice-cold water

FOR THE CUSTARD
2 ounces/scant ½ cup/50 g cornstarch (cornflour)
3 ounces/⅓ cup/80 g sugar
1 vanilla bean (pod)
17 fl oz/2 cups/500 ml almond milk

TO DECORATE
14 ounces/2 cups/400 g strawberries
Confectioners' (icing) sugar, for dusting
Edible flowers

EQUIPMENT NEEDED
8 × 4-inch/10-cm fluted tartlet pans (tins)
Food processor
Measuring cup or jug
Zester
Plastic wrap (cling film)
Bowls
Electric whisk
Saucepan
Rolling pin
Baking sheet
Parchment paper
Baking beans
Cooling rack
Immersion (stick) blender
Small strainer (sieve) or dusting spoon

Preheat the oven to 350°F/180°C/160°C Fan/Gas 4. Grease the tartlet pans (tins) with a little butter.

To make the pastry, place the flour, sugar, oil, grated lemon zest, and salt into a food processor, then blitz to coarse crumbs. Pour the water into the processor and continue to blitz until a dough forms that sticks to the blades. Shape the dough into a small block, wrap in plastic wrap (cling film), and leave to rest for 30 minutes at room temperature.

To make the custard, place the cornstarch (cornflour) in a bowl, add the sugar and the seeds from the vanilla bean (pod). Slowly pour the almond milk into the bowl, mixing continuously with an electric whisk as you do so, until combined. Transfer the mix to a saucepan and bring to a boil over low heat, stirring, then simmer for about 5 minutes, or until the cream is thick enough to coat the back of a spoon and when you draw a finger through the custard, it doesn't flow back immediately. The custard should not have a floury taste. Pour into a bowl and cover with plastic wrap, ensuring the wrap is touching the surface of the custard, and leave to cool.

On a lightly floured surface, roll out the pie dough (pastry) to ⅛ inch/3 mm thick. Using a tartlet pan as a guide, cut out pastry disks slightly larger than the prepared tartlet pans. If necessary, re-roll any scraps to give enough disks. Press down firmly on the base and sides, then prick the base of the dough with a fork. Using a sharp knife, trim away any excess dough that is overhanging the sides of the tart pan to neaten.

Line the pastry cases with parchment paper, fill with baking beans, and place in the lower part of the preheated oven for 20 minutes to blind bake. After 20 minutes, remove the baking beans and parchment paper and return to the oven for a further 10 minutes, or until the pastry cases are golden. Remove from the oven and leave to cool slightly in the pans, then remove the pastry cases from the pans and leave to cool completely on a cooling rack.

Using an immersion (stick) blender, blitz the custard until light and smooth, then pour into the tart cases.

Wash and hull the strawberries, if they are large cut them into slices, or leave whole if they are small, and arrange on top of the custard. Leave to rest in the refrigerator for 30 minutes, then dust with confectioners' sugar and decorate with some edible flowers before serving.

CHOCOLATE AND LEMON BALM BAVARIAN CREAM

Bavarian al cioccolato e melissa

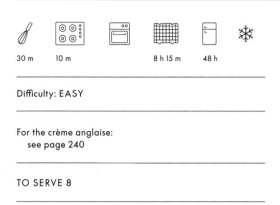

30 m   10 m   8 h 15 m   48 h

Difficulty: EASY

For the crème anglaise:
   see page 240

TO SERVE 8

FOR THE BAVARIAN CREAM
1 quantity (24 fl oz/scant 3 cups/700 ml) of crème anglaise
   prepared following the base recipe on page 240 and
   flavored with 15 lemon balm leaves
½ ounce/10 g platinum gelatin sheets
5 ounces/150 g bittersweet (dark) chocolate
7 fl oz/scant 1 cup/200 ml heavy (whipping) cream

TO DECORATE
7 fl oz/scant 1 cup/200 ml heavy (whipping) cream
¾ ounce/20 g bittersweet (dark) chocolate
2 ounces/½ cup/50 g confectioners' (icing) sugar
Edible flowers

EQUIPMENT NEEDED
Fine-mesh strainer (sieve)
Bowls
Silicone spatula
Electric whisk
Measuring cup or jug
8 × 3-inch/8-cm brioche, dariole, or pudding molds
Grater with large holes

Prepare the crème anglaise following the instructions on page 240, adding the lemon balm leaves when heating the milk. Turn off the heat and leave to infuse for 15 minutes. Strain the milk through a fine-mesh strainer (sieve) and continue following the instructions on page 240 up to stage (6).

Soak the gelatin in cold water for 5 minutes. Finely chop the chocolate and add to the hot crème anglaise, stirring until it has melted. Squeeze the water from the gelatin. Add to the chocolate crème anglaise and stir until it has dissolved. Remove from the heat and set aside to cool. When cool, whip the heavy (whipping) cream with the electric whisk until soft, add 3–4 tablespoons of whipped cream to the chocolate custard, and fold in using a silicone spatula.

Fold in the remaining cream until you obtain a smooth, even mixture, then pour into the molds. Place in the refrigerator for 6–8 hours. To unmold the Bavarian creams, dip one mold at a time into a bowl containing hot water, for a few seconds, then invert the mold on a serving dish. Return to the refrigerator for 15 minutes. Meanwhile, whip the cream and grate the chocolate. Serve the Bavarian creams with a quenelle of whipped cream and decorated with chocolate flakes and edible flowers.

VARIATIONS
If you cannot find lemon balm, use a mixture of lemon verbena and regular mint leaves.

WHITE CHOCOLATE CREMOSO WITH GRAPEFRUIT

Cremoso bianco con pompelmo e crumble

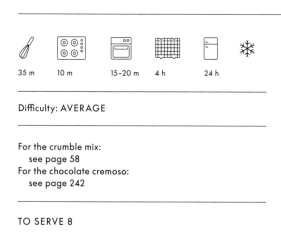

35 m   10 m   15–20 m   4 h   24 h

Difficulty: AVERAGE

For the crumble mix:
   see page 58
For the chocolate cremoso:
   see page 242

TO SERVE 8

FOR THE CRUMBLE
2 ounces/¼ cup/50 g rice flour
2 ounces/½ cup/50 g almond flour (ground almonds)
Pinch of salt
2 ounces/4 tablespoons/50 g unsalted butter
1 ounce/¼ cup/30 g confectioners' (icing) sugar
1 ounce/⅓ cup/30 g almond flakes, skin on

FOR THE WHITE CHOCOLATE CREMOSO
12 ounces/350 g white chocolate
7 fl oz/scant 1 cup/200 ml heavy (whipping) cream
1¾ fl oz/3 tablespoons/50 ml whole (full-fat) milk
3 egg yolks
1 vanilla bean (pod)
1 ounce/7 teaspoons/30 g superfine (caster) sugar

TO SERVE
2 pink grapefruit

EQUIPMENT NEEDED
Baking sheet
Parchment paper
Paring knife
Paper towel
8 serving glasses or ramekins
Measuring cup or jug

Preheat the oven to 350°F/180°C/160°C Fan/Gas 4 and line the baking sheet with parchment paper.

Using the ingredient quantities listed on this page, prepare the crumble mix following the instructions on page 58. Transfer the mix to the lined baking sheet and bake in the preheated oven for 15–20 minutes, or until golden.

Using a paring knife, peel the grapefruit and remove the pith around each segment. Arrange the grapefruit segments in the bottom of the serving glasses or ramekins.

Using the ingredient quantities listed on this page, prepare the white chocolate cremoso following the instructions on page 242—however, there is no need to add gelatin to this mixture as it will softly set without it.

Pour the cremoso over the grapefruit, dividing it equally between the glasses. Place in the refrigerator for 4 hours. Just before serving, sprinkle the crumble topping over the cremoso and serve immediately.

FROZEN YOGURT ICE POPS WITH LEMON CURD

Ghiacciato di yogurt con lemon curd

20 m   3–4 m   6 h   30 d

Difficulty: AVERAGE

For the lemon curd:
   see page 244

TO SERVE 8

FOR THE ICE POPS
5 fl oz/scant ⅔ cup/150 ml heavy (whipping) cream
1 teaspoon/2 g agar agar
7 ounces/generous ¾ cup/200 g plain (natural) whole-milk
   (full-fat) yogurt
⅔ quantity (10½ ounces/300 g) of lemon curd prepared
   following the base recipe on page 244

EQUIPMENT NEEDED
Small saucepan
Measuring cup or jug
Hand whisk
Bowls
8 ice-pop bar molds
8 wooden ice-pop sticks

Pour the cream into a small saucepan, then add the agar agar. Mix with a hand whisk and bring to a boil over medium–low heat. Cook for 1 minute, then remove from the heat. Pour the warm cream into a bowl, add the yogurt, and stir to combine.

In a separate bowl, mix half the lemon curd with one-third of the cream and yogurt mixture.

Pour a layer of the plain cream and yogurt mixture into the base of each ice-pop bar mold, followed by a layer of the lemon curd mixture. Continue alternating the two mixtures until the molds are almost filled. Ripple the remaining lemon curd through the surface of each ice pop. Insert a wooden ice-pop stick into each mold.

Transfer the ice-pop molds to the freezer and chill for 6 hours or until frozen. To unmold, dip one ice-pop mold at a time into boiling water for 20 seconds, then remove the ice pop from the mold by gently pulling on the stick. Serve immediately.

FRUIT AU GRATIN WITH CHANTILLY CREAM

Frutta gratinata con crema Chantilly

15 m   10 m

Difficulty: EASY

For the Chantilly cream:
    see page 246

TO SERVE 8

FOR THE FRUIT AU GRATIN
1 vanilla bean (pod)
3 ounces/⅓ cup/80 g turbinado (demerara) sugar
8 small bananas
Juice of 1 lime
1 papaya
7 ounces/2 cups/200 g seedless Muscat grapes

TO SERVE
¾ quantity (1 pound 12 ounces/800 g) of Chantilly cream
    prepared following the base recipe on page 246

EQUIPMENT NEEDED
Baking sheet
Parchment paper
Bowl
Juicer
Cook's blowtorch (optional)

Line a baking sheet with parchment paper.

Remove the seeds from the vanilla bean (pod) and place in a bowl with turbinado (demerara) sugar, then stir to combine.

Peel the bananas, then slice four of them in half lengthwise and cut the other four into thick slices. Place on the lined baking sheet. Drizzle the bananas with half of the lime juice.

Cut the papaya in half, remove the seeds, peel, and cut into wedges. Arrange on the baking sheet alongside the bananas.

Wash and dry the grapes, divide into small bunches, and add to the other fruit on the baking sheet.

Drizzle the fruit with the remaining lime juice and sprinkle over the vanilla sugar.

Preheat the broiler (grill) to high. Position the baking sheet 3–4 inches/7–10 cm away from the heat source and cook until the sugar has caramelized. Alternatively, use a cook's blowtorch to caramelize the fruit. Leave the fruit to cool.

Divide the caramelized fruits between small plates and serve with the Chantilly cream.

TART WITH CHIBOUST CREAM, WALNUTS, AND APPLES

Tarte con crema chiboust, noci e mele

1 h 15 m   25 m   25 m   4 h 30 m   48 h

Difficulty: ADVANCED

For the classic pie dough (shortcrust pastry):
    see page 52
For the Chiboust cream:
    see page 248

TO SERVE 8

FOR THE CLASSIC PIE DOUGH
  (SHORTCRUST PASTRY)
4 ounces/1 cup/120 g type "00" flour or all-purpose
    (plain) flour
3½ ounces/7 tablespoons/100 g unsalted butter
3 ounces/⅔ cup/80 g confectioners' (icing) sugar
3 ounces/¾ cup/80 g walnuts, finely chopped
Pinch of salt
1 egg

FOR THE CALVADOS APPLES
4 Royal Gala apples
2 ounces/4 tablespoons/50 g unsalted butter
1 bay leaf
2 ounces/¼ cup/50 g superfine (caster) sugar
1½ tablespoons Calvados

TO DECORATE
1 quantity of Chiboust cream prepared following the base
    recipe on page 248
¾ ounce/¼ cup/20 g walnuts, roughly chopped
Edible flowers, such as rose petals

EQUIPMENT NEEDED
6-inch/15-cm round loose-bottomed or springform cake
    pan (tin)
Acetate sheet
Baking sheet
Parchment paper
Rolling pin
8-inch/20-cm round cake pan (tin)
Non-stick skillet (frying pan)
Plastic wrap (cling film)

Line the inner sides of the cake pan (tin) with an acetate sheet then pour in the Chiboust cream. Leave to set in the refrigerator for 4 hours.

Using the ingredient quantities listed on this page, prepare the classic pie dough (shortcrust pastry) following the instructions on page 52, stirring the finely chopped walnuts into the flour and butter mixture before the egg is added. Leave to rest in the refrigerator for 30 minutes.

Preheat the oven to 350°F/180°C/160°C Fan/Gas 4 and line the baking sheet with parchment paper.

Roll out the dough on a sheet of parchment paper to form a round sheet ¼ inch/½ cm thick. Using the 8-inch/20-cm cake pan as a template, cut the dough into a circle the same size as the base of the pan. Place the parchment paper and dough on the baking sheet and bake in the preheated oven for 25 minutes, until the pastry is golden around the edges, looks set, and is dry in the center. Leave to cool.

To make the Calvados apples, wash, quarter, and core the apples, then chop into small pieces. Melt the butter in a non-stick skillet or deep frying pan, add the apples and the bay leaf, and cook over high heat for 5 minutes. Sprinkle with the sugar and continue to cook until the sugar starts to caramelize. Pour in the Calvados, let it evaporate, then turn off the heat and leave to cool.

Remove the Chiboust cream from the cake pan and place on top of the base, then remove and discard the acetate. Arrange the chopped apples around the exposed outer section of the base. Finely chop the walnuts and sprinkle over the Chiboust cream, then decorate with the edible flowers. Serve immediately.

TIPS AND TRICKS
By baking the pastry base on a baking sheet, rather than in a cake pan (tin), the pastry will brown and crisp more easily. When cooked in a pan, the pastry will take on less color and be softer.

FRAISIER

Fraisier

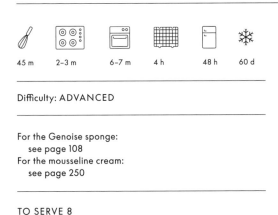

45 m	2–3 m	6–7 m	4 h	48 h	60 d

Difficulty: ADVANCED

For the Genoise sponge:
  see page 108
For the mousseline cream:
  see page 250

TO SERVE 8

FOR THE CAKE
1 quantity (23 ounces/600 g) of Genoise sponge mix
  prepared following the base recipe on page 108
1 pound 5 ounces/600 g large strawberries
1 quantity (1 pound 13 ounces/800 g) of mousseline cream
  prepared following the base recipe on page 250 and
  flavored with the grated zest of 1 unwaxed lemon

FOR THE SYRUP
5½ ounces/⅔ cup/160 g superfine (caster) sugar
5 fl oz/scant ⅔ cup/150 ml water
1 vanilla bean (pod)
7 ounces/200 g strawberries

TO DECORATE
3½ ounces/100 g small strawberries
Confectioners' (icing) sugar, for dusting

EQUIPMENT NEEDED
18 × 12-inch/45 × 30-cm shallow jelly roll pan (Swiss roll tin)
  or baking sheet
Parchment paper
Saucepan
Measuring cup or jug
Food processor
Silicone spatula
Clean dish towel (tea towel)
8-inch/20-cm round springform pan (tin)
Pastry brush
Acetate sheet
Pastry (piping) bag fitted with ½-inch/1-cm plain piping
  tip (nozzle)
Small strainer (sieve) or dusting spoon

Preheat the oven to 400°F/200°C/180°C Fan/Gas 6. Line the baking sheet with parchment paper. Line the base of the springform pan (tin) with parchment paper and the sides with an acetate sheet.

To make the strawberry syrup, place the sugar in a saucepan with the water and vanilla pod, cut lengthwise. Bring to a boil over medium heat, then turn off the heat and leave the syrup to cool.

Meanwhile, wash and hull the strawberries, then blend to a puree in a food processor. When the syrup is cool, remove the vanilla pod, add to the puréed strawberries, and blend well.

Pour the prepared sponge mix into the lined baking sheet to form an even layer. Bake in the preheated oven for 6–7 minutes, until golden and firm to the touch—a skewer inserted into the center comes out clean. Cover with a dish towel (tea towel) and leave to cool.

When cool, cut two disks out of the sponge using the springform pan (tin) as a template. Carefully place one of the sponge disks on the base of the pan and brush with the strawberry syrup.

Slice the large strawberries in half and arrange them in the pan so they line the inner sides, with the tips pointing upwards and the cut sides facing outwards. Set aside any leftover strawberries.

Fit the piping tip (nozzle) to the pastry (piping) bag and fill the bag with the prepared mousseline cream. Pipe the cream around the edge of the pan to hold the strawberries in place. Fill the central cavity with the reserved strawberries and finish with the remaining mousseline cream.

Place the second sponge disk on top of the mousseline cream and brush with some more strawberry syrup. Place the cake in the refrigerator and chill for 4 hours.

When ready to serve, unmold the cake and transfer it to a serving plate. Carefully remove and discard the acetate. Dust the cake with confectioners' (icing) sugar and decorate the top with a handful of small strawberries, either left whole or sliced in half depending on their size. Serve with the remaining strawberry syrup.

TIPS AND TRICKS
The Genoise sponge is cooked at a high temperature, which works because the baking sheet is large and the baking time is short. Alternatively, baking the sponge for 15–20 minutes at the lower oven temperature of 350°F/180°C/160°C Fan/Gas 4.

FROZEN SABAYON WITH LIMONCELLO

Zabaione ghiacciato al limoncello

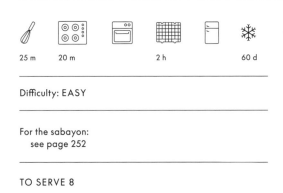

25 m   20 m   2 h   60 d

Difficulty: EASY

For the sabayon:
   see page 252

TO SERVE 8

FOR THE CANDIED LEMONS
1 unwaxed lemon
3½ ounces/scant ½ cup/100 g superfine (caster) sugar
3½ fl oz/scant ½ cup/100 ml water

FOR THE SABAYON
6 egg yolks
7 ounces/scant 1 cup/200 g superfine (caster) sugar
7 fl oz/scant 1 cup/200 ml limoncello
7 fl oz/scant 1 cup/200 ml heavy (whipping) cream

EQUIPMENT NEEDED
Paper towels
Small saucepan
Measuring cup or jug
Electric whisk
Silicone spatula
8 serving glasses or ramekins

Wash and dry the lemon and cut into slices ⅛ in/3 mm thick. Place the sugar in a small saucepan, add the water and bring to a boil over medium heat. Add the lemon slices and cook over low heat for 7–8 minutes, until they become transparent. Turn off the heat and set aside to cool.

Using the ingredients quantities listed on this page, but replacing the Marsala wine with the limoncello and reserving the cream to use later, prepare the sabayon following the instructions on page 252 and leave to cool.

Whip the cream and fold into the cooled sabayon. Pour into the serving glasses or ramekins and place in the freezer for 2 hours. Drain the candied lemons, arrange them on the sabayon and serve immediately.

CHOCOLATE AND COFFEE MOUSSE CAKE

Torta di mousse al cioccolato e caffè

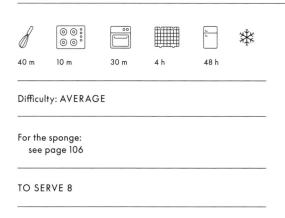

40 m	10 m	30 m	4 h	48 h	

Difficulty: AVERAGE

For the sponge:
   see page 106

TO SERVE 8

FOR THE CAKE
1 quantity (23 ounces/600 g) of chocolate sponge mix
   prepared following the base recipe variation on
   page 106

FOR THE SOAKING LIQUID
2 ounces/½ cup/50 g unsweetened cocoa powder
3½ fl oz/scant ½ cup/100 ml whole (full-fat) milk
3½ fl oz/scant ½ cup/100 ml freshly brewed espresso coffee

FOR THE WHITE CHOCOLATE MOUSSE
7 ounces/200 g white chocolate
13 fl oz/1⅔ cups/400 ml heavy (whipping) cream

TO DECORATE
1 teaspoon coffee beans
½ ounce/4 teaspoons/10 g unsweetened cocoa powder
½ ounce/10 g cacao (cocoa) nibs

EQUIPMENT NEEDED
8-inch/20-cm square cake pan (tin)
Parchment paper
Fine-mesh strainer (sieve)
Bowls
Small saucepan
Measuring cup or jug
Hand whisk
Cooling rack
Pastry brush
Bain-marie or double boiler
Electric whisk
Silicone spatula
Metal spatula or palette knife
Mortar and pestle
Small strainer (sieve) or dusting spoon

Preheat the oven to 350°F/180°C/160°C Fan/Gas 4. Grease the cake pan (tin) with a little butter and line with parchment paper.

To make the soaking liquid, sift the cocoa powder into a bowl. Pour the milk and coffee into a small saucepan, heat until almost at boiling point, then pour onto the cocoa powder, stirring continuously with a hand whisk as you do so. Set aside to cool.

Pour the sponge mix into the prepared cake pan and bake in the preheated oven for 30 minutes, or until risen and firm to the touch—a skewer inserted into the center should come out clean. Put the pan on a cooling rack and let the cake cool completely in the pan.

To make the white chocolate mousse, finely chop the white chocolate, place in a bain-marie or double boiler, and melt over gentle heat. Pour the melted chocolate into a bowl and leave to return to room temperature. In a separate bowl, whip the cream using an electric whisk. Carefully fold the whipped cream into the cooled, melted chocolate using a silicone spatula.

Once cool, remove the cake from the pan and cut it horizontally into three layers. Place the bottom layer on a serving plate and brush it with one-third of the soaking liquid to moisten. Spread one-third of the chocolate mousse over the bottom sponge layer. Brush the second sponge layer with another one-third of the soaking liquid and place it on the mousse layer. Spread the sponge layer with another one-third of the mousse. Brush the final top layer of sponge with the remaining soaking liquid and place it on top of the second layer of mousse. Using a metal spatula or palette knife, spread the remaining mousse over the top sponge layer. Place the cake in the refrigerator for 4 hours.

Coarsely crush the coffee beans using a mortar and pestle. Decorate the top of the cake with a dusting of cocoa powder, the cacao (cocoa) nibs, and the crushed coffee beans.

CHOCOLATE AND CHESTNUT CRÈME BRÛLÉE

Crème brûlée cioccolato e castagne

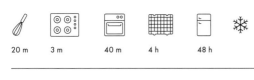

20 m   3 m   40 m   4 h   48 h

Difficulty: EASY

TO SERVE 8

FOR THE CRÈME BRÛLÉE
11½ fl oz/scant 1½ cups/350 ml heavy (whipping) cream
1 vanilla bean (pod)
4 egg yolks
2 ounces/¼ cup/60 g superfine (caster) sugar
8 ounces/scant 1 cup/220 g unsweetened chestnut puree
1 ounce/30 g bittersweet (dark) chocolate, finely chopped
2 ounces/¼ cup/50 g turbinado (demerara) sugar

EQUIPMENT NEEDED
Saucepan
Measuring cup or jug
Hand whisk
Silicone spatula
8 individual baking dishes
Deep-sided roasting pan (tin)
Cook's blowtorch

Preheat the oven to 325°F/160°C/140°C Fan/Gas 3.

Pour the cream into a saucepan, add the vanilla bean (pod) sliced lengthwise, and heat until just before boiling point. Remove from the heat and set aside to cool then remove the vanilla bean.

Using a hand whisk, beat the egg yolks with the superfine (caster) sugar until light and fluffy. Add the chestnut puree and vanilla-flavored cream, then mix with a silicone spatula to combine.

Arrange the baking dishes in a deep-sided roasting pan (tin). Fill the dishes with the prepared chestnut cream and sprinkle the finely chopped chocolate on top. Carefully pour boiling water into the roasting pan so that the water comes two-thirds up the sides of the dishes and bake in the preheated oven for 40 minutes, or until just set.

Remove the dishes from the roasting pan and leave to cool. Place in the refrigerator to chill for 4 hours.

Sprinkle the dishes with the turbinado (demerara) sugar and caramelize with a cook's blowtorch. Leave the caramel to cool slightly before serving.

MATCHA TEA MUFFINS WITH CRÈME BRÛLÉE

Muffin al tè matcha con crème brûlée

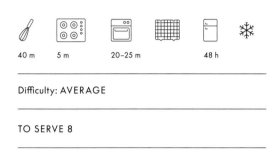

40 m	5 m	20–25 m		48 h	

Difficulty: AVERAGE

TO SERVE 8

FOR THE MUFFINS
3½ ounces/7 tablespoons/100 g unsalted butter, plus extra
   for greasing
2 eggs
4 ounces/½ cup/120 g superfine (caster) sugar
Pinch of salt
4 ounces/1 cup/120 g type "00" flour or all-purpose
   (plain) flour
1 teaspoon/5 g baking powder
2½ teaspoons/5 g powdered matcha green tea (optional)

FOR THE CRÈME BRÛLÉE
10 fl oz/1¼ cups/300 ml heavy (whipping) cream
4 fl oz/½ cup/120 ml whole (full-fat) milk
1 vanilla bean (pod)
3 egg yolks
1 ounce/¼ cup/30 g cornstarch (cornflour)
2 ounces/¼ cup/50 g superfine (caster) sugar
¾ ounce/5 teaspoons/20 g turbinado (demerara) sugar

EQUIPMENT NEEDED
2½-inch/6-cm muffin pans (tins)
Small saucepan
Bowls
Electric whisk
Fine-mesh strainer (sieve)
Silicone spatula
Saucepans
Measuring cup or jug
Pastry (piping) bag fitted with ½-inch/1-cm plain piping
   tip (nozzle)
Cook's blowtorch

Preheat the oven to 350°F/180°C/160°C Fan/Gas 4. Grease the muffin pans (tins) with a little butter.

Melt the butter in a small saucepan and set aside to cool. Break the eggs into a bowl, add the sugar and salt, and beat with an electric whisk until you obtain a light and fluffy mixture. Sift the flour, baking powder, and matcha green tea (if using) into the bowl, and mix with a silicone spatula to combine.

Add the melted butter and stir until incorporated, then pour the mixture into the muffin pans. Bake the muffins in the preheated oven for 20–25 minutes, or until golden, risen, and firm to the touch—a skewer inserted into the center comes out clean. Leave to cool.

To make the crème brûlée, pour the cream into a saucepan with the milk and vanilla bean (pod) sliced lengthwise, and heat until just before boiling point. In a separate bowl, beat the egg yolks with the cornstarch (cornflour) and the superfine (caster) sugar, then remove the vanilla bean (pod) from the cream and slowly pour the hot vanilla cream into the bowl, continuously stirring with the hand whisk as you do so.

Pour the mixture into a clean saucepan and cook over low heat for 5–6 minutes, stirring continuously, until it is thick enough to coat the back of a spoon. Transfer to a bowl, place it in an ice bain-marie and leave to cool, stirring from time to time.

Using a pastry (piping) bag fitted with a plain piping tip (nozzle), pipe the crème brûlée on top of the upturned muffins, sprinkle with the turbinado (demerara) sugar and caramelize with a cook's blowtorch. Leave the caramel to cool slightly before serving.

VARIATIONS
If you prefer to omit the matcha tea, instead add 1 teaspoon of vanilla extract to the eggs at the same time as the sugar is added to the mixture.

CRÈME CARAMEL

Flan di latte

| 15 m | 5 m | 40 m–1 h | 6 h | 48 h | |

Difficulty: EASY

TO SERVE 8

FOR THE CRÈME CARAMEL
3 ounces/⅓ cup/80 g superfine (caster) sugar
⅞ ounce/scant ¼ cup/25 g cornstarch (cornflour)
13 fl oz/1⅔ cups/400 ml whole (full-fat) milk
14-ounce/397-g can of sweetened condensed milk
Grated zest of 1 unwaxed lemon
4 eggs
Edible flowers for decoration

EQUIPMENT NEEDED
Small saucepan
8-inch/20-cm shallow baking dish or
 8 × 3-inch/8-cm pudding molds
Bowl
Hand whisk
Measuring cup or jug
Zester
Immersion (stick) blender
Deep-sided roasting pan (tin)

Preheat the oven to 325°F/160°C/140°C Fan/Gas 3.

Place the sugar in a small saucepan with 3 tablespoons of water and heat until you obtain an amber-colored caramel. Pour enough into the baking dish or individual molds to cover the base.

Place the cornstarch (cornflour) in a bowl and mix with the milk using a hand whisk. Add the sweetened condensed milk, lemon zest, and eggs, then blitz with an immersion (stick) blender.

Arrange the baking dish or molds in a deep-sided roasting pan (tin), and fill with the crème. Carefully pour boiling water into the roasting pan so that the water comes two-thirds up the side of the dish or molds. Bake in the preheated oven for 1 hour for a large dish and 40 minutes for individual dishes, or until just set.

Remove the dish or molds and leave to cool, then put in the refrigerator for 6 hours. If cooking in a single baking dish, serve slices on individual serving plates with some caramel from the base of the dish spooned over the top. If cooked in individual molds, turn out the crème caramels onto individual serving plates, pouring over any caramel in the base of the molds. Decorate with edible flowers before serving.

CHOCOLATE FRANGIPANE TART WITH SPICED PEARS

Crostata di pere e cioccolato con frangipane

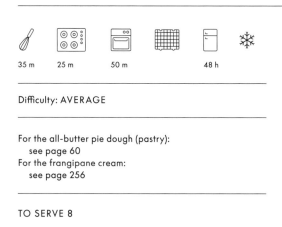

35 m   25 m   50 m   48 h

Difficulty: AVERAGE

For the all-butter pie dough (pastry):
   see page 60
For the frangipane cream:
   see page 256

TO SERVE 8

FOR THE SPICED PEARS
17 fl oz/2 cups/500 ml water
2-inch/4-cm cinnamon stick
2 whole cloves
4 ounces/½ cup/120 g superfine (caster) sugar
2–3 firm, white pears, such as Bosc or Conference

FOR THE FRANGIPANE
7 ounces/½ cup plus 5 tablespoons/200 g unsalted butter
7 ounces/1⅔ cups/200 g confectioners' (icing) sugar
2 eggs
7 ounces/scant 1 cup/200 g almond flour (ground almonds)

FOR THE TART
Butter, for greasing
1 quantity all-butter pie dough (pastry) with egg, prepared
   following the base recipe on page 60
3 ounces/80 g bittersweet (dark) chocolate, finely chopped

EQUIPMENT NEEDED
Saucepan
Bowls
Hand whisk
Silicone spatula
10-inch/23-cm round tart pan (tin)
Rolling pin
Parchment paper
Baking beans
Measuring cup or jug
Cooling rack

To make the spiced pears, pour the water into a saucepan with the cinnamon, cloves, and sugar, then bring to a boil over medium heat. Halve the pears and then core them. Add the pear halves to the saucepan, turn the heat down to low and poach for 20 minutes, or until soft. Leave the pears to cool in the syrup, then drain and cut into thin slices.

To make the frangipane, cut the butter into small cubes, place in a bowl, and leave to soften. Using a hand whisk, beat the softened butter with the confectioners' (icing) sugar to a smooth, velvety consistency. Add one egg and a tablespoon of almond flour (ground almonds) and continue beating. Add the remaining egg and 2 tablespoons of almond flour, stir together with a silicone spatula, then add the remaining almonds and stir to incorporate.

Preheat the oven to 350°F/180°C/160°C Fan/Gas 4. Grease the tart pan (tin) with a little butter.

On a lightly floured surface, roll out the pie dough (pastry) to ⅛ inch/3 mm thick. Carefully lift the rolled-out pie dough and use it to line the prepared tart pan. Press down firmly on the base and sides, then prick the base of the dough with a fork. Using a sharp knife, trim away any excess dough that is overhanging the sides of the tart pan to neaten.

Line the pastry case with parchment paper, then fill with baking beans and place it in the lower part of the preheated oven for 15 minutes to blind bake. After 15 minutes, remove the baking beans, and remove and discard the parchment paper.

Finely chop the chocolate and scatter it over the base of the partly cooked pastry case. Pour the frangipane into the pastry case, level it with the back of a spoon, then arrange the spiced pear slices on top. Return the tart to the oven and bake for a further 35 minutes, or until the filling has puffed up slightly, is golden brown on top, and just set in the center. Leave the tart to cool in the pan on a cooling rack.

LEMON RICOTTA MOUSSE WITH CHOCOLATE CENTER

Limoni di ricotta con cuore di cioccolato

45 m   5 m   6 h 30 m   48 h   30 d

Difficulty: ADVANCED

For the simple ganache:
   see page 192

TO SERVE 6

FOR THE MOUSSE
½ ounce/10 g platinum gelatin sheets
10½ ounces/1¼ cups/300 g sheep's ricotta (or use whole
   milk ricotta)
3 ounces/⅓ cup/80 g superfine (caster) sugar
1 unwaxed lemon
7 fl oz/scant 1 cup/200 ml heavy (whipping) cream

FOR THE GANACHE
2½ fl oz/5 tablespoons/80 ml heavy (whipping) cream
3½ ounces/100 g bittersweet (dark) chocolate

TO DECORATE
Raspberry sugar or dried raspberry powder
Candied lemon slices
Candied lemon peel

EQUIPMENT NEEDED
Bowls
Zester
Juicer
Strainer (sieve)
Immersion (stick) blender
Small saucepan
Fine-mesh strainer (sieve)
Silicone spatula
Measuring cup or jug
Electric whisk
3-inch/7.5-cm silicone half-sphere molds

Using the ingredient quantities listed on this page, prepare the simple ganache following the instructions on page 192, omitting the butter. Place in the refrigerator and leave to cool until the ganache becomes almost solid.

To make the lemon mousse, soak the gelatin in cold water for 5 minutes. Place the ricotta in a bowl with the sugar, add the grated zest of the lemon and the juice of half the lemon, poured through a strainer (sieve). Blitz with an immersion (stick) blender until you obtain a smooth, even mixture.

Heat 2 fl oz/¼ cup/60 ml of the cream in a small saucepan over low heat until hot but not boiling. Squeeze the water from the gelatin. Add to the hot cream and stir until it has melted. Pass the gelatin mixture through a fine-mesh strainer (sieve) into the ricotta mixture and stir with a silicone spatula.

Using an electric whisk, whip the remaining cream to soft peaks and fold it into the lemon mousse using a spatula. Pour half the mix into the molds, then place in the freezer for 20–30 minutes. Arrange a spoonful of chocolate ganache in the middle of each mold, then top with the remaining lemon mousse. Place in the freezer and leave to freeze for 6 hours.

Remove from the molds, then transfer to individual serving dishes. Leave to return to room temperature for 30 minutes before serving. Decorate with a sprinkling of raspberry sugar or powder and top with the candied lemon slices and peel.

CHOCOLATE, AVOCADO, AND COCONUT MOUSSE

Mousse di cioccolato, avocado e latte di cocco

20 m   5 m   1 h   24 h

Difficulty: EASY

TO SERVE 8

FOR THE MOUSSE
7 ounces/200 g bittersweet (dark) chocolate (dairy-free)
14 ounces/400 g ripe avocados
Juice of ½ lime
4 fl oz/½ cup/120 ml coconut milk
2 tablespoons acacia or wildflower honey
1½ ounces/40 g fresh coconut flesh

EQUIPMENT NEEDED
Bain-marie or double boiler
Silicone spatula
Bowl
Plastic wrap (cling film)
Immersion (stick) blender
Measuring cup or jug
8 serving glasses or ramekins
Peeler

Finely chop the chocolate, place in a bain-marie or double boiler and melt over gentle heat, stirring with a silicone spatula. When the chocolate has melted, transfer to a bowl and set aside to cool a little.

Cut the avocados in half, remove the pits (stones), and scoop out the flesh using a spoon. Puree the flesh with an immersion (stick) blender until it is smooth and creamy. Place 2 tablespoons of the avocado puree in a small bowl, add 1 teaspoon of lime juice, and mix to incorporate. Press a piece of plastic wrap (cling film) on the surface of the avocado puree and set aside in the refrigerator.

Mix the melted chocolate with the rest of the avocado puree, add the coconut milk and honey, then blitz with the immersion blender for a few seconds to make a mousse.

Divide the mousse equally between the individual glasses or ramekins. Leave in the refrigerator for 1 hour, until the mousses have set slightly.

When ready to serve, decorate each mousse with a little of the reserved avocado puree. Using a peeler, shave the coconut flesh into fine slivers and use them to garnish each mousse before immediately before serving.

STRAWBERRY MOUSSE ON PISTACHIO SPONGE

Mousse di fragole con biscotto ai pistacchi

Difficulty: ADVANCED

For the fruit mousse:
  see page 258

TO SERVE 6

FOR THE PISTACHIO SPONGE BASE
2 eggs, separated
2 ounces/¼ cup/60 g superfine (caster) sugar
1½ ounces/⅓ cup/40 g type "00" flour or all-purpose
  (plain) flour
1 ounce/¼ cup/25 g pistachios chopped with
  ¾ ounce/2 tablespoons/20 g sugar

FOR THE STRAWBERRY MOUSSE
½ ounce/10 g platinum gelatin sheets
14 ounces/3¼ cups/400 g small strawberries
3½ ounces/scant ½ cup/100 g superfine (caster) sugar
Juice of 1 large lemon
1 vanilla bean (pod)
7 fl oz/scant 1 cup/200 ml heavy (whipping) cream

FOR THE GLAZE
½ ounce/10 g platinum gelatin sheets
9 ounces/2 cups/250 g small strawberries
3 ounces/scant ⅓ cup/80 g superfine (caster) sugar

TO DECORATE
1 ounce/¼ cup/30 g shelled pistachios, finely chopped

EQUIPMENT NEEDED
Baking sheet
Parchment paper
Bowls
Electric whisk
Silicone spatula
3-inch/7-cm round pastry cutter
Food processor
Saucepan
Juicer
Fine-mesh strainer (sieve)
Measuring cup or jug
3-inch/7-cm silicone half-sphere molds
Cooling rack

Preheat the oven to 425°F/220°C/200°C Fan/Gas 7. Line the baking sheet with parchment paper.

To make the sponge base, place the egg whites and half the sugar in a bowl and beat with an electric whisk until fluffy and frothy, and the sugar has dissolved. Beat the egg yolks with the remaining sugar and a tablespoonful of water, until light and frothy. Add one-quarter of the egg whites to the yolk mixture. In a separate bowl, combine the flour with the pistachios chopped with sugar, then fold it into the yolk mixture with a silicone spatula. Fold in the remaining egg whites. Pour the mixture into the prepared baking sheet and bake in the preheated oven for 10 minutes, until golden and firm to the touch —a skewer inserted into the center should come out clean. Leave to cool, then cut 6 disks out of the sponge with the pastry cutter.

To make the mousse, soak the gelatin in cold water for 5 minutes. Hull the strawberries, then puree them in a food processor. Transfer to a saucepan and add the sugar. Strain the lemon juice and add to the pan along with the vanilla bean (pod), cut lengthwise. Cook over low heat for 5 minutes, or until the sugar has dissolved, then remove the vanilla bean. Squeeze the water from the gelatin, add to the saucepan, and stir until dissolved. Pour through a fine-mesh strainer (sieve) into a bowl and leave to cool, stirring occasionally. Whip the cream to soft peaks and the whisk in the strawberry puree. Pour the mixture into the silicone molds. Place the molds in the refrigerator and leave to set overnight.

To make the glaze, soak the gelatin in cold water for 5 minutes. Hull the strawberries and puree in a food processor, then transfer to a saucepan and add the sugar. Squeeze the water from the gelatin, add to the pan, place on very low heat and cook for 2–3 minutes, stirring continuously until the gelatin and sugar have dissolved—do not let the puree boil. Pour through a fine-mesh strainer into a bowl and leave to cool to room temperature, stirring occasionally.

Once set, remove the mousses from the molds and place them on a cooling rack. Pour over the glaze and transfer to the refrigerator for 30 minutes to set. To serve, place the pastry bases on a serving plate, sit the mousses on top, and scatter over the pistachios.

MISTAKES TO AVOID
As the fruit puree cools, stirring the mixture stops it setting too quickly. If set rapidly, a skin can form leaving streaks in the mousse.

TIPS AND TRICKS
If you do not have a silicone mold then brush the insides of a metal mold with a little flavorless vegetable oil before using. Then, when unmolding the mousse, dip the mold in hot water for 10 seconds.

PAPAYA AND PASSION FRUIT MOUSSE

Mousse di papaya e frutti della passione

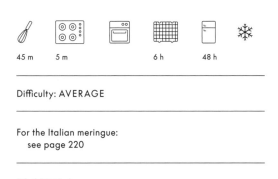

45 m	5 m		6 h	48 h	

Difficulty: AVERAGE

For the Italian meringue:
   see page 220

TO SERVE 6

FOR THE MOUSSE
¾ ounce/16 g platinum gelatin sheets
1 pound 5 ounces/600 g papaya flesh
8 passion fruit
Grated zest of 1 unwaxed lime
13 fl oz/1⅔ cups/400 ml heavy (whipping) cream

FOR THE ITALIAN MERINGUE
4 egg whites
5 ounces/¾ cup/160 g superfine (caster) sugar
2½ fl oz/5 tablespoons/70 ml water

TO DECORATE
½ ounce/10 g thin papaya slices

EQUIPMENT NEEDED
Bowls
Fine-mesh strainer (sieve)
Saucepan
Immersion (stick) blender
Zester
Silicone spatula
Measuring cup or jug
Electric whisk
6 individual serving glasses

Soak the gelatin in cold water for 5 minutes. Cut the papaya in half lengthwise, remove the flesh, and set aside. Halve the passion fruit, remove the flesh from all but one, and using the back of a spoon, pass it through a fine-mesh strainer (sieve) to remove the seeds and collect all the juice.

Heat the passion fruit juice in a saucepan over low heat until it boils, then remove from the heat and add to the papaya flesh.

Puree with an immersion (stick) blender, then pour the puree into a saucepan with the lime zest and bring to a boil over a medium–low heat.

Squeeze the water from the gelatin, add to the saucepan, turn off the heat, and stir until the gelatin has dissolved. Transfer to a bowl and leave to cool to room temperature, stirring occasionally.

Using the ingredient quantities listed on this page, prepare the Italian meringue following the instructions on page 220. Gently fold the meringue into the fruit mixture.

Using an electric whisk, whip the cream to soft peaks and fold it into the fruit mixture using a silicone spatula.

Spoon the fruit mousse into the serving glasses, dividing the mixture equally. Leave in the refrigerator to set for 6 hours. Decorate each mousse with the reserved passion fruit pulp and slivers of papaya.

GRAPEFRUIT AND PINK PEPPER MOUSSE

Spuma al pompelmo e pepe rosa

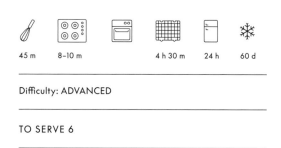

| 45 m | 8–10 m | | 4 h 30 m | 24 h | 60 d |

Difficulty: ADVANCED

TO SERVE 6

FOR THE MOUSSE
6 ounces/¾ cup/170 g superfine (caster) sugar
2½ fl oz/5 tablespoons/75 ml water
3 egg whites
⅛ ounce/7 g platinum gelatin sheets
3 pink grapefruit
1 level teaspoon dried pink peppercorns
6 fl oz/¾ cup/170 ml heavy (whipping) cream

EQUIPMENT NEEDED
Small saucepans
Measuring cup or jug
Kitchen thermometer
Stand mixer fitted with whisk attachment
Bowl
Mortar and pestle
Juicer
Fine-mesh strainer (sieve)
Electric whisk
Silicone spatula
3-inch/7.5-cm silicone donut molds

Place the sugar in a small saucepan with the water and warm over low heat until the sugar dissolves. Increase the heat to medium and bring to a boil. Use a kitchen thermometer to continuously monitor the temperature and when it reaches 230°F/110°C, start to whisk the egg whites to soft peaks in the stand mixer. When the syrup reaches 250°F/121°C, remove it from the heat and slowly pour into the egg whites, continuously whisking as you do so, until the meringue has cooled.

Soak the gelatin in cold water for 5 minutes and crush the peppercorns using a mortar and pestle. Squeeze 2 of the grapefruit to give 4 fl oz/½ cup/120 ml of juice. Pour through a strainer (sieve) into a small saucepan, add two-thirds of the crushed pink peppercorns, and heat until just below boiling point.

Squeeze the water from the gelatin. Add to the saucepan, turn off the heat, and stir until the gelatin has dissolved. Add the juice of the third grapefruit and mix to combine, then pour the mixture through a fine-mesh strainer (sieve) set over a bowl and leave to cool to room temperature, stirring occasionally.

Using an electric whisk, whip the cream to soft peaks and fold it into the grapefruit mixture using a silicone spatula. Pour the mixture into the molds and place in the freezer for 4 hours.

Unmold onto individual serving plates and leave at room temperature for 30 minutes before serving. Decorate the mousses with the remaining crushed pink peppercorns.

SEMIFREDDOS

Pâte à bombe

Pâte à bombe

15 m   10 m

Difficulty: EASY

MAKES 1 QUANTITY
(8 OUNCES/225 G PÂTE À BOMBE)

FOR THE PÂTE À BOMBE
6 egg yolks
5 ounces/⅔ cup/140 g superfine (caster) sugar
4 teaspoons/20 ml water

EQUIPMENT NEEDED
Stand mixer fitted with whisk attachment
Small saucepan
Kitchen thermometer
Measuring cup or jug

AS USED IN
– Mirror-Glazed Mango and Raspberry Hearts
  (see page 302)
– Semifreddo-Cassata with Orange Marmalade
  (see page 306)

Place the egg yolks in the bowl of the stand mixer with half the sugar (1).

Whisk until the volume has trebled and you have a very light and fluffy mousse-like mix, which is paler in color (2).

Place the remaining sugar in a small saucepan, add the water, and set over low heat (3–4). Let the sugar dissolve, gently swirling the pan from time to time. Once the sugar has dissolved completely, increase the heat to medium and bring to a boil. Using a kitchen thermometer, continuously monitor the temperature and when the syrup reaches 250°F/121°C (5), remove from the heat. Very slowly pour the sugar syrup into the yolk mix, continuously whisking as you do so. Keep whisking until the mixture has cooled down to room temperature (6).

TIPS AND TRICKS
When making the pâte à bombe, the sugar must be fully dissolved before bringing the syrup to the boil. If the sugar has not completely dissolved then the syrup can quickly crystallize as it is poured into the whisked egg yolks, which results in a lumpy mousse.

The purpose of whipping the yolks with the boiling sugar syrup is to pasteurize them. Alternatively, you can whip the yolks with the water and sugar over a boiling water bain-marie until the mix reaches 185°F/85°C.

As you pour the boiling sugar syrup onto the whisked egg yolks, do not let the hot syrup touch the beaters of the stand mixer as it will harden on the beaters. If you do not have a stand mixer, ask someone else to hold and operate an electric hand mixer while you very slowly and carefully pour in the hot syrup, making sure the syrup does not splash.

 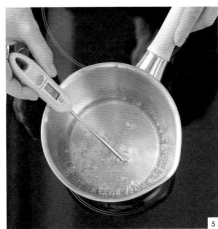 

MIRROR-GLAZED MANGO AND RASPBERRY HEARTS

Cuore di mango e lamponi con glassa lucida

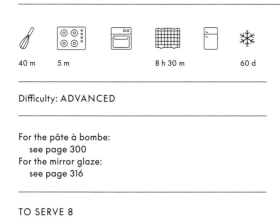

40 m   5 m   8 h 30 m   60 d

Difficulty: ADVANCED

For the pâte à bombe:
   see page 300
For the mirror glaze:
   see page 316

TO SERVE 8

FOR THE MANGO PARFAIT
⅛ ounce/5 g platinum gelatin sheets
2–3 large ripe mangos, at room temperature
17 fl oz/2 cups/500 ml heavy (whipping) cream
1 quantity of pâte à bombe prepared following the base
   recipe on page 300

FOR THE RASPBERRY JAM
6 ounces/1½ cups/170 g raspberries
1 ounce/2 tablespoons/30 g superfine (caster) sugar
1 level teaspoon/3 g powdered pectin

FOR THE GLAZE
1 quantity of mirror glaze prepared following the base
   recipe on page 316
1 teaspoon pink or red gel paste food coloring

EQUIPMENT NEEDED
Bowls
Immersion (stick) blender
Fine-mesh strainer (sieve)
Saucepan
Food processor
Measuring cup or jug
Electric whisk
Silicone spatula
8 × 3-inch/7-cm silicone heart-shaped molds or
   medium springform heart-shaped mold
Cooling rack

To make the jam, blitz the raspberries to a puree with the immersion (stick) blender. Pass the puree through a fine-mesh strainer (sieve), pressing down using the back of a spoon, to remove the seeds. Place the puree in a small saucepan with the sugar and pectin. Put over low heat until the sugar has dissolved, stirring occasionally. Once dissolved, turn up the heat and boil for 1–2 minutes or until thickened. To check the jam is the correct consistency, place a little of the mixture onto a chilled small plate and draw a teaspoon through—it should flow back very slowly.

To make the parfait, soak the gelatin in cold water for 5 minutes. Remove the pits (stones) from the mangoes, then place the flesh in a food processor and blitz to a puree. Measure out 1 pound/scant 2 cups/450 g. Warm 4 ounces/½ cup/125 g of the puree in a pan over low heat until just boiling. Remove from the heat. Squeeze the water from the gelatin. Add to the puree and stir until dissolved. Transfer to a bowl and stir in the remaining measured puree. Using an electric whisk, whip the cream to soft peaks. Using a silicone spatula, carefully fold the pâte à bombe into the mango puree, followed by the whipped cream.

Half fill the silicone molds or mold with the mango parfait. Tap the base of each mold on a work surface to remove any air bubbles. Place the molds in the freezer for 1 hour in order to get a firmer surface to spread the raspberry jam layer over.

Once firm, add a layer of raspberry jam, leaving 1¼ inch/3 cm below the rim. Carefully pour the remaining mango parfait on top to fill the molds. Place in the freezer for 10–12 hours, until frozen. Unmold the frozen semifreddo hearts and place on parchment paper. Return to the freezer while you make the mirror glaze.

Prepare the mirror glaze following the instructions on page 316. Add the food coloring to get the desired shade, then leave to cool.

Place a semifreddo heart on an upturned dish that is slightly smaller than the dessert placed on a cooling rack with a baking sheet underneath. When it has reached 89.5°F/32°C, pour the mirror glaze over the top of the dessert, ensuring it is completely covered. If the mirror glaze becomes too thick to pour, gently warm it in a heatproof bowl over a saucepan of hot water.

Once the glaze has set, transfer the dessert to a serving plate, and leave to rest at room temperature for 5–10 minutes before serving.

TIPS AND TRICKS
When making a mousse, always fold the lightest ingredient in last. Here the light whipped cream is folded in after the mango puree.

CITRUS AND SAFFRON SEMIFREDDO

Semifreddo di agrumi e zafferano

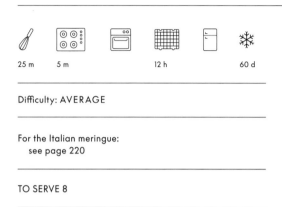

25 m   5 m   12 h   60 d

Difficulty: AVERAGE

For the Italian meringue:
    see page 220

TO SERVE 8

FOR THE SEMIFREDDO
2½ fl oz/5 tablespoons/75 ml water
Large pinch of saffron threads
5 ounces/¾ cup/150 g superfine (caster) sugar
2 egg whites
Grated zest and juice of 1 unwaxed lemon
Grated zest and juice of 1 unwaxed orange
10 fl oz/1¼ cups/300 ml heavy (whipping) cream

TO DECORATE
1 unwaxed orange
2 unwaxed limes
Large pinch of saffron threads

EQUIPMENT NEEDED
Small saucepans
Measuring cup or jug
Fine-mesh strainer (sieve)
Kitchen thermometer
Stand mixer fitted with whisk attachment
Zester
Juicer
Electric whisk
Silicone spatula
2-lb/900-g loaf pan (tin)

To make the meringue, heat the water in a small saucepan, add the saffron, and leave to infuse for 10 minutes.

Place 3½ ounces/½ cup/100 g of the sugar in a small saucepan. Pour the saffron-infused water through a strainer (sieve) into the pan and warm over low heat until the sugar dissolves. Increase the heat to medium and bring to a boil. Use a kitchen thermometer to continuously monitor the temperature and when it reaches 230°F/110°C, start to whisk the egg whites to soft peaks in the stand mixer. When the syrup reaches 250°F/121°C, remove it from the heat and slowly pour into the egg whites, whisking continuously as you do so, until the meringue has cooled.

Grate the zest of the orange and lemon, then juice them. Pour the juices through a strainer into a bowl with the remaining sugar and zests. In a separate bowl, whip the cream to soft peaks then whisk in the citrus sugar. Carefully fold in the meringue, using a silicone spatula, and pour the mixture into the loaf pan (tin). Place in the freezer for 12 hours.

When ready to serve, dip the loaf pan in boiling water for a few seconds to loosen the semifreddo. Place a serving plate over the loaf pan, turn it upside down, and lift the pan off the semifreddo. Decorate with the remaining orange, peeled and cut into thin slices, the very thinly sliced lime, saffron threads, and citrus zest.

SEMIFREDDO-CASSATA WITH ORANGE MARMALADE

Semifreddo-cassata con marmellata di arance

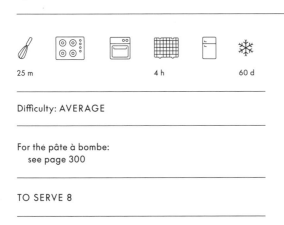

25 m   4 h   60 d

Difficulty: AVERAGE

For the pâte à bombe:
  see page 300

TO SERVE 8

FOR THE SEMIFREDDO

10½ ounces/1¼ cups/300 g sheep's ricotta (or use whole-milk ricotta)

2 ounces/scant ½ cup/50 g confectioners' (icing) sugar

2 ounces/50 g bittersweet (dark) chocolate (minimum 70% cocoa solids)

7 ounces/1 cup/200 g chopped mixed candied fruit

7 fl oz/scant 1 cup/200 ml heavy (whipping) cream

1 quantity (8 ounces/225 g) of pâte à bombe prepared following the base recipe on page 300

TO DECORATE

3½ ounces/⅓ cup/100 g bitter orange marmalade

1 fl oz/2 tablespoons/30 ml boiling water

1 unwaxed orange, thinly sliced

EQUIPMENT NEEDED

Bowls

Measuring cup or jug

Immersion (stick) blender

Electric whisk

Silicone spatula

8 freezer-safe individual serving glasses

Place the ricotta in a bowl with the confectioners' (icing) sugar and blitz with the immersion (stick) blender to a smooth, even cream.

Finely chop the chocolate and add to the ricotta mix along with the chopped candied fruit, then stir to mix. Using an electric whisk, whip the cream to soft peaks. Mix one-quarter of the pâte à bombe into the ricotta cream, then fold in the remainder using a silicone spatula. Fold in the whipped cream.

Divide the mixture between the individual serving glasses, level the surface with the back of a teaspoon, and then place in the freezer for 4 hours.

Dilute the orange marmalade with the boiling water and stir to mix. Just before serving, pour the diluted marmalade over the semifreddos and decorate with thin slices of orange.

SEMIFREDDO WITH PINE NUTS AND PEACH SAUCE

Semifreddo ai pinoli con salsa di pesche

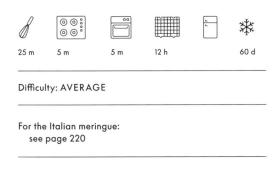

25 m   5 m   5 m   12 h   60 d

Difficulty: AVERAGE

For the Italian meringue:
  see page 220

TO SERVE 8

FOR THE SEMIFREDDO
4 ounces/scant ¾ cup/120 g pine nuts
5 ounces/¾ cup/150 g superfine (caster) sugar
2½ fl oz/5 tablespoons/75 ml water
2 egg whites
10 fl oz/1¼ cups/300 ml heavy (whipping) cream

FOR THE PEACH SAUCE
1 ounce/2½ tablespoons/30 g superfine (caster) sugar
2 lemon balm sprigs (or use a mixture of lemon verbena
  and mint)
4 peaches
Juice of ½ lemon

EQUIPMENT NEEDED
Baking sheet
Food processor
Small saucepan
Bowls
Measuring cup or jug
Electric whisk
Silicone spatula
2-lb/900-g loaf pan (tin)
Immersion (stick) blender
Saucepan
Juicer
Strainer (sieve)

Preheat the oven to 350°F/180°C/160°C Fan/Gas 4.

Place the pine nuts on a baking sheet and toast in the preheated oven for 5 minutes or until golden. If not golden after 5 minutes, check them every minute as they can burn quickly. Set aside to cool then reserve ¾ ounce/2 tablespoons/20 g of the pine nuts to garnish the finished dessert. Place the remainder in a food processor and blitz briefly until coarsely chopped.

Place the sugar in a small saucepan with the water and warm over low heat until the sugar dissolves. Increase the heat to medium and bring to a boil. Use a kitchen thermometer to continuously monitor the temperature and when it reaches 230°F/110°C, start to whisk the egg whites to soft peaks in the stand mixer. When the syrup reaches 250°F/121°C, remove it from the heat and slowly pour into the egg whites, continuously whisking as you do so, until the meringue has cooled.

Using an electric whisk, whip the cream to soft peaks. Using a silicone spatula, gently fold the whipped cream into the cooled meringue along with the chopped pine nuts. Pour into the loaf pan (tin) and place in the freezer for 12 hours.

When ready to serve, make the peach sauce. Blitz the sugar with the leaves from the lemon balm sprigs until finely chopped using an immersion (stick) blender. Bring a saucepan of water to a boil then blanch 3 of the peaches for 30 seconds. Drain, leave to cool, then remove the skin and pits (stones). Blitz the peach flesh to a puree, along with the lemon balm sugar and lemon juice.

Dip the loaf pan in boiling water for a few seconds to loosen the semifreddo. Place a serving plate over the loaf pan, turn it upside down, and lift the pan off the semifreddo. Decorate with the remaining peach, cut into thin slices, and the reserved pine nuts. Serve with the peach sauce.

ICING AND FROSTING

Glacé icing
Glassa a freddo di acqua e zucchero

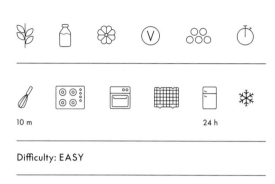

10 m   24 h

Difficulty: EASY

MAKES 1 QUANTITY
(7 OUNCES/200 G FROSTING)

FOR THE FROSTING
7 ounces/1⅔ cup/200 g confectioners' (icing) sugar
2 fl oz/4 tablespoons/60 ml water
Flavors to taste (2 tablespoons liqueur, ½ teaspoon vanilla
    extract, ½ teaspoon grated zest of 1 unwaxed orange
    or lemon)

EQUIPMENT NEEDED
Bowl
Hand whisk

AS USED IN
– Frosted Spiced Cookies
  (see page 326)

Place the confectioners' (icing) sugar in a bowl and combine with the water (1).

Beat with a hand whisk until you obtain a smooth and dense mix (2–3).

HOW TO USE
Glacé icing can be used to cover cakes or biscuits or, by reducing the quantity of liquid added, for piping decorative designs or writing. It dries more slowly than royal icing and is also runnier, so is unsuitable for piping intricate decorations.

To cover a cake with glacé icing, place the cake on a cooling rack and spread the frosting over the cake with a metal spatula or palette knife. To make the frosting shine, place the cake in a preheated oven at 350°F/180°C/160°C Fan/Gas 4 for just a few seconds.

TIPS AND TRICKS
The required consistency of the frosting (icing) will depend on how it is to be used and can be adjusted by adding more or less water. It can also be colored using food colorings of any shade, to suit the cake and the occasion. Any coloring used must be water soluble and should be added once the sugar and water have been whisked together. Add any food coloring to the icing just one drop at a time until you reach the desired strength of color.

VARIATIONS
Glacé icing can be flavored with many different flavorings. Instead of mixing the icing with water, use 2 tablespoons of fruit juice or liqueur plus 2 tablespoons of water. If preferred, flavor the icing to taste with ½ teaspoon of vanilla extract or ½ teaspoon of grated zest of an unwaxed orange or lemon. If using vanilla extract, the icing will not be bright white as the vanilla will give it a slight tint.

Royal icing with egg whites
Glassa reale con albume

10 m   24 h

Difficulty: EASY

MAKES 1 QUANTITY
(12 OUNCES/325 G FROSTING)

FOR THE FROSTING
3 egg whites
10½ ounces/2½ cups/300 g confectioners' (icing) sugar
Juice of ½ lemon

EQUIPMENT NEEDED
Bowls
Electric whisk
Juicer
Fine-mesh strainer (sieve)
Measuring cup or jug

AS USED IN
– Date and Apple Cake
(see page 328)

Place the egg whites in a bowl and start to beat with an electric whisk on a low speed, adding the confectioners' (icing) sugar a little at a time (1).

Continue to beat the mix until the sugar has been completely incorporated and you obtain a smooth, thick mixture (2).

Squeeze the lemon and pour the juice through a fine-mesh strainer (sieve) to filter it, then slowly pour 2 teaspoons of the juice into the frosting mix, whisking continuously as you do so (3). Continue whisking until the frosting (icing) is very thick. If you lift the beaters and let some frosting drop back into the bowl, the trail should remain on the surface for about 10 seconds (4).

You can add a few drops of food coloring (liquid, powder, or gel), a little at a time, while you continue to work the mixture, until you obtain the desired color.

Its thick consistency makes royal icing suitable for use with a pastry (piping) bag with a very small piping tip (nozzle), or a paper cone, to create decorations and writing on cookies and cakes.

TIPS AND TRICKS
The consistency of the frosting can be adjusted by varying the quantity of lemon juice added—the more juice added the runnier the frosting. If the frosting is too thin, you can also add some extra confectioners' sugar. You can use thicker frosting for piped decorations and more fluid frosting to pour directly onto a cake to cover it. When it dries, royal icing becomes hard and crunchy.

VARIATIONS
This frosting contains uncooked egg white, which is not recommended for certain groups of people (see page 359). If preferred, use pasteurized egg white from a carton.

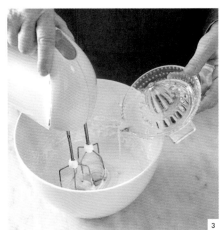

Mirror glaze

Glassa lucida

15 m   5 m

Difficulty: AVERAGE

MAKES 1 QUANTITY
(1 POUND 15 OUNCES/850 G MIRROR GLAZE)

FOR THE GLAZE
¾ ounce/20 g platinum gelatin sheets
5 fl oz/scant ⅔ cup/150 ml water
6 ounces/¾ cup/150 g superfine (caster) sugar
7 ounces/⅔ cup/200 g sweetened condensed milk
13 ounces/380 g good-quality white chocolate
    (minimum 30% cocoa butter), finely chopped
Gel food coloring

EQUIPMENT NEEDED
Bowls
Small saucepan
Measuring cup or jug
Heatproof bowl
Hand whisk
Immersion (stick) blender

AS USED IN
– Mirror-Glazed Mango and Raspberry Hearts
  (see page 302)

Soak the gelatin in cold water for 5 minutes.

Meanwhile, pour the measured water into a small saucepan with the sugar and condensed milk and gently warm over low heat until the sugar has dissolved. Turn up the heat only slightly to low-medium and bring to a boil. Do not turn the heat up too high as the sugar can easily catch and burn. Remove the pan from the heat.

Squeeze the water from the gelatin. Add it to the pan with the milk mixture and stir continuously until the gelatin has dissolved.

Add the chopped white chocolate to the pan with the gelatin mixture (1). Briefly blend with an immersion (stick) blender or gently stir with a wooden spoon until the chocolate has melted and you have a smooth, even mixture (2).

Add your chosen food coloring (3) and blitz with an immersion blender until you obtain an even color (4–5) and the mixture is smooth. Repeat with a little extra food coloring if necessary to obtain your preferred shade.

Transfer the glaze to a bowl and leave to cool, stirring occasionally, until it starts to set and thicken slightly. The temperature of the glaze must cool to 89.5°F/32°C before it can be used (6).

Mirror glaze is used to impart a shine to mainly cold desserts, usually those with a surface that is not too porous or absorbent.

TIPS AND TRICKS
When blending the glaze with an immersion (stick) blender, keep the blade at the bottom of the bowl and do not move it around in order to avoid creating too many air bubbles in the glaze. If full of bubbles, the mirror effect of the glaze will be spoiled. To ensure there are no bubbles, you can sieve the glaze before pouring it.

To obtain a marbled effect, divide the glaze into two halves and add a different coloring to each half. Pour the two colored frostings (icings) into a bowl but do not mix, then pour onto the cake.

Any leftover mirror glaze can be stored in the refrigerator for up to 2 days. To use, simply reheat in a heatproof bowl over a saucepan of hot water and pour as instructed above.

MISTAKES TO AVOID
When glazing a cake, avoid spoiling the glazed edges of the cake by lifting it a little way above the rack. Do this by placing a bowl with a slightly smaller diameter than the cake underneath it. This way, the glaze will drip from the edges without sticking to the rack, making it easier to transfer the cake and to achieve an even glaze.

White chocolate is temperature sensitive and can seize easily if the temperature is too high. By stirring the gelatin into the condensed milk mixture first, it gives the mixture a chance to cool slightly before being poured over the white chocolate. White chocolate melts at 86°F/30°C and so the mixture will still be warm enough for the chocolate to melt.

Cocoa mirror glaze

Glassa lucida al cacao

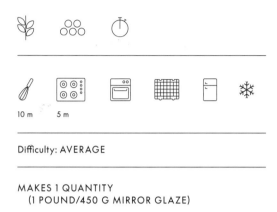

10 m   5 m

Difficulty: AVERAGE

MAKES 1 QUANTITY
(1 POUND/450 G MIRROR GLAZE)

FOR THE GLAZE
¾ ounce/20 g platinum gelatin sheets
3½ fl oz/scant ½ cup/100 ml heavy (whipping) cream
3½ fl oz/scant ½ cup/100 ml water
6½ ounces/generous ¾ cup/180 g superfine (caster) sugar
2½ ounces/scant ⅔ cup/75 g unsweetened cocoa powder

EQUIPMENT NEEDED
Bowls
Small saucepan
Measuring cup or jug
Hand whisk
Fine-mesh strainer (sieve)

Soak the gelatin in cold water for 5 minutes. Pour the cream into a small saucepan, then add the water and sugar. Bring to a boil over low heat, stirring frequently with a hand whisk (1–2–3).

Turn off the heat, squeeze the water from the gelatin, then place in the saucepan (4), stirring with the whisk until it has dissolved.

Pour the mix through a fine-mesh strainer (sieve) into a measuring cup or jug (5) then sift the cocoa powder directly into a bowl (6).

Pour the warm liquid mix, very slowly, onto the sifted cocoa, stirring continuously with the whisk as you do so (7). Continue to mix until you obtain a smooth, even glaze.

HOW TO USE
To cover a cake with the glaze, place the cake on a cooling rack set over a baking sheet. When the glaze has cooled to 88°F/31°C, pour the glaze onto the center of the cake so that it trickles over the top surface and the edges. Spread the glaze out with a metal spatula or palette knife, if necessary, to cover the entire cake.

TIPS AND TRICKS
It is very important to sift the cocoa to eliminate any lumps. Add the liquid to the cocoa a little at a time to ensure it mixes evenly.

Dolci al cucchiaio (the Italian term for desserts that need to be eaten with a spoon, such as semifreddos) need to be completely frozen before being glazed, to ensure their surface is very cold and the glaze will set quickly. For the same reason, sponge cakes need to be chilled thoroughly in the refrigerator for 30 minutes before glazing.

Butter frosting (icing)

Glassa al burro

10 m

Difficulty: EASY

MAKES 1 QUANTITY
(14 OUNCES/400 G BUTTER FROSTING)

FOR THE FROSTING
5 ounces/⅔ cup/150 g unsalted butter
1 vanilla bean (pod)
9 ounces/2 cups/250 g confectioners' (icing) sugar
2 tablespoons whole (full-fat) milk

EQUIPMENT NEEDED
Bowl
Fine-mesh strainer (sieve)
Electric whisk

Cut the butter into small cubes, place in a bowl and set aside to bring to room temperature. Slice the vanilla bean (pod) lengthwise, open it and scrape the inside with the tip of a knife to remove the seeds (1).

Place the vanilla seeds in a bowl with the softened butter and sift the confectioners' (icing) sugar into the bowl (2). Beat with the electric whisk until you have a very soft and fluffy cream that can be easily spread (3).

Add the milk (4), and beat until incorporated.

HOW TO USE
To ensure the butter frosting (icing) adheres properly, spread the surface of cakes or pastries with a very thin layer of fruit preserves (jam) then spread the butter frosting using a metal spatula or palette knife.

MISTAKES TO AVOID
The ideal temperature to whip butter is about 68°F/20°C—not cold straight out of the refrigerator, or too warm. Do not be tempted to warm it in a microwave oven as this will prevent it from incorporating air, meaning it cannot be whipped. Instead, ensure you have removed it from the refrigerator in good time for it to reach room temperature when you need it.

When making butter frosting, it is important always to sift the confectioners' sugar, otherwise there may be small lumps of sugar in the frosting.

VARIATIONS
For a lighter frosting, you can replace half the quantity of butter with cream cheese (fresh, soft, spreadable cheese). First, beat the butter and confectioners' sugar together, at the same time adding 1 teaspoon of cornstarch (cornflour) per 3½ ounces/100 g cream cheese. Stir the cream cheese first to soften it slightly, then whisk it into the butter and sugar mixture to make the frosting.

Buttercream
Crema al burro

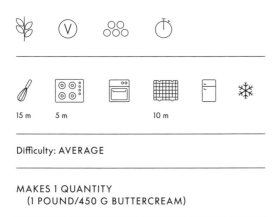

15 m   5 m   10 m

Difficulty: AVERAGE

MAKES 1 QUANTITY
(1 POUND/450 G BUTTERCREAM)

FOR THE BUTTERCREAM
9 ounces/1 cup/250 g unsalted butter
4 ounces/scant ⅔ cup/130 g superfine (caster) sugar
3 tablespoons/40 ml water
4 egg yolks
1 vanilla bean (pod)

EQUIPMENT NEEDED
Bowl
Small saucepan
Measuring cup or jug
Kitchen thermometer
Stand mixer fitted with whisk attachment

AS USED IN
– Buckwheat Cake with Buttercream
  (see page 338)

Cut the butter into small cubes, place in a bowl and set aside to bring to room temperature.

Place the sugar in a small saucepan and pour in the water. Set the pan over low heat. Let the sugar dissolve, gently swirling the pan from time to time. Once the sugar has dissolved completely, increase the heat to medium and bring to a boil. Using a kitchen thermometer, continuously monitor the temperature and when the syrup reaches 250°F/121°C (1), remove from the heat.

Meanwhile, slice the vanilla bean (pod) lengthwise, open it and scrape the inside with the tip of a knife to remove the seeds. Place the vanilla seeds in the bowl of a stand mixer with the egg yolks, then beat until pale and fluffy.

Very slowly pour the hot sugar syrup into the beaten yolk mix, continuously whisking as you do so (2). Continue to whisk the mixture until it has cooled to about 68°F/20°C and then, while still whisking, add the softened butter, one tablespoon at a time (3) until you have a pale and fluffy cream (4). Place in the refrigerator for 10 minutes before using.

HOW TO USE
Buttercream can be used as a frosting (icing) for cupcakes, to fill cakes or as a thin coat of frosting where cakes are to be decorated with sugar paste.

MISTAKES TO AVOID
It is important that the temperature of the butter is about 68°F/20°C when it is added to the whipped mix. It must be added one tablespoon at a time, without adding the next until the previous one has been completely incorporated. Do not whip the mix for too long after all the butter has been added to ensure the yolk mix does not separate.

The egg mixture and the butter both need to be at the same temperature. If the egg mixture is too warn then the butter will melt as it is whisked in.

Caramel decorations
Caramello e decorazioni

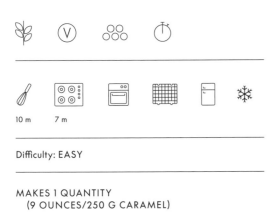

10 m   7 m

Difficulty: EASY

MAKES 1 QUANTITY
(9 OUNCES/250 G CARAMEL)

FOR THE CARAMEL
9 ounces/generous 1 cup/250 g superfine (caster) sugar
2 fl oz/¼ cup/60 ml water

EQUIPMENT NEEDED
Bowls
Small saucepan
Measuring cup or jug
Pastry brush
Kitchen thermometer
Ice bain-marie
Spun sugar whisk

AS USED IN
– Chocolate Tartlets with Caramel Mousse
  (see page 74)
– Gianduja Chocolate and Coffee Cake
  (see page 208)

Place the sugar in a small saucepan (1), and pour in the water (2). Set the pan over medium heat. Stir briefly to dissolve the sugar. As the syrup heats up, frequently brush the insides of the saucepan with cold water to remove any sugar deposits that may cause the syrup to crystallize (3). Without stirring, continue to heat the syrup, monitoring the temperature with a kitchen thermometer until it reaches 330°F/165°C (4). The caramel will be a medium amber color and may smoke slightly. Immediately place the base of the saucepan in the ice bain-marie to stop the cooking process (5). Leave for a few minutes without stirring until the caramel has thickened a little. To check if the caramel is ready to use, dip a fork in and lift it up. If the caramel drips quickly into the pan, let it cool and thicken for a little longer. When the caramel starts to fall in visible threads, it is ready to use.

The color of caramel is dependent on the cooking temperature of the sugar—a light caramel color is obtained at a temperature of between 313°F/156°C and 330°F/165°C, getting darker at higher temperatures, up to 347°F/175°C. Above this, the sugar will burn.

There are various techniques that can be used to create spun sugar decorations with caramel. A spun sugar whisk (6) or two forks used together will allow you to create decorations of various types, consistency and shape. One of the simplest ways is to use a large sheet of parchment paper on a work surface, dipping the spun sugar whisk into the caramel and letting the caramel drop from the whisk directly onto the paper, until you form a small sugar bundle.

It is possible to use a dish for more wispy results. Stretch threads of caramel between opposite edges of the dish, which has been lightly greased with a flavorless oil (7). Working quickly, lift the threads from the dish (8) and arrange into the desired shape, for example a small nest. Do this while the caramel threads are still warm, if they cool too much then they will then snap when you try to shape them.

Alternatively, use different shaped objects as supports for caramel threads, such as a small half-sphere cake pan (tin) to make a caramel cage (9). Using a fork, let threads of caramel drip directly onto the oiled half-sphere pan (10–11–12). Once the caramel has set, it can be carefully removed from its support before using.

It is simple to make shaped caramel decorations, whether drops, flakes, or squiggles. In this case it is sufficient to use parchment paper, a tablespoon, or even small molds, such as cookie cutters.

Caramel decorations, especially those made of thin threads, don't like humidity and therefore they cannot be stored in the refrigerator. For best results, prepare at the last minute, just before use.

VARIATIONS
To prevent the sugar from crystallizing when heated add 3 tablespoons of liquid glucose. To obtain a runny caramel sauce, carefully add 4 tablespoons of boiling water to the pan (the caramel may bubble up and spit a little) when the syrup has reached 330°F/165°C and continue to cook until all the caramel has dissolved. Leave to cool and store in the refrigerator. Caramel can also be prepared dry, by cooking the sugar directly without any water. In this case, it is used to add flavor to sauces.

FROSTED SPICED COOKIES

Biscotti speziati glassati

35 m   15 m   6 h

Difficulty: EASY

For the glacé icing:
   see page 312

TO SERVE 8 (MAKES 40–50 COOKIES)

FOR THE COOKIES
1 pound/3⅔ cups/450 g type "00" flour or all-purpose
   (plain) flour
1 teaspoon baking soda (bicarbonate of soda)
4 ounces/½ cup plus 1 tablespoon/130 g unsalted butter
1 teaspoon ground ginger
1 teaspoon ground cinnamon
Pinch of grated nutmeg
Pinch of ground allspice
Pinch of salt
7 ounces/1 cup/200 g dark brown sugar
3 ounces/¼ cup/80 g acacia honey
1 egg

FOR THE FROSTING (ICING)
1 quantity (7 ounces/200 g) of glacé icing prepared
   following the base recipe on page 312

EQUIPMENT NEEDED
Fine-mesh strainer (sieve)
Bowls
Hand whisk
Plastic wrap (cling film)
Baking sheet
Parchment paper
Rolling pin
Pastry cutters in various shapes
Cooling rack
Pastry (piping) bag fitted with a small plain piping
   tip (nozzle)

Sift the flour with the baking soda (bicarbonate of soda) directly into a bowl, add the cold butter cut into small cubes, the spices, and a pinch of salt. Working quickly to ensure the ingredients do not become too warm, rub the ingredients together using your fingertips until the mixture resembles breadcrumbs. In a separate bowl, whisk together the sugar, honey, and egg, then add to the flour mixture.

Mix until you obtain a soft and smooth dough, then wrap in plastic wrap (cling film) and leave to rest in the refrigerator for 2 hours.

Preheat the oven to 325°F/160°C/140°C Fan/Gas 3. Line a baking sheet with parchment paper.

On a lightly floured surface, roll out the dough to ⅛ inch/3 mm thick. Cut out cookies using pastry cutters in different shapes.

Baking the cookies in batches. Place them on the lined baking sheet, leaving ½ inch/1 cm between each cookie to allow for them to spread. Bake in the preheated oven for 15 minutes, or until slightly darker around the edges and dry on top. Transfer the cookies to a cooling rack and leave to cool completely.

Prepare the glacé icing following the instructions on page 312. For an easy way to decorate the cookies, simply drizzle or splatter the frosting over using a teaspoon. Alternatively, fill a pastry (piping) bag fitted with a small plain piping tip (nozzle) with the frosting and decorate the biscuits in whatever pattern you prefer. Leave the frosting to dry for 3–4 hours before serving.

These cookies can be stored in an airtight container for up to 7 days.

TIPS AND TRICKS
When cutting out the cookies, dip the pastry cutter in flour every time so that it doesn't stick to the dough (pastry).

If piping the decoration onto the cookies, then use less water when mixing the glacé icing for a piping consistency. Alternatively, use royal icing for more definition (see page 314).

DATE AND APPLE CAKE

Torta di datteri e mele glassata

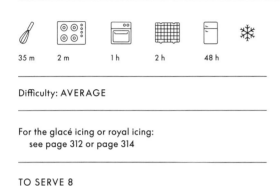

35 m   2 m   1 h   2 h   48 h

Difficulty: AVERAGE

For the glacé icing or royal icing:
    see page 312 or page 314

TO SERVE 8

FOR THE CAKE
5 ounces/½ cup plus 2 tablespoons/150 g unsalted butter
1 pound/2 cups/450 g dried dates
6 fl oz/¾ cup/180 ml black tea
1 teaspoon baking soda (bicarbonate of soda)
2 Golden Delicious apples
6½ ounces/1½ cups/180 g type "00" flour or all-purpose
    (plain) flour
1 teaspoon baking powder
4 eggs
1 teaspoon ground cinnamon
3¼ ounces/scant ½ cup/90 g soft light brown sugar

FOR THE ICING
1 quantity of glacé icing prepared following the base
    recipe on page 312 or 1 quantity of royal icing prepared
    following the base recipe on page 314

EQUIPMENT NEEDED
2-lb/900-g loaf pan (tin)
Parchment paper
Bowls
Measuring cup or jug
Immersion (stick) blender
Fine-mesh strainer (sieve)
Silicone spatula
Cooling rack
Pastry (piping) bag fitted with star piping tip (nozzle)
    (optional)

Preheat the oven to 325°F/160°C/140°C Fan/Gas 3. Line the loaf pan (tin) with parchment paper.

Cut the butter into small cubes, place in a bowl and set aside to bring to room temperature. Pit (stone) the dates and place in a bowl with the boiling tea and baking soda (bicarbonate of soda), and leave to steep for 15 minutes. Meanwhile, peel the apples and cut into small cubes. Puree the steeped dates with the immersion (stick) blender until you have a smooth paste. Add the softened butter, the flour sifted with the baking powder, the eggs, cinnamon, chopped apples and sugar, and mix with a silicone spatula until combined.

Pour the mixture into the loaf pan and bake in the preheated oven for 1 hour. Leave the cake to rest for 10 minutes to cool slightly, then remove it from the pan and leave on a cooling rack to cool completely.

Prepare the glacé or royal icing following the instructions on page 312 or 314. For an easy way to decorate the cake, simply drizzle the glacé icing over using a jug or spoon. Alternatively, fill a pastry (piping) bag fitted with a star piping tip (nozzle) with the royal icing and pipe small roses over the surface of the cake. Leave the frosting to set before serving.

CHOCOLATE TRUFFLE CAKE WITH RASPBERRY GLAZE

Tutto cioccolato con glassa lucida di lamponi

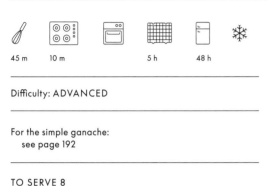

45 m   10 m   5 h   48 h

Difficulty: ADVANCED

For the simple ganache:
    see page 192

TO SERVE 8

FOR THE BASE
9 ounces/250 g graham crackers or digestive biscuits
3½ ounces/7 tablespoons/100 g butter, melted

FOR THE GANACHE
10½ ounces/300 g bittersweet (dark) chocolate (minimum
    70% cocoa solids)
12½ fl oz/1½ cups/370 ml heavy (whipping) cream

FOR THE RASPBERRY MIRROR GLAZE
¾ ounce/20 g platinum gelatin sheets
14 ounces/3¼ cups/400 g raspberries
2 ounces/3 tablespoons/60 g glucose syrup (liquid glucose)
12 ounces/1¾ cups/350 g superfine (caster) sugar
7 fl oz/scant 1 cup/200 ml heavy (whipping) cream
1¾ fl oz/3 tablespoons/50 ml lemon juice

TO DECORATE
3½ ounces/¾ cup/100 g raspberries
Pinch of freeze-dried raspberries

EQUIPMENT NEEDED
Strong, clean plastic bag
Rolling pin
7-inch/18-cm round loose-bottomed or springform cake
    pan (tin)
Parchment paper
Bowls
Electric whisk
Immersion (stick) blender
Fine-mesh strainer (sieve)
Saucepan
Measuring cup or jug
Kitchen thermometer
Cooling rack

Line the cake pan (tin) with parchment paper.

To make the base, place the graham crackers or digestive biscuits in a strong, clean plastic bag. Using a rolling pin, crush the crackers or biscuits into fine crumbs. Place the crumbs in a bowl, pour on the melted butter, and mix until fully combined. Spoon the crumb mixture into the lined cake pan and press down with the back of the spoon or base of a glass to achieve an even layer. Place in the refrigerator for 1 hour, or until firm.

Prepare the chocolate ganache following the instructions on page 192 to step (4). Place in the refrigerator for 1 hour, or until cool and starting to thicken.

Using an electric whisk, whip the ganache until it is lighter and thicker. Pour into the cake pan over the base, then place in the refrigerator for 4 hours or until set.

To make the raspberry mirror glaze, soak the gelatin in cold water for 5 minutes. Puree the raspberries using an immersion (stick) blender, then push through a fine-mesh strainer (sieve) using the back of a spoon to remove the seeds. Place the puree in a saucepan, add the glucose syrup (liquid glucose), sugar, and cream. Warm over low heat until it just starts to boil, then remove from the heat. Squeeze the water from the gelatin and add to the pan with the lemon juice, then stir until the gelatin has dissolved.

Pass the glaze through a fine-mesh strainer then leave to cool to 89°F/32°C. Remove the cake from the pan, place it on an upturned plate or bowl that is slightly smaller than the cake and then onto a cooling rack. Completely cover the cake with the glaze and leave to set. Transfer to a serving plate and refrigerate until ready to serve. Decorate with both fresh and freeze-dried raspberries just before serving.

TIPS AND TRICKS
If you are nervous about transferring the finished cake to a serving plate after it has been glazed, it is possible to glaze the cake on the serving plate or cake stand. Tear off strips of parchment paper and place them around the serving plate. Sit the cake on top of the paper so that just a little of each strip is underneath the cake. Pour the glaze over the top of the cake and, if necessary, use an offset spatula or palette knife to spread the glaze down the sides of the cake. Let the glaze set slightly and then slide the paper strips away to leave a clean edge around the cake.

CHOCOLATE TORTE

Torta Sacher

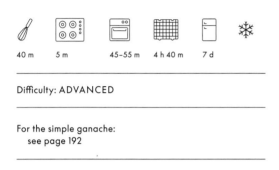

40 m 5 m 45–55 m 4 h 40 m 7 d

Difficulty: ADVANCED

For the simple ganache:
  see page 192

TO SERVE 10–12

FOR THE SPONGE
5 ounces/140 g bittersweet (dark) chocolate (minimum
  70% cocoa solids), finely chopped
5 ounces/½ cup plus 1 tablespoon/140 g unsalted butter,
  softened, plus extra for greasing
¼ teaspoon salt
3½ ounces/1 cup/100 g confectioners' (icing) sugar, sifted
6 eggs, separated
1 teaspoon vanilla extract
2 ounces/scant ½ cup/55 g all-purpose (plain) flour
2 ounces/heaping ½ cup/55 g almond flour or meal (ground
  almonds)
1 ounce/⅓ cup/30 g unsweetened cocoa powder, sifted
3 ounces/heaping ⅓ cup/80 g superfine (caster) sugar

FOR THE FILLING AND TOPPING
7 ounces/scant 1 cup/200 g apricot preserves (jam) without
  fruit chunks
1 tablespoon orange juice or rum
1 quantity of simple ganache prepared with bittersweet
  (dark) chocolate following the base recipe on page 192

TO SERVE
6¾ fl oz/scant 1 cup/200 ml heavy (whipping) cream,
  whipped (optional)

EQUIPMENT NEEDED
Bain-marie or double boiler
Stand mixer fitted with flat beater attachment
Bowls
Electric whisk
Silicone spatula
Fine-mesh strainer (sieve)
9-inch/23-cm round springform cake pan (tin)
Cooling rack
Metal spatula or palette knife
Saucepan
Measuring cup or jug

Preheat the oven to 325°F/160°C/140°C Fan/Gas 3. Grease the cake pan (tin) with butter and then line with parchment paper.

Place the chopped chocolate in a heatproof bowl set over a saucepan of hot water, making sure the bowl is not touching the water. Melt the chocolate, stirring occasionally. Set aside.

Place the softened butter, salt, and confectioners' (icing) sugar in the bowl of a stand mixer. Beat until pale and smooth. Add the egg yolks, one at a time, beating after each addition. Add the vanilla extract and melted chocolate and mix to combine. Combine the flour, almonds, and cocoa powder, then add to the bowl and mix until just combined—the mixture will be quite thick at this stage.

Place the egg whites in a grease-free bowl and whisk until frothy. Slowly whisk in the superfine (caster) sugar, a little at a time. Continue until the egg whites form soft, shiny peaks, but do not overwhisk them. Using a silicone spatula, gently fold one-quarter of the egg whites into the chocolate mixture. Add the remaining egg whites and gently fold in until just combined, taking care not to deflate the mixture.

Scrape the mixture into the pan and bake in the preheated oven for 45–55 minutes or until risen, firm to the touch, and a skewer inserted into the center of the cake comes out with a few damp crumbs attached, but no uncooked batter. Let cool in the pan for 15 minutes, then release from the pan and transfer to a rack to cool completely.

Cut the sponge cake in half horizontally to make two equal layers. Place the top layer upside down on a cooling rack and spread the cut side with two-thirds of the preserves. Sandwich with the bottom layer so the flat base of the sponge is now on the top of the cake.

Warm the remaining apricot preserve until it becomes runny, then stir in the orange juice or rum. Brush the thinned preserves over the top and sides of the sponge. Let dry on the cooling rack for 1 hour.

Place the cake, on the rack, over a large baking sheet. Pour the warm chocolate ganache over the cake and then use an offset spatula or palette knife to spread the ganache down the sides. If the chocolate ganache is too thick to pour, place the heatproof bowl over a saucepan of hot water, making sure the bowl does not touch the water, and stir until the ganache is a thick but pourable consistency. Transfer the cake to a serving plate and leave to set for at least 3 hours, or preferably overnight.

When ready to serve, slice the cake into generous wedges and serve with whipped cream, if desired.

SPICED PUMPKIN CAKE
Torta di zucca speziata

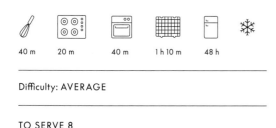

| 40 m | 20 m | 40 m | 1 h 10 m | 48 h | |

Difficulty: AVERAGE

TO SERVE 8

FOR THE CAKE
7 ounces/½ cup plus 5 tablespoons/200 g unsalted butter
1 pound 5 ounces/600 g Mantua pumpkin or Turban
    squash flesh (or use butternut squash or 2½ cups canned
    pumpkin puree)
10½ ounces/1⅓ cups/300 g superfine (caster) sugar
1 teaspoon five-spice powder
Pinch of salt
3 eggs
11 ounces/2⅔ cups/330 g type "00" flour or all-purpose
    (plain) flour
1½ teaspoons baking powder
1½ teaspoons baking soda (bicarbonate of soda)

FOR THE SWISS MERINGUE BUTTERCREAM
14 ounces/1¾ cups/400 g unsalted butter
4 egg whites
7 ounces/1 cup/200 g superfine (caster) sugar

TO DECORATE
3½ ounces/100 g candied citron (or use crystallized lemon
    or orange peel)

EQUIPMENT NEEDED
8-inch/20-cm round springform cake pan (tin)
Parchment paper
Bowls
Steamer
Immersion (stick) blender
Stand mixer fitted with whisk attachment
Fine-mesh strainer (sieve)
Cooling rack
Bain-marie or double boiler
Electric whisk
Metal spatula or palette knife

Preheat the oven to 350°F/180°C/160°C Fan/Gas 4. Line the springform cake pan (tin) with parchment paper.

Cut the butter into small cubes, place in a bowl and set aside to bring to room temperature.

If using fresh pumpkin, cut the pumpkin flesh into cubes and steam for 15 minutes or until soft. Leave to cool, then puree using an immersion (stick) blender.

Place the softened butter in the bowl of the stand mixer with the sugar, five-spice powder, and a pinch of salt. Whip at medium speed until pale and fluffy. Add the eggs, one at a time, alternating with a spoonful of flour until all the eggs are combined. Add the pumpkin puree and remaining flour sifted with the baking powder and baking soda (bicarbonate of soda). Mix gently, then pour into the lined cake pan.

Bake the cake in the preheated oven for 40 minutes, or until risen and firm to the touch—a skewer inserted into the center comes out clean. Let rest in the pan for 10 minutes to cool slightly. Remove from the pan and place on a cooling rack to cool completely.

To make the Swiss meringue buttercream, cut the butter into small cubes, place in a bowl, and set aside to bring to room temperature. Place the egg whites in the grease-free bowl of the stand mixer, add the sugar, and set over a bain-marie to heat gently. Using an electric whisk, beat for 5–6 minutes until the sugar has dissolved completely and the egg whites form stiff peaks. Remove the bowl from the bain-marie and position it on the stand mixer. Once the egg whites have cooled to room temperature, continue to whisk slowly, adding the softened butter a little at a time.

Cut the cake horizontally into three layers. Using a metal spatula or palette knife, spread one-third of the Swiss meringue buttercream onto the bottom layer. Place the middle layer of cake on top and spread with another one-third of the buttercream. Top with the final layer of cake and spread the remaining buttercream on top. Place in the refrigerator for 1 hour.

To decorate, scatter the candied citron over the top of the cake just before serving.

VARIATIONS
The Swiss meringue buttercream contains only lightly cooked egg white, which is not recommended for certain groups of people (see page 359). If preferred, use pasteurized egg white from a carton.

CARROT, WALNUT, AND CANDIED GINGER CAKE

Torta di carote, noci e zenzero candito

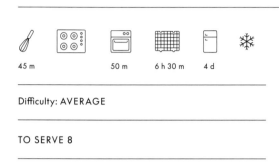

45 m   50 m   6 h 30 m   4 d

Difficulty: AVERAGE

TO SERVE 8

FOR THE CAKE
4 eggs
1 vanilla bean (pod)
Grated zest of 1 unwaxed lemon
10½ ounces/1⅓ cups/300 g superfine (caster) sugar
8 fl oz/scant 1 cup/220 ml sunflower oil
10½ ounces/2¼ cups/300 g type "00" flour or all-purpose (plain) flour
1 heaping teaspoon baking powder
1 teaspoon baking soda (bicarbonate of soda)
Pinch of salt
1 pound/450 g carrots
3¼ ounces/¾ cup/90 g walnuts
3 ounces/80 g candied (crystallized) ginger

FOR THE FILLING AND TOPPING
7 ounces/1 cup plus 5 tablespoons/200 g unsalted butter
1 pound 2 ounces/2 cups/500 g fresh cream cheese
3½ ounces/generous ¾ cup/100 g confectioners' (icing) sugar

TO DECORATE
2 ounces/½ cup/50 g walnut halves
¾ ounce/20 g candied (crystallized) ginger

EQUIPMENT NEEDED
9-inch/22-cm round springform cake pan (tin)
Parchment paper
Stand mixer fitted with whisk attachment and flat beater attachment
Zester
Fine-mesh strainer (sieve)
Silicone spatula
Peeler
Grater
Cooling rack
Plastic wrap (cling film)
Metal spatula or palette knife

Preheat the oven to 325°F/160°C/140°C Fan/Gas 3. Line the springform cake pan (tin) with parchment paper.

Break the eggs into the bowl of the stand mixer fitted with the whisk attachment, add the seeds from the vanilla bean (pod), the grated zest of the lemon and the sugar, and whisk until pale and mousse-like. With the stand mixer still going, slowly pour the oil into the mixture, and keep whisking for 1 minute.

Add the flour sifted with the baking powder, the baking soda (bicarbonate of soda) and a pinch of salt and mix with a silicone spatula until combined. Peel the carrots, then coarsely grate. Finely chop the walnuts, and chop the ginger into small cubes. Add the carrots, walnuts, and candied (crystallized) ginger to the cake mix and stir to incorporate.

Pour the mix into the lined springform pan and bake in the preheated oven for 50 minutes, or until golden, risen, and firm to the touch—a skewer inserted into the center comes out clean. Let the cake cool in the pan for 10 minutes, then remove from the pan and leave on a cooling rack to cool completely. Once cool, wrap in plastic wrap (cling film) and place in the refrigerator for 5–6 hours.

To make the frosting (icing), bring the butter and cream cheese to room temperature. Beat the butter in the stand mixer using a flat beater until it becomes fluffy, then add the confectioners' (icing) sugar and beat for a further 3–4 minutes. Stir the cream cheese to soften then add to the buttercream and mix until just combined.

Remove the cake from the refrigerator and cut it into two layers. Using a metal spatula or palette knife, spread the bottom sponge layer with one-half of the frosting to make a generous filling. Place the second sponge layer on top and spread with the remaining frosting. Leave to rest in the refrigerator for 30 minutes. When ready to serve, decorate with walnuts and candied ginger.

MISTAKES TO AVOID
To ensure the butter and cream cheese for the frosting (icing) blend together perfectly, both must be at room temperature, otherwise the frosting will separate, creating lumps.

BUCKWHEAT CAKE WITH BUTTERCREAM

Torta di grano saraceno con crema al burro

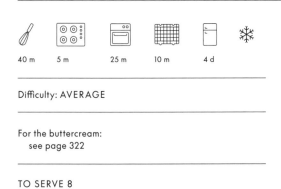

40 m   5 m   25 m   10 m   4 d

Difficulty: AVERAGE

For the buttercream:
  see page 322

TO SERVE 8

FOR THE CAKE
7 ounces/2 cups/200 g pecans
7 ounces/½ cup plus 5 tablespoons/200 g unsalted butter
8 ounces/scant 2 cups/230 g type "00" flour or all-purpose
  (plain) flour
7 ounces/1⅓ cups/200 g buckwheat flour
1½ teaspoons baking powder
½ teaspoon baking soda (bicarbonate of soda)
7 ounces/1 cup/200 g soft light brown sugar
4 eggs
11½ fl oz/scant 1½ cups/350 ml whole (full-fat) milk
Pinch of salt

FOR THE FILLING AND TOPPING
1 quantity of buttercream prepared following the base
  recipe on page 322

TO DECORATE
1 ounce/¼ cup/30 g pecans, roughly chopped
A few ripe Cape gooseberries (physalis)

EQUIPMENT NEEDED
2 × 7-inch/18-cm deep round cake pans (tins)
Parchment paper
Food processor
Skillet (frying pan)
Paper towel
Fine-mesh strainer (sieve)
Bowls
Electric whisk
Measuring cup or jug
Silicone spatula
Cooling rack
Metal spatula or palette knife

Preheat the oven to 350°F/180°C/160°C Fan/Gas 4 and line the springform cake pans (tins) with parchment paper.

Coarsely chop the pecans in a food processor. Melt 1½ ounces/3 tablespoons/40 g of the butter in a skillet (frying pan), add the chopped pecans and toast over low heat for 3–4 minutes. Transfer onto some paper towel and leave to cool.

Sift the flours with the baking powder and baking soda (bicarbonate of soda) into a bowl. In a separate bowl, beat the remaining butter with the sugar, using the electric whisk, until you obtain a soft and fluffy mixture. Add one egg and a spoonful of the sifted flours and mix with the electric whisk. Add the remaining eggs, one egg at a time, alternating with a spoonful of flour and continuously whisking as you do so. Continue to whisk as you add the remaining flour and pour in the milk very slowly.

Add the toasted pecans, stir with a silicone spatula and pour into the lined cake pans. Bake in the preheated oven for 25 minutes, or until golden, risen, and firm to the touch—a skewer inserted into the center should come out clean. Leave the cakes to cool in the pans for 10 minutes, then remove from the pans and place on a cooling rack to cool completely.

Sandwich the two sponge layers together, using one-third of the buttercream between the layers. Using a metal spatula or palette knife, spread the remaining buttercream over the top of the cake. Decorate with the roughly chopped pecans and the Chinese lantern berries (physalis).

VARIATIONS
Finish the cake in the "naked" style by spreading the buttercream thinly over the entire cake, allowing some of the cake crumb to show through the buttercream around the edges of the cake.

GLOSSARY

AGAR AGAR

A vegetable-based, tasteless thickener derived from a red seaweed. It is available in powder form, in flowers, or in bars. Thanks to its high gelling-thickening power, it is used in confectionery for the preparation of desserts, ice creams, puddings, creams, etc. A teaspoon of this seaweed is equivalent to about 8 sheets of gelatin and, on average, the proportion to use is 1 teaspoon to 0.5 litre of liquid. It is used by dissolving it in water or other liquids brought to a boil.

BAIN-MARIE COOKING

A cooking method that involves immersing a container with the preparation to be cooked in another larger one, which is full of hot water that is kept constantly at just boiling. In particular, it is used for delicate sauces or, more frequently, to heat a preparation without altering its taste and texture.

BASTARDELLA

A metal container, quite deep and equipped with two handles. The bottom must be flat and wide, while the shape is mostly semi-spherical. It is mainly used to mix creams and sauces or used in a bain-marie.

BAVARIAN

With a frothy and light appearance, it is a spoon dessert very similar to a pudding, characterized by a base of custard and whipped cream set with gelatin and flavored with fruit, preserves (jam), chocolate, coffee, or vanilla.

BLIND BAKING

When the empty "shell" of a pie dough (pastry) case is baked in the oven with no filling, it is said to be blind-baked. Later on, this blind-baked pastry case becomes a filled tart or quiche. A tart pan (tin) is lined with dough, the base is covered with parchment paper, then the pastry case is filled with ceramic "baking beans"—this prevents the pastry swelling excessively during cooking, thereby losing its shape. In the absence of these ceramic beans, dried pulses or coarse salt can be used. After the initial baking, remove the pan from the oven, remove the paper and baking beans, then return the pan to the oven, so that the dough dries out in the center and takes on a light golden color.

BUCKWHEAT FLOUR

Buckwheat is not actually part of the wheat family, but related to rhubarb. Its grains are used both whole and peeled. Gluten-free, buckwheat flour is used in the production of breads, focaccia, and fresh pasta. It has a consistency similar to barley. Buckwheat is rich in amino acids and mineral salts such as iron, zinc, and selenium.

CANDY

The process of making candied fruits involves dipping the fruit several times in a sugar solution, until the sugar is absorbed. Depending on the type of fruit, this process may preceded by a cooking phase. During the process, the water content of the fruit is progressively replaced by sugar, which gives the candied fruit its texture, aroma, and shelf life. The candying of citrus peel is very common.

CARAMEL

The process consists of melting the sugar with a little water, then boiling the syrup until it reaches an amber color and using it to make decorative shapes, spun sugar or for coating nuts and sometimes fruits. It can also be used as the base for a caramel sauce. It requires a lot of attention, to prevent the sugar from burning or crystallizing.

CHARLOTTE

Spoon dessert of French origin, it has many variations. It is made with a special round and flared mold, lined with sponge biscuits or sponge cake soaked in liqueur, then filled with mousses, creams, and fruit compotes.

CHEESECAKE

Cheesecakes are usually made with cream cheese (fresh, spreadable while cheese) that can be flavored with fruit, chocolate, and vanilla. They have a base made from cookie crumbs or sponge cake.

CHESTNUT FLOUR

Rich in carbohydrates and mineral salts, low in fat, it is a particularly versatile flour for both sweet and savory preparations. It has the advantage of being gluten-free though usually needs to be mixed with regular flour to make a pastry dough.

CITRUS ZESTER

Sometimes called a citrus stripper, this tool pares long, thin strips of zest from citrus fruits. The strips can be used, raw or cooked, as decorations. The tool can also be used to make decorative patterns on the surface of citrus fruits.

COCONUT FLOUR

Improperly called "flour," coconut flour is the dried white pulp of the coconut that has been reduced to very fine flakes or powder. It is bought both loose and packaged; it can be kept for a long time and is used for various dishes and desserts, as well as to prepare "homemade" coconut milk: the flour is boiled in water or milk, then left to infuse while cooling, then filtered.

COOK'S BLOWTORCH
An instrument with an adjustable flame used for heating different types of surfaces. In confectionery, a blowtorch is used to caramelize shaped surfaces, for example, meringue, custard cream, and crème brûlée. There are professional blowtorches for use in commercial kitchens, with high power and an adjustable flame, then there are smaller domestic blowtorches suitable for home use, with non-adjustable flame intensity.

CORNSTARCH (CORNFLOUR)
It is a fine white flour obtained from the processing of maize. Its function in patisserie is mainly that of thickener, along with potato starch.

COULIS
In French, it means "concentrated." In confectionery it indicates a puree obtained mostly from fruit, basically in two ways: raw, by blending the ingredients and filtering the mixture obtained, or by briefly cooking the fruit or vegetables. In confectionery it is used as a sauce, to garnish or accompany desserts of various kinds.

CREAM OF TARTAR
It is a natural acidic leavening agent obtained usually from grapes and tamarind. It is a white potassium salt which has the characteristic of being odorless and tasteless. It is usually mixed with baking soda (bicarbonate of soda) to make baking powder, used for leavening cakes, muffins, and cookies. It is widely used in natural and vegan cuisine due to the certainty of its non-animal origin and the total absence of stabilizers that could contain fatty acids of animal origin. It can also sometimes replace brewer's yeast for people with intolerances.

CUPCAKE
Also known as a fairy cake in the UK and a patty cake in Australia, a cupcake is a small sweet sponge baked in a baking pan (tin) with cups that is similar to a muffin mold. The classic cupcake recipe calls for a topping—royal icing, glacé icing, sugar paste, or buttercream—and some decoration, which can be candied (glacé) cherries, nuts, fruits, or more elaborate sugar-paste figures.

DATES
Rich in sugar plus minerals (such as potassium, iron, magnesium, phosphorus, calcium, and vitamin B) means that they are widely used in confectionery as a sweetener. They are readily available in any season both fresh and dried, although check that they are not treated with glucose syrup.

GELATIN
It is the most common gelatin substance of animal origin, once obtained from the processing of fish (hence the name) but now more commonly derived from animal sources. Easily available, it generally comes in the form of thin and transparent sheets weighing a few grams. To use, it is softened for a few minutes in cold water, then drained and squeezed, then combined with the mixture to be thickened.

GLAZE
From the French glacer, "to freeze," glazing involves covering the surface of cakes, cookies, or other sweets with a shiny and sugary layer. Glazes can be flavored with chocolate, cocoa, caramel, syrups, liqueurs, and other flavorings, or enriched with other ingredients, such as egg whites, and colored with food dye.

GOMASIO
Hailing from Japan, gomasio is a mixture of toasted sesame seeds (goma) and salt (shio). It can be used as a condiment, instead of salt, to flavor various culinary preparations, including confectionery.

GRATINATING
It is a type of cooking that takes place in the oven or under the broiler (grill) by intensely heating the surface of a dish to obtain a golden crust. In order for gratinating to take place, the surface to be gratinated must contain fatty ingredients such as butter, cheese, oil or cream, or compounds such as sauces or creams that contain these ingredients.

INCORPORATING
The term "incorporating" is used when a solid ingredient is mixed into a liquid or semi-liquid. It is best to carry out this process in several stages to obtain a homogeneous mixture: small quantities of each ingredient are combined, with more of each being added only when the previous additions are fully mixed together.

MAKING A MOUND
This is the way to prepare the flour on a clean work surface before mixing: a small conical mound of flour is made, a well is dug in the center, and then eggs are cracked directly into the well or other ingredients are added.

MANITOBA FLOUR
Obtained from a type of Canadian wheat, manitoba flour is a protein-rich flour used for bread and baked goods that require long leavening. It is defined as a "strong" flour. Its main characteristic is that it contains a high quantity of insoluble proteins which, in contact with a liquid in the mixing phase, produce gluten. It is therefore a flour rich in gluten and low in starches. The gluten is capable of retaining the leavening gases, allowing a considerable rise during cooking.

MELON BALLER
A tool with a hemispherical head that can be used to make balls from firm fruits. It can also be used to remove seeds from fruits such as papaya and cores from apples and pears.

MELTING
Melt ingredients such as butter or chocolate in a bain-marie, microwave oven, or over low heat. A low temperature is important so that the ingredients just melt and do not boil, as boiling could affect the flavor and texture.

MUFFINS
Muffins are individual sponge cakes that differ from cupcakes in that they usually contain a higher proportion of liquid and are chemically leavened with baking powder and/or baking soda (bicarbonate of soda).

MUSCOVADO SUGAR
A type of unrefined dark brown sugar with a caramel flavor. It is grainier and moister than other cane sugars. As well as providing flavor and sweetness, muscovado sugar can help to make baked goods moister and stay fresh slightly longer.

PANCAKES
Pancakes have long been a staple in many countries. A thin crêpe batter is made with flour, eggs, and milk and cooked on a hot pan or plate. Crêpes can be served with sweet or savory fillings. Adding a raising agent results in thicker pancakes with a fluffy center. They are often served with fruit and maple syrup.

PECTIN
Pectin is a natural substance contained in fruit and causes preserves (jam) to thicken. The concentration of pectin varies according to the type of fruit: the level of pectin is high in apples and plums, whereas it is much lower in pears and peaches. In this latter case, adding a little lemon juice, some apple peels, plus some extra sugar can help with setting.

PIE
A pie is a pastry case baked in the oven that contains either a savory or sweet filling. Traditionally, a pie uses particular types of pie dough (pastry), which can be a classic pie dough (shortcrust pastry), sweet shortcrust pastry, or puff pastry. Sweet pies can have a variety of fillings, such as fruit, custards, ganache, or frangipane.

POTATO STARCH
It is the starch extracted from potatoes and is a very light, flavorless, and odorless fine white flour. It is used, like wheat flour and cornstarch (cornflour), to thicken creams or sauces and also in the preparation of cakes and other baked desserts, making them soft and light.

RICE FLOUR
Rice flour is made by removing the outer husk and grinding the white grain to a fine flour. Rice flour is gluten-free so can be used to replace wheat flour in some cakes and pastries. It can also be used as a thickener for sauces and creams and to coat fried foods, instead of breadcrumbs.

RUBBING IN
The action of mixing fat and flour for pastry. This can be done in a food processor or by hand, with a pastry cutter or with the fingertips, and gives a mixture that looks like breadcrumbs or coarse sand. It should be done as quickly as possible, so that the butter doesn't become too warm and start to melt.

SIFTING
Dry ingredients, such as flour and cocoa, can be passed through a fine-mesh strainer (sieve) to remove lumps and to aerate the ingredients. It is also possible to sift ingredients with a special hand-held sifter.

SIMPLE SYRUP
A mixture of sugar and water, which can be flavored with fruits. Simple syrup is made from equal quantities of sugar and water, cooked until the sugar has dissolved, then briefly brought to a boil. It can be used for desserts and fruit salads.

SLURRY/SLAKE
The process of mixing dry ingredients, such as cornstarch (cornflour), or yeast, with a liquid, such as water or milk, to make a thick liquid mixture.

SOFTENED BUTTER
Butter brought to room temperature, around 68°F/20°C. It can then be beaten until pale and soft, to use in cakes or to add to some doughs, such as brioche.

SPELT FLOUR
An ancient species of wheat that has regained popularity. It is easily digestible, low in calories, and rich in proteins, carbohydrates, vitamin B, and fiber. It contains gluten.

STEVIA
Derived from a plant native to South America, stevia has a very high sweetening power and, for this reason, it should be used with care (approximately, half a teaspoon of stevia powder is equivalent to one teaspoon of sugar). It has a slight licorice flavor.

TEMPERING
A technique that puts melted chocolate through three different temperature points. The process of tempering aligns the cocoa and fat molecules in chocolate, giving the chocolate shine and a certain brittleness (called "snap"). Chocolate is tempered to be used for chocolates and chocolate decorations.

THICKENING
The term "thickening" is used when a sauce, cream, gravy, or cooking juices are made more concentrated and viscous. Thickening can be done by adding a binding ingredient, such as flour or cornstarch (cornflour), or by adding a protein, such as egg yolks, or a fat, such as cream or butter. Reducing the water content in a liquid also has a thickening effect. This reduction can be done by boiling or simmering the liquid until the water evaporates.

WAFFLES
Also known as a gaufre, waffles are crunchy on the outside and soft on the inside. They are cooked on double hotplates, which give waffles their characteristic grid surface. There are many variations from Belgium to France, from Germany to Scandinavia and the Netherlands. In the Abruzzese and Molise regions of Italy they have a very thin version called ferratella, or pizzelle.

WHEAT STARCH
Very fine and powdery flour made from the endosperm of wheat grains. Like other starch powders, such as potato starch and cornstarch (cornflour) it has strong thickening qualities. Substituting a proportion of wheat flour with wheat starch in baked goods can give a softer, finer crumb.

WHIPPING OR WHISKING
Incorporating air using a fork, hand whisk, or electric stand mixer. It will make the ingredients, such as cream and egg whites, more frothy and increase the volume. When whisking egg whites, start on low speed and gradually increase the speed to help the whites reach maximum volume and create a stable foam.

INDEX

RECIPE NOTES

Flour is type "00" or all-purpose (plain) flour, unless specified otherwise.

Sugar is white superfine (caster) sugar, unless specified otherwise.

Butter is unsalted butter, unless specified otherwise.

Milk is whole (full-fat) milk, unless specified otherwise.

Cream is fresh heavy (whipping) cream, unless specified otherwise.

Eggs are assumed to be US size large (UK size medium) and preferably organic and/or free-range, unless specified otherwise.

Gelatin is platinum gelatin sheets, unless specified otherwise.

Chocolate is bittersweet (dark) chocolate and with a minimum of 70% cocoa solids, unless specified otherwise.

Breadcrumbs are fresh unless specified otherwise.

Individual fruits, such as apples and pears, are assumed to be of medium size, unless specified otherwise, and should be peeled and/or washed, unless specified otherwise.

When the zest of a citrus fruit is used, always use unwaxed organic fruit.

Herbs are fresh herbs, unless specified otherwise.

Cooking and preparation times given are for guidance only, as individual ovens vary.

If using a convection (fan) oven, follow the manufacturer's instructions concerning oven temperatures.

Exercise a high level of caution when following recipes involving any potentially hazardous activity. This includes the use of high temperatures and open flames, such as using a cook's blowtorch. In particular, when deep-frying, slowly and carefully lower the food into the hot oil to avoid splashes, wear long sleeves to protect your arms, and never leave the pan unattended.

When deep-frying, heat the oil to the temperature specified, or until a cube of bread browns in 30 seconds. After frying, drain the fried foods on paper towels.

When sterilizing jars for preserves, wash the jars in clean, hot soapy water and rinse thoroughly. Heat the oven to 275°F/140°C/120°C Fan/Gas Mark 1. Place the jars on a baking sheet and place in the oven to dry.

When no quantity is specified for an ingredient—for example, strips of citrus zest, chocolate shavings, or edible flowers for decorating finished dishes—then quantities are discretionary and flexible.

Imperial and metric measurements, as well as volumetric cup measurements, are given for each recipe. Follow only one set of measurements throughout a recipe, and not a mixture, as they are not interchangeable.

All volumetric cup measurements given are level. Flour cup measures are spooned and leveled. Brown sugar cup measures are packed, while other dry ingredient measures are loosely packed.

All tablespoon and teaspoon measurements given are level, and not heaping, unless otherwise stated.
1 teaspoon = 5 ml
1 tablespoon = 15 ml
Australian standard tablespoons are 20 ml, so any Australian readers are advised to use 3 teaspoons in place of 1 tablespoon when measuring small quantities.

Some recipes include uncooked or very lightly cooked eggs. These should be avoided by the elderly, infants, pregnant women, convalescents, and anyone with an impaired immune system.

Phaidon Press Limited
2 Cooperage Yard
London E15 2QR

Phaidon Press Inc.
65 Bleecker Street
New York, NY 10012

phaidon.com

First published 2021
© 2021 Phaidon Press Limited

The recipes in this book were first published as *Il Cucchiaio d'Argento: Scuola di pasticceria*, first published in 2019
© Editoriale Domus

Translation from Italian: Franca Simpson in association with First Edition Translations Ltd.

ISBN 978 1 83866 314 8

A CIP catalogue record for this book is available from the British Library and the Library of Congress.

Commissioning Editor: Emily Takoudes
Project Editor: Lisa Pendreigh
Production Controllers: Jane Harman and Adela Cory
Artworker: Ana Teodoro

Cover designed by Julia Hasting
Designed by Hans Stofregen

Photography by Haarala Hamilton, except pages 29–43, 53–67, 107–113, 133–135, 147–149, 161–165, 189–193, 219–225, 239–259, 301, 313–327 (Editoriale Domus S.p.A. and Il Cucchiaio d'Argento S.r.l)

Printed in China

The publisher would like to thank Hattie Arnold, Vanessa Bird, Jo Ireson, Sarah Kramer, João Mota, Max Robinson, Ellie Smith, Tracey Smith, Caroline Stearns, and Emilia Terragni for their contributions to this book.